# R THE EENTRY TEAM

## CARING FOR YOUR RETURNING MISSIONARIES

# RThe EENTRY Team

*CARING FOR YOUR*
*RETURNING MISSIONARIES*

## NEAL PIROLO

**Emmaus Road International**
7150 Tanner Court    San Diego, CA 92111    (858) 292-7020

Copyright ©2000
Emmaus Road International
All Rights Reserved

Published by Emmaus Road International
7150 Tanner Court, San Diego, California 92111-4236 USA

Printed in the United States of America
ISBN 1-880185-07-5

## *Dedication*

To the many
cross-cultural workers
whose reentry experiences
are shared in an attempt
to improve the care of
missionaries.

# Acknowledgements

The first acknowledgement must go to the Holy Spirit, our Divine Teacher. Without Him, our quest for Truth would be fruitless. Second, to my wife Yvonne who has been a faithful encourager through the producing of this book and for her contribution to the final edit.

What a privilege it has been to work with the many returning missionaries who wrote their stories. Each has given a perspective of the awesome picture of missionary reentry. We gratefully acknowledge their contributions.

To Arlene Knickerbocker, who did much of the initial research. To Kim Hanselman who spent hours typing and retyping the stories. To Dennis Upshur whose own experience on the field and subsequent reentry gave him a perspective to wisely edit this work. To my brother Paul who used his grammatical editing skills to meticulously comb through the final manuscript. To Larry Chan who took another "comb" to correct my corrections! To the Emmaus Road Prayer Support Team who have invested hours of prayer that this resource will result in the better care of returning missionaries.

And finally and foremost, *"unto Him who by His power within us is able to do infinitely more than we even dare to ask or imagine; to Him be glory throughout all ages"* (Ephesians 3:20-21).

# Contents

**Section I: DISCOVERING THE PROBLEM & THE SOLUTION**     **9**

       Introduction     11

   *One.*   A Shared Responsibility     15

   *Two.*   A Scriptural Foundation     22

   *Three.*   The Human Dilemma     33

**Section II: REENTRY STORIES**     **49**

   *Four.*   Mission Accomplished     51

   *Five.*   Short-Term Missions     102

   *Six.*   Listen to Me; Please, Listen     121

   *Seven.*   Silly Little Things     144

   *Eight.*   MKs, Third World Kids     106

   *Nine.*   On Furlough     210

   *Ten.*   Home, Not By Choice     242

       Epilogue     298

**Section III: RESOURCES**     **299**

       Further Thoughts     301

       Resources     313

       Index to Reentry Stories     317

       Resources of Emmaus Road     318

# Section I

## Discovering the Problem
## &
## the Solution

# Introduction

When George Verwer, Founding Director of Operation Mobilization, heard that I was attempting a study speaking specifically to the issues of missionary reentry, he fired a quick e-mail to me. "You aren't going to have just a collection of 'horror' stories, are you?" I assured him that my goal was quite the contrary.

Yes, I wanted a collection of real stories about real reentry issues by real missionaries. Yes, I wanted the missionaries to be open and honest in telling their stories. And, yes, I expected more "horror" stories than positive ones. But, I told him, I have three objectives:

1) I want the reader to hear the bad and the good—the agony and the ecstasy of reentry;

2) I want the reader to understand thoroughly the feelings and thoughts behind the stories—to grapple with the issues real missionaries deal with; and

3) I want the reader to relate that understanding to any potential problem of similar nature their own missionary friend might encounter upon his return.

Ultimately, I want to see a Church educated in the Biblical model of reentry care so simply stated in the Book of Acts. So simply stated, yet as diversely complex as the individual personality of each returning missionary, whether adult or child, whether married or single, whether coming home to other work or returning to the field.

This is not a bedtime storybook! Nor is it a book about the mighty deeds of faithful missionaries filled with intrigue and excitement. It is a book of stories—stories about that critical time in the life of a missionary called reentry. If all you do is read the stories and say, "Oh, my! That's too bad!," to one and "Oh, my! That's nice!," to another, I will be terribly disappointed.

We have formatted the book to be studied. The ideas must be understood and digested. They must become a part of you as you concern yourself with the privileged opportunity to be a reentry caregiver.

In Section I, we establish the need for a cooperative relationship between the Church and mission agency. We lay a foundation in Scripture. Yet, we also relate to the human dilemma. Why is it so difficult to follow such a simple solution? What are the areas of challenge a missionary faces on reentry? How do the other five areas of missionary care impact reentry? What are the typical reentry patterns? What dangers lie in them?

In Section II, we have missionaries who were able to tell their stories, do so honestly.

Through mission links on the Internet and other Christian sources, I requested stories to be told of the good and the bad of missionary reentry. I am overwhelmed by the honesty with which many have responded. I am also grieved by many who said they would tell their story, but couldn't.

All were promised the strictest confidentiality by changing or omitting names of people and places. All stories included in this work were returned to the writers for final approval of the edited version.

On first reading of a number of the stories, I considered laying them aside. Through much prayer and soul searching to present an honest picture of reentry issues, however, I have included a number that may appear trivial or bizarre, or even non-Christian.

I was amazed (yet I shouldn't have been) that time and again when I talked with a missionary that I knew had a particularly difficult reentry, he would express a willingness to write his story. He was glad a study like this was being made to help others to avoid going through what he did. However, when it came time for him to write it down, the memory of the pain was still too great for him to do so. (*Throughout our study, we'll be referring to your missionary with a generic "he"— though at times we may mean he, she, or they.*)

My heart cried as I saw the need for reentry care for so many. Some had been home for years without beginning to resolve their reentry issues. I wanted to give my time to them. Yet, my priorities would not allow me to do so. I had to pass them by! Even as I write these words, I groan at the thought of so many hurting returned missionaries.

Thus, in this writing there are as many (or more) positive stories of reentry as negative. This is only because those with positive stories were more willing to write them.

I had thought to try to coerce the still-hurting missionaries into writing their stories, but that would have only added to the pain they are already experiencing. I have to leave it to you, after reading this book, to find those who are living on the fringes of church—or have left the church—and help to restore them.

The stories have been divided into seven divisions, each one dealing with issues of a particular nature or representing a particular group of missionaries.

Following each story, we have a section called, FOR FURTHER UNDERSTANDING. In it we try to pull out specific feelings and concerns expressed. As you progress through the stories, you'll gain skill in "reading between the lines" and see areas of need that might not be written in this section. You will see symptoms of "trouble ahead" that will make you a knowledgeable reentry caregiver.

After that, we have placed a section called, FOR FURTHER ACTION. In it we give you some activities that should help you relate the incident of this missionary to what your friend might encounter.

Throughout the stories, we've inserted the issues talked about in Section I. They form the standard by which to measure the problems and the solutions to the issues of reentry. Keep them in mind as you read the stories. Let them become "second nature" to you. Then, as you talk with your returning missionary friend, you will perceive more readily and easily the issues he needs to confront—with *your* help!

My talking and relating with many people on this subject has led me to believe it is *not* a matter of the Church not *wanting* to care for their missionaries on reentry. Rather, it is a matter of ignorance. Not in the "dumb" sense of that word, but just a lack of knowledge. Here are stories and exercises to help you become more aware of the issues and solutions to reentry.

In Section III, we have included articles and resources to assist you in your becoming a reentry care giver.

As deeply as I can search my motivation, it is my heart's desire to see missionaries better cared for. And that requires people like you. Our goal is to help you become a valuable reentry support team member. It will not be an easy task for you. It will take effort. You will expend energy. You will cry—and you will probably laugh! You will be puzzled by what seems (to you) so elementary, but to your friend is a tangled web of mystery. You may even "miss" the real issue and make a mistake, pressing in an area that really isn't a problem to your friend! But, take heart, you are going in the right direction. You will pray—a lot! You will ask God for wisdom and understanding—for a perceptive and listening heart. And your friend will be grateful.

Fruitful reading and diligent study lies before you!

Neal Pirolo

Emmaus Road International

San Diego, CA 92111 USA

Chapter One

# A Shared Responsibility

A number of years ago it was my privilege to put some ideas into a book titled, *SERVING AS SENDERS: How to Care for Your Missionaries*. The concepts are rooted in First Century missionary endeavor, yet vital for every cross-cultural worker today. The six areas of care we discuss were all asked for (sometimes received; sometimes not) by Paul, the Apostle, a missionary statesman of that era. The book deals with missionary care during the months of preparation, the time on the field and upon return.

As the ideas began to be put into practice in churches, pastors began focusing the theme of their mission conferences on *SERVING AS SENDERS*. And began inviting me to do the book as a seminar as a part of that conference.

It has been my privilege to see missionary after missionary being better cared for. This, after all, was the "bottom line" of my heart for that resource. Many thrilling reports have come back to me. One missionary, having been home for several weeks into his second furlough commented, "I thought I was in a different church! Their care for my family and me was 180 degrees from what it had (hadn't) been four years earlier!"

While I was doing a "turbo-charged" seminar at another church (for they had already been applying the principles to their 29 missionary families), one missionary stated, "I wanted my Quest Team to literally carry me up the aisle to the platform when it was my time to speak! This is exactly how I felt they had cared for me this last term. They carried me through by their total support!"

However, However... (and my pen doesn't want to write further because it is so much "fun" to just bask in the positive stories). However, from every quarter I am still observing that reentry care is being grossly neglected. People—the missionary as well as the committed caregivers—do not seem to understand the complex issues of reentry. Nor the simple steps of the solution.

I see it in the missionary, already on home assignment for three years, still not quite sure where or how he fits back into the social, material and spiritual lifestyle of his community.

I see it in the once "best friend" who doesn't know how to relate to this (new) person who is now more concerned for the lost than for the local sports team's national standing.

I see it in the missionaries who want to pour out their heart to me on a ten-minute break after I share the reentry segment in a seminar. My heart cries for their desperation. Yet I know I am not the one to help— other than to listen kindly and tell them they have to find a person who will listen to them share their heart, a person who will let them pour out all of their thoughts and feelings in a "safe" environment. And, at a time when *they* need to share.

I see it in the pastor who "pedestals" the returning missionary, flaunting the missionary's successes as marks on a score card or "notches" on his own Bible!

I see it in the missionary, receiving a new wardrobe of clothes from a well-meaning, generous caregiver. Yet he remembers how his national partner refused a few shirts he wanted to leave with him with the words, "I have one shirt to wear while I am washing my other one. What would I do with a third shirt?"

Can you imagine the ambivalence—the tension, the frustration, the excitement, the stress on this missionary? He is certainly thrilled with the new image he sees in the full length mirror. Yet he surely wouldn't want to look into the eyes of his national partner right now!

But I am getting ahead of myself. The intent of this book is to expose this too-long "closeted" issue of missionary care. We have collected true, real life stories written by returning missionaries. We believe that by your reading about the diverse situations they face, you will become sensitive to your missionary at this time.

## A SHARED RESPONSIBILITY

The care of a missionary on reentry must be a shared responsibility by their mission agency and their home church. (Though most missionaries have many "supporting" churches, i.e., they receive financial support from many, they should have one "home" church—the church who heard the Holy Spirit say, *"Separate unto Me* (this individual, couple or family) *for the work which I have ordained for them to do"* (Acts 13:2).

Yet, the reentry time in the life of a missionary remains shrouded in ignorance. I believe the mission agency is more aware of the problems of reentry, but personnel-challenged as they usually are, they do not have the staff to deal with the issues. One regional office of a large agency, after a tragic suicide of a returned missionary, established a tremendous program of education in the churches of that district. But personnel were reassigned, others retired, and the program "died" (no pun intended). It probably will not be revived until another tragedy awakens them to the vital need for caregiving during this critical time.

Shortly after *SERVING AS SENDERS* was published, I was given the opportunity to share its concepts with the Director of Member Care of a rather large mission agency. (This is the department of a mission agency that is counterpart to the caregiving provided by a missionary's sending church.)

"It would certainly be an asset for our missionaries," a couple in his department told him. An appointment was set for me to meet with him. The book was given to him to read. The couple who had arranged this meeting called to say he hadn't yet read the book. Could another appointment be set? Again, he had not read the book. Yet a third time he had not found the time to read the book. At their encouragement, we agreed to keep the third appointment, anyway.

My concern now was how I would succinctly present the thesis of this book to the director. I decided to give a brief overview of the six areas of care and then tell the story of Beth, the lady who struggled through several months of reentry stress, finding no help—anywhere! In a final, desperate appeal, one Sunday morning she again approached her pastor. His reply: "Beth, I am busy! But if you must, call and set an appointment for a week from next Wednesday." In that moment she "realized" she wasn't worth anybody's time. She went home and swallowed a bottle of Valium! By God's grace, and a roommate sensitive to the Spirit's leading, Beth was found and taken to the hospital. She recovered.

A bit dramatic, for sure. And this is not the end of most reentry stories. But certainly this Director of Member Care would be aware of the seriousness of the issues missionaries face on Home Assignment (a new name for *furlough*) or when they come home to stay.

His response struck me with as much impact as Beth's pastor's had on her. "Neal, this sort of thing doesn't really happen!"

What should I say? What *could* I say? This person

obviously is not in touch with the reality of reentry, I thought. A few words were mumbled about what a great work his organization is doing. And the appointment was over. Not until months later did I learn that a lady from that organization had succeeded in committing suicide just months previous to our appointment.

Now, I acknowledge that stories about the stress of reentry do not make for good recruiting material. It's a subject (some think) that must be avoided at all costs. It's like when one is leading a person to Christ. For fear you might "lose" them, you don't tell them that upon trusting in Christ, they will be automatically conscripted into the Army of God—a Soldier of the Cross! No! We use the "warm, fuzzy" terms instead.

Rather, a part of "opening their eyes" is to prepare them for battle; to give them some basic training in spiritual warfare. Likewise, in recruiting new missionaries, rather than keeping the subject of reentry in the dark closet of secrecy, we need to prepare them for the realities of war. (For, after all, true missionary work is war!) And casualties are a real part of war. But there are also solutions which will help avoid casualty.

In William Taylor's book, *TOO VALUABLE TO LOSE*, an attempt is made to place statistics to the casualties of the spiritual warfare of missionary work. Though there are many factors, one conclusion of this study of 453 mission agencies from fourteen sending countries pointed to the need for better ongoing support and pastoral care. Many agencies are attempting to provide this care. And some are finding a measure of success. Yet, so much better are those who recognize this as a shared responsibility and are encouraging the Church to participate in this vital time of caregiving.

I believe the Church, on the other hand, is basically ignorant of the issues missionaries face on reentry. After all, "What's the big deal? They're just coming home!" This posture of ignorance, along with a number of attitudes we will discuss in Chapter Three, has fostered the dilemma: Lack of care for returning missionaries.

At this point, I need to tell one more story. For it is this situation that became the final "push" of motivation for me to attempt this writing.

The issues of reentry were already heavy on my heart. At one missions conference I was given Friday evening to share an impassioned appeal for caregivers to step forward and become their missionary friend's "intensive care unit" in this needy time of reentry. After the service came the typical hand-shaking and comments about how great—how needed—how timely!

Saturday evening we were divided into groups to go to various homes. It was a dessert/coffee time to focus on the one missionary assigned to that home. It was to be a time to get a little closer—a little more real with that missionary.

Bill... *(Here and throughout the book all names of missionaries, churches, agencies and countries are changed—or omitted—to protect the confidentiality of the parties involved.)* Bill and I sat in the dining area. The ladies were happily exchanging "favorite" recipes of this or that dessert. Where were the men? Oh! They were in the family room engrossed in the final quarter of an NBA playoff game.

Yes, they knew Bill had a video to show of (what was left of) his work. You see, for the third time now the government and rebel forces had pushed back and forth through the region he was working in. Everything in their path had been destroyed. And Bill had a video to show these people in his "supporting" church.

Well, when the game was over, they slipped his video in. Yes, truly the destruction was complete. Fortunately there was no loss of life to any of the workers— this time. On a previous raid a family member had been killed. The video ended. It was rewound. And handed back to Bill.

"What blend of coffee is this? It's really good!" Through heart-broken grief and utter disbelief, I held my tongue! I did try to direct a question or two to Bill loud enough for others to hear. But the various blends of coffee and tasty desserts won the people's attention. And a pair of feisty thousand-dollar puppies who were tearing up the carpet were a terribly fun distraction.

It was then that I knew, if the Lord would so enable me, that I had to make an attempt at addressing this issue a bit more directly.

You might ask, "Why didn't Bill just speak up? Why didn't he just say, 'Listen! I need to tell you my story'?"

Several days before, I had heard a brief synopsis of his story. Thus, on an appropriate occasion, I had asked him, "How's it going?"

His reply was picture-perfect! With a smile he said, "Great!" He *had* to. This is the image a missionary must portray to the people back home. How else can he be sure they will continue to fund his efforts overseas?!

But I got in his face. Our noses must not have been more than three inches apart. I whispered, "You don't need to fool me!" Immediately he broke down. Through sobs of grief he lamented, "I can't believe this is the third time everything has been destroyed. Even the Christians we had been discipling were looting the buildings along with the rebels."

Herein lies your answer: One in such pain is hard-pressed to take any initiative to share the deep issues of his heart unless he is assured of a "safe" environment. He can't risk being judged as "unstable." He might be forced to stay home until he "gets over it!"

My prayer: May your reading of these stories—and focusing on the action steps that follow—so captivate your mind and heart that in your sphere of influence Bill's story (and a thousand like his) will never be repeated.

Let's begin with a Scriptural foundation.

Chapter Two

# A Scriptural Foundation

*"From there they sailed back to Antioch (in Syria) where they had first been commended to the grace of God for the task which they had now completed. When they arrived there they called the church together and reported to them everything about how God had worked with them and how He had opened the door of faith to the Gentiles. And at Antioch they stayed with the disciples for a good long time.... Paul and Barnabas continued in Antioch, teaching and preaching the Word of the Lord, in the company of many fellow-workers"* (Acts 14:26-28; 15:35).

The writers of the New Testament continually referred to their Scriptures to give authority to statements they made. Peter, on the Day of Pentecost, quoted from Moses and David several times. Stephen gave a whole history of Judaism. Paul, in establishing the missions process in Romans 10, began by quoting Joel.

Following their good pattern, we wish to lay a Scriptural foundation for this most critical of times in the life of a missionary: REENTRY.

It was in the days of Claudius Caesar. Agabus had

prophesied the famine that was now ravaging the Empire. The Christians in Antioch, as each family determined in their heart, had laid in store supplies for the believers in Jerusalem. Now the famine was at its height. Barnabas and Saul accompanied the caravan of food to the Holy City.

Their conversation with the Apostles, no doubt, turned to the words of Jesus: "Jerusalem *and* Judea *and* Samaria *and* the uttermost parts." Reports of praise made it clear: "You have filled Jerusalem with this Man's doctrine," the enemies of Christ testified. Peter had had his rooftop sheet-of-unclean-animals experience in Joppa resulting in the first (recorded) cross-cultural conversion. Cornelius, the Roman Centurion, and many of his relatives had trusted in Christ. Philip, the deacon, and his four prophetess daughters were in Caesarea. And he had had his Ethiopian eunuch experience.

BUT! Who had gone to the uttermost parts? At this point Antioch, where Barnabas and Saul were ministering, was the farthest city to which anyone had gone as a result of the persecution that arose after the martyrdom of Stephen.

Somewhere on their journey back from Jerusalem, Barnabas and Saul must have gotten excited about those regions beyond. For, on their return, the church at Antioch put five men forward to be considered for a mission. Next: Prayer *and* fasting! Then the Holy Spirit said, "I want Barnabas and Saul. I have a work for them to do." More prayer *and* fasting. The church laid their hands on them and sent them out. "So they, being sent forth by the Holy Spirit...," began a two-year missionary venture. (See Acts 11-13.)

However, not only did this church use wisdom in sending out their missionaries, they knew what they needed to do to bring them home! In just four brief verses (which can be overlooked so easily), the five vital

issues of reentry are modeled for us:
1) *They finished their assignment,*
2) *They returned to their sending church,*
3) *They received the church's hospitality,*
4) *They rehearsed **all** that God had done in and through them,* and
5) *They ministered again in their church.*

Because these five phrases can be so simply stated and because they focus on the returning missionary, the work of a reentry care group could be underestimated. Let's look a bit more closely at each of these five steps to successful reentry.

THEY COMPLETED THEIR ASSIGNMENT
*"And when they had fulfilled the work for which they had been sent out to do...."* Wow! To be guided by the Spirit! The church had heard the Holy Spirit say, "I want Barnabas and Saul for the work I have for them to do." And now, two years later, they sensed by the Holy Spirit that the work had been completed. Had everyone gotten saved? No! Had they covered the whole of the Roman Empire? No! It is true that Paul had been acclaimed Mercury and Barnabas, as Jupiter. And Paul had been stoned. And they had been thrown out of a few synagogues. And out of a few cities. And a few churches had been planted! And now they discerned that the work that God had sent them to do was completed.

How great when churches and agencies and missionaries today clearly hear from God, the Holy Spirit to know when to come home. Unfortunately, many don't. Uncomfortable statistics (garnered by those who gather such data) suggest that up to fifty percent of all missionaries are doing work that could be done *better* by nationals! (That is not if/when the nationals get more training. It is by using currently available nationals.)

Another category of unproductive field workers are

those who have "crashed" on the field but are too proud to come home. Not only are they ineffective on the field, but they are draining the energies of other missionaries who are trying to buoy them up.

Other categories of those who don't know when to come home are those who are fighting at non-decisive points of battle, are working at tasks for which they are not suited, or have made the nationals so dependent on them that they don't see how they could *ever* come home!

However, guided by the Holy Spirit, Paul and Barnabas, knowing that what He had sent them to do was now fulfilled, came home.

THEY RETURNED TO THEIR HOME CHURCH
*"And they returned to Antioch."* They did eventually go up to Jerusalem (and other cities along the way), but they first returned to their home church—the church from which they had been commissioned. (I tried to expand this paragraph, but there was no need. It is as simple as that: They returned to the church that had sent them out! I could say it again: They returned to the church that had sent them out!)

Experiences—good and bad—that I have listened to have confirmed in my heart that not only is it crucial for a missionary to have a home church from which to be sent, but that upon reentry, it should be their first stop.

If your missionary friend's agency has a required time of debriefing at their headquarters first—great! There can be value to both your friend and the agency. Also, some families have found value in a week's holiday before coming home, so they may "regroup" as a family. Maybe the children have been at boarding school; Dad has been focused on one assignment; Mom on another. There is wisdom in allowing—encouraging—requiring!—them to reintroduce themselves to each other as a family again during a brief retreat alone. A good theme for them to discuss is how they will function as a family in their new setting.

However, as good as those activities may be, there is still work for you to do. After all, you are the Body of Christ. An agency is just that—an agent to assist the Church in fulfilling Christ's command to the Church! If you sent out your missionary with a commissioning, recognizing that as your "cross-cultural parts" leave, the entire Body is going to be stretched to embrace the world; if you have cared for your missionary while he was on the field, relating with him in the joys and sorrows of cross-cultural ministry, then you have to be there when he returns home, providing the hospitality and debriefing he so greatly needs. I repeat: If you are diligent in properly sending out your missionary, you also need to carve out the time and energy to bring him home safely.

I realize that I included in this writing a story expressing exactly the opposite of what I just so strongly advocated. But, as you read it, also consider the other supporting factors in that story that made it a wise choice for the couple to *not* return to their home church. There are also several stories which relate to the splitting of home churches and the effect that has on a returning missionary.

THEY RECEIVED THE CHURCH'S HOSPITALITY
*"And they abode a long time with the disciples there."*
Why did they abide *with* the disciples? Why didn't they just rent an apartment, get the needed clothes, furniture and appliances from the mission boutique and settle in? After all, they're just coming home, aren't they?

To our individualistic society, this may be the most difficult aspect of reentry to understand. Your missionary has been experiencing community! He has been relating with, working with, enjoying life with people of many ethnic, cultural and even theological differences. He needs to find at home that same security of community.

When Paul and Barnabas came home, they abode. It is noteworthy that of the twelve Greek words scholars translate "abide," the one used here is defined *to wear through by rubbing; to rub away!* In other words, their stay with the disciples in Antioch was of such a duration that all the strangeness of relationship had come to be "rubbed away!"

When your missionary friend "abides" with you, he knows where the extra light bulbs are stored. He even feels free to "raid the fridge" when he is hungry! He isn't just camped out in your front hallway. He talks; you talk—you relate. You live there; he lives there—until he again feels comfortable in his *new* home environment.

Whether he stays with you, other friends, in a house provided by your church, or with family, be sure to check with him before he returns. Let him be prepared for the accommodations you are providing for him. (For the most fabulous story on "abiding" accommodations, read the last story in Chapter Four. On second thought, maybe you shouldn't. If you see how well this church did, you may be discouraged. Or worse, you may not want to read the rest of the book! You will have all of your answers in that story.)

THEY REHEARSED **ALL**
*"And when they gathered the church together, they rehearsed all that God had done with them and how He had opened the door of faith to the Gentiles."* Some years later Doctor Luke had joined Paul on his missionary journeys. Paul was still "rehearsing" events from that first trip! "We ministered in synagogues—a really mixed reception! Usually it lasted only one Sabbath. But through that we heard the Lord say, 'I have set you as a light to the Gentiles.' We led the proconsul of the Island

of Pathos to the Lord. Elymas, a sidekick of the deputy, was messing with him. I had to ask the Lord to blind him for a season. Yes, they tried to stone me in Iconium, but we caught wind of their plot and escaped to Lystra. The Lord miraculously healed a crippled man there. They thought we were gods! Can you imagine that? The priest of Jupiter almost sacrificed an ox to us. We had to rip off our clothes to show them that we were really human! (It was my favorite tunic!)

"Then certain Jews from Iconium found out where we were. They got me there. Stoned me. Dragged me out of the city. Left me for dead. I waited until they were gone. (The disciples still stood around me.) Then I got up, brushed myself off, and went back into the city. Talk about some tough times! But out of that I heard the Lord confirm, 'through much tribulation we must enter the Kingdom of God.' A real sobering thought! Not too popular with those satisfied to stay in their 'comfort zones!' But, hey, after two years of this, we sensed by the Holy Spirit that we had completed what He sent us out to do, so we returned to Antioch."

Two years! The brief summary Luke gave in Acts 13 and 14 do not tell the tales of Pisidia and Pamphylia, of Perga and Attalia. Nor of everything that happened in the other cities that were mentioned. But Scripture assures us that they *"rehearsed **all**...."*

Your missionary friend needs the opportunity to *"rehearse **all**!"* There are two levels of debriefing needs that your friend has: Public and private. In our training of missionaries, we encourage them not even to ask for the "ten minutes on Sunday morning." For this often truncates opportunity for other sharing. In our "sound-bite" society, when the people hear the "ten minutes," they come to believe that they have thus "heard it all." Why would they want to hear it again? What more could be said?

For the hearer and the speaker we rather recommend multiple meetings with many different age groups and venues, both Christian and secular. You need to set meetings for your returning friend with preschoolers, primary, middle, upper elementary kids, high school and college students, career people and homemakers, and all the way to senior citizens. Rotarians and Kiwanians—a radio talk show, a newspaper article. Why? One obvious reason: All different age groups are further challenged to "lift up their eyes...."

But far more critical than that is the benefit to your missionary. Consider, if you set ten meetings with ten different college/career groups, your missionary friend has to rethink all that happened to him on the field only *once!*—through the mind of that audience.

However, in having to share with many different age groups and in a variety of venues, he has to rethink his experiences that many times. This is good. To be able to process and process again what he did, telling one story to preschoolers, yet another to the Rotary Club gives your missionary the opportunity to *debrief!* In verbalizing *all*, he is able to sort through his experiences, identifying the positive—and noting the negative. He is reinforcing his memories of the good and the bad so that he maintains a sane reality of his time on the field.

The second level of debriefing is done in private. A missionary needs to share in the safe environment of a close friend those deep experiences not easily understood in a public gathering. Name them? Impossible! They will be different with each missionary. And they will be different for the same missionary at various times of remembrance. These are the phone-calls-in-the-middle-of-the-night times when your missionary friend is remembering events totally out of context with your culture, yet so vivid to your friend because they happened to him. (In the stories that follow, you'll find many situations of this type.)

We need to allow our missionary to *"rehearse all!"*

THEY MINISTERED AGAIN
*"Paul and Barnabas, however, stayed on at Antioch, teaching and preaching the Word of the Lord in company with many others."* The Second Church Council had taken place. The issue of Gentile Christians having to be circumcised had been "settled." (A religious/cultural issue that would rise again! And again!) But Paul and Barnabas, Judas and Silas (and probably Barnabas' nephew, John Mark) returned to Antioch. When the church heard the good news of the Council's decision in the letter sent by James, they rejoiced at the report.

Judas and Silas, after a time of ministry, were given permission to return to Jerusalem. Judas left; Silas remained.

As things settled down again, Paul and Barnabas found themselves fully integrated back into the life at Antioch. New Bible studies were started; new opportunities to minister were found.

(Just a thought: Maybe one reason why returning missionaries don't fully integrate back home is because they were not active in ministry in the church before they left. If this is true, it pushes the issues of reentry way back to the caliber of person a church sends to the field. Many church missions leaders require—yes! require—their missionaries to function in a position of responsibility in the church *before* they send them to an agency or to the field.)

It is imperative that the reentry process is allowed to run its course to full integration *before* your friend moves on to other activity. Some missionaries acknowledge that years later there remain unresolved issues. "A careless word spoken on reentry is still stinging ten years later," one missionary reports.

Just being asked about their missionary experiences can stir up buried feelings of hurt, anger, sadness, or disappointment. A twenty-year-old cries as he remembers a thoughtless slighting of his need when he returned home at thirteen years of age. Life plans have changed course because of unresolved, buried issues of reentry.

But something that has challenged the hearts of thousands of missionaries ever since was already stirring in Paul's heart. For, once a person has ministered cross-culturally, he will never be the same again! "Hey! Barney! Let's go check up on those churches we got planted in all the cities where we preached the Word," Paul proposed.

And whether your returned, fully integrated missionary friend resumes ministry at home or goes back to the field, your job as a reentry caregiver is complete only at such time that he is ready to move on.

SUMMARY

How is it that we can write pages to explain something when Scripture can say it so succinctly?

*"From there they **sailed back to Antioch** (in Syria) where they had first been commended to the grace of God for the **task which they had now completed.** When they arrived there they called the church together and **reported to them everything** about how God had worked with them and how He had opened the door of faith to the Gentiles. And at Antioch **they stayed with the disciples a good long time.** Paul and Barnabas continued in Antioch, **again teaching and preaching** the Word of the Lord, in the company of many fellow workers"* (Acts 14:26-28; 15:35).

I can say—unequivocally—that as you and the whole reentry team provide the environment to help your returning missionary friend follow this simple, five-point prescription, his reentry experience will be one of minimal frustration and hurt:

1) They came home at the Holy Spirit's direction,
2) They returned to their sending church,
3) They *abode a long time* with them there,
4) They rehearsed *all*, and
5) They were again active in ministry.

If your friend is just coming home on furlough and plans to return to the field, providing the care these five principles requires will make his time more satisfying. If your friend is not planning to return to the field, helping him follow this prescription will allow him more quickly to get involved in other areas of ministry back home.

This is the simply stated solution to the issues of re-entry. However, culture and society, the temperament of missionaries and interpersonal relationships have a tendency to complicate the issues. We need to look at the dilemma of human experience.

Chapter Three

# The Human Dilemma

Though in an ideal world the Scriptural solution could be applied so easily to all returning missionaries, there are mitigating factors that preclude such ease. This is the human dilemma. There are four areas of concern that complicate the process: 1) The nine issues determining the length of time for the reentry process to be completed; 2) The nine areas of life in which your returning missionary will find stressful challenges; 3) The four wrong reentry behavior patterns to which your friend's personality might be drawn; and 4) How successfully the support team has served in the other five areas of care during preparation for the field and while your missionary friend was on the field.

HOW LONG SHOULD THIS PROCESS TAKE?
Scripture does not let us know how long Paul and Barnabas' reentry process took. We do know they had some pretty wild adventures! And Scripture does say that they abode for "a *long* time."

Today, experience tells us that it usually takes longer than expected. One lady, whose story you will read, said it took her "nine months to feel at home again." She had been gone for a year! How long your missionary friend will need the warm gift of hospitality extended will vary by any number of circumstances:

1) *The length of time your friend has been gone.*

Certainly the longer he has had opportunity to relate with and minister among people of another culture, the more he will adapt to their ways. Thus, the more difficult it will be for him to readjust to "our" ways.

But, if your friend is gone only for a short time (even just a weekend), dramatic changes can also take place in his life, creating the need for sensitive reentry care. People's hearts have been moved with compassion for the lost in just one afternoon as we have taken them across the border from us into Tijuana, Mexico.

2) *The degree of change in his home environment.*

The people, the places, the things! We all change, but how radical have been those changes? If your missionary friend left a "sleepy little hollow," ministered in a sleepy little hollow and returns to the same, it likely will be easier for him to become comfortable again. On the other hand, if his home town has doubled in size, friends have moved away, the church has experienced a "split"—good or bad, or his favorite "greasy spoon" restaurant has become a freeway interchange, he might experience a greater degree of frustration.

Realize that you saw these changes take place as they were happening. Your mouth was drooling as you drove to that restaurant. What?! The building is boarded up! Remember the surprise? But it was still several weeks before it was bulldozed down. And you watched the progress of the freeway being built. For you it was positive; it meant a faster route to work. You had a long time to process this change as it was happening.

But your friend came home with his mouth watering for those greasy French fries. Yet, when he saw the freeway interchange (even though you wrote and told him), it was difficult for him to accept that he will never again order fries at that favorite spot. Whereas if he, like you, could have come to that realization day-by-day, he would not have experienced such shock.

If you are wondering how such a little thing could cause difficulty in your friend's reentry, you will especially want to read the chapter titled, SILLY LITTLE THINGS. For it can be "silly little thing" after "silly little thing" that will exhaust your missionary's tolerance. And possibly lead to devastating results.

3) *The degree of change in him.*

Likewise, the changes that have taken place in your friend's life, while they came gradually for him (thus making them seem not so dramatic to him), are radically *impossible* for you to process. He is now more interested in a prayer meeting for the lost of the world than in prime tickets for his (previously) favorite sports team. You find this difficult to handle, especially because you paid for the tickets! Yet, he sees it as only natural that the lost of the world are a higher priority than sports. "How come *you* can't see *that*?" he wonders.

But he has also changed in more ways than just spiritually. Aspects of his physical, emotional, mental, social and cultural being have probably undergone radical change, as well. A damaged liver from hepatitis or malaria can have long-lasting effect. Having enjoyed living in a community-centered society can produce ill feelings to one coming home to a highly individualistic culture. One man cried out, "I was only gone ten weeks, but where is the community I grew to appreciate there?"

4) *The attitude of the church toward your missionary friend.*

If your church has "pedestaled" him as some great, almost-right-there-next-to-God being, it will be impossible for him to be honest with anybody about any problem. All his responses will have to be—*Great! Wonderful! Fabulous! Couldn't be better!*

Another factor, closely related, is the realization that money comes from "success stories!" Anything less than success will have the missions committee questioning whether or not to continue financially supporting your friend. After all, we want to be a part of something "great!" The trouble comes when we set secular goals as the measure of success. Seventeen years spent on a New Testament translation for fifty indigenous people without one conversion does not seem as *successful* as 4500 "decisions for Christ" at a three-night crusade!

Honestly, are you more interested in a report of "one hundred computers that were kept repaired" or of "six indigenous churches that were planted and the new believers are now going to neighboring tribes with the Good News of Jesus Christ?" Which is more critical to the fulfillment of the Great Commission? If you want to say the latter, you may be honestly "wrong!" For, it is very possible that one of those "repaired computers" was used by the Bible translator who brought God's Word to that indigenous group so that they would be saved, thus becoming the missionaries to those neighboring tribes!

Until false images of how we measure "who is the greatest among us" are broken down or until we completely destroy the process of "comparing ourselves among ourselves," you will have to be there to help your friend deal with the impossibilities of adjusting.

On the other hand—more likely if yours is a large church—the missionary, rather than being exalted, may be "lost in the crowd." The full program of events may not allow for any acknowledgement of his return. Other "more important" personalities may deny any recognition for your friend.

5) *The amount of time given to your friend to prepare for reentry before leaving the field.*

Most missionaries have spent a considerable time preparing to go *to* the field. Training for the task can take several years. Partnership development can take a year or more. Even the final "closing up" of his home country affairs can take a while. And then comes the practical pre-field training of how to live and minister in a second culture. During this lengthy time your friend has been thinking consciously and subconsciously about *going!*

He left—finally! He enjoyed fruitful ministry on the field. Now it is time to come home. "Already?" he exclaims! Rather than taking time to think about the adjustments needed for life back home, he is putting even greater energy into doing all he can in the ministry before leaving. His thoughts are: What will happen while I'm gone? Have I spent enough time in training the national leaders who will assume my responsibilities? Tickets have been purchased. A hurried letter has been sent. But not until he is on the plane, taking a deep breath, does he begin thinking about *you* and home.

6)  *The length of time it takes to return home.*

Modern means of transportation, though gratifying to our sense of comfort and convenience, play a detrimental role in easing a missionary back into his home culture. We can board a jetliner and be anywhere in the world in less than twenty-four hours.

One missionary relates the shock of her experience: Her jungle village accommodations had been secured for her absence; in other words, her hammock had been folded and stored. She had taken her final bath in the river with the village ladies. Whisked away by a jungle pilot on a fifty-minute plane ride to the mission's regional headquarters, she enjoyed the modest comforts of her still-jungle-surrounded home. (It may be noted that before the convenience of an airstrip near her village location, it took three weeks of travelling by truck, boat, dugout canoe and trekking to get there.) She bussed to the capital city. And now, less than forty-eight hours after her river bath, she was dressed in her British finery, sitting in the Queen's palace in London, sipping tea with a friend!

Until well into the Twentieth Century, missionaries had the "luxury" of travelling home by boat and train. It could take weeks to arrive. What did they do during those long hours and days? They began the reentry process. They were able to put their work into a broader perspective. They were able to think about you and what to expect back home. They prayed for wisdom to share the passion of their hearts. They relaxed.

But your friend, jet-lagged and exhausted, must face the welcoming committee at the airport with tailor-fresh attire and smiles of success written across his face. Had he been given the luxury of travelling by ship, for example, or had he had the opportunity for a few days of holiday to ease the transition, reentry for him might have been smoother.

7)   *The uniqueness of your friend's personality.*

The individuality of your friend will affect the length of time for the reentry process. His nature and the nature of his ministry may one time make reentry more difficult; whereas, on another occasion of reentry, he may sense less or no trauma. Then, even within the same family there can be a wide divergence of characteristics affecting their reentry. Each member is unique. Caregiving is a very personalized ministry. One "shoe" does not fit all!

8)   *The disadvantaged position your friend is in to take authority over the situation.*

It is easy to recognize in physical situations: A friend is trapped under a fallen tree. He is immobilized. Without help from another, he will remain pinned under that tree trunk.

When your friend is "trapped" under the frustration of the clashing of cultures, he needs your help. Even when the "tree" is lifted off, the injuries sustained may need the care of a "physician." In this case, prayerfully *you* will be there to offer your knowledgeable care!

9) *The attitude of "It won't—it can't happen..." by him and/or by you is "suicidal!"*

"It's no big deal! I'm just going home!" is often met on reentry by the attitude of the people back home, "It's no big deal! He's just coming home!" This attitude on anyone's part will stall the process of adjustment. Reentry stress does happen. It will happen. It happens to seasoned missionaries. It happens to weekend missionaries! The only deterrent from being devastated by it, is being prepared for it.

The awesome privileged responsibility of being a part of a reentry team is yours. And that opportunity for you to minister to him continues until your friend has been fully integrated and is ministering again. Or until he returns to the field.

AREAS OF CHALLENGE

The areas of challenge which your friend may find stressful are many. Your missionary friend needs to be helped to face the ambivalence of each. Some issues may be more frustrating than others, but each should be "talked through." And some will come up more than once. Consider the following areas of stress:

1) *Physical*

The very first issue of reentry is the effect of the travel on the physical nature of your missionary friend. In Santiago, Chile, I saw written on an airport billboard: "Jet lag is intended to make you look like your passport photo!" Seriously, it is said that a six- to eight-hour transcontinental flight is equivalent to a full day's physical labor.

But jet lag is just the beginning. Change of climate, change of elevation, change of season, change of diet, change of pace—change! Change in modes of transportation and speed. Can you imagine this? For four years your missionary's fastest means of transportation was a Honda 50, the "baby" of motorcycles. Over the jungle trails, the top speed had been twenty miles per hour!

Now your missionary has been hurled at jet speeds of five to six hundred miles per hour from one continent to another in less than twelve hours to face the challenges of a metropolitan freeway system. He is driving a Ford Expedition at an outrageous seventy miles per hour, with cars around him honking for him to get out of the way! "You're going too slow!" they yell.

Changes! In time schedules. Or just in his attitude toward time. All of the effects on your missionary friend's physical being will need adjustment and/or accommodation. Can you imagine needing to put a sweater on because you're "chilled" at 75 degrees Fahrenheit? But if your body had adjusted to triple digit temperatures, 75 degrees could be cold!

2) *Professional*

All the ramifications of "earning a living" need to be reviewed. Work ethic, production being more important than people, the closer supervision of a "boss," loss of job skills while on the field—just to name a few.

Another factor for missionaries on Home Assignment (a new name for *furlough*) is that of being put into a position for which they are not at all qualified. When a computer technician who is not a good public speaker is asked to share the vision of his mission before a congregation of 300, he will likely experience stress! Or, the lady who contributed greatly to the mission work, having had a maid to do all her housework and cooking, now facing a two-story house with no outside help could become traumatized!

3) *Financial*

Having lived without all the gadgets of materialism, two extremes could present themselves: a) He may try to continue an austere lifestyle in a society of opulence, or b) He may indulge himself in every "new and improved" trinket of hedonism!

Doubting that your friend will go to either extreme,

caution must still be exercised in watching for the symptoms of jealousy or signs of lusting. Getting him to express his thoughts about all he sees and desires is a first step to resolution.

(It has been years since we purchased our new carpet, but at times, I still feel I must defend replacing it, though it had been faded and threadbare for fifteen years!)

4) *Cultural*

New beliefs, values, attitudes and behaviors have become a part of your returning friend. Perhaps he has adapted to a culture with a slower pace, a more relaxed atmosphere. Or perhaps, he has lived in an environment of continually being on guard for some kind of danger. Maybe his Christian activity had to be covert.

The cultural differences that your friend may try to hold on to are innumerable. When schedules and attitudes of the people back home don't allow for them, he needs you to help him process his feelings.

5) *Social*

To be acclaimed "our missionary" can place an ungodly halo over your friend's head. If he has come home feeling that maybe he didn't really do that well overseas, he may grasp the significance of "our missionary" for some sense of security or esteem. The conflict that festers in his own mind will have to be dealt with—hopefully with your listening ear and wise counsel.

Or, if it is a particularly large church, or there is a new pastor, or most of his friends have moved, your friend may return, not having been missed and the new usher may hand him a visitor's card to fill out!

6) *Linguistic*

The new language your missionary friend has learned may be far more descriptive than his mother tongue. He may try to express himself in his limited home language and feel inadequate. Then, think of all the new words and jargon that have been added in his absence. He needs time to learn (or learn to avoid) this new vocabulary.

7)　*National/Political*

Possibly he has found a government more responsive to the needs of people. New laws and new leadership back home have possibly brought undesired changes. Having seen the other side of his country's foreign policy may give him a new perspective on his own country. These issues must be dealt with.

8)　*Educational*

The formal and informal educational standards of the world vary greatly. Social skills may be considered more important than academic lessons. Principles of reason may be regarded with higher value than rote memorization of facts. The pursuit of excellence may still motivate the educational system where your friend was ministering. Your friend, whether student, parent or just one concerned for educational excellence may find reason for concern with his home country's educational standards.

9)　S*piritual*

More critical than any (or even all) of the previous issues, your friend will face the stress of the spiritual tenor of his home country. Whether real or perceived, he will sense a lower level of spirituality in his church at home. He has focused his mission on the salvation of the lost and the discipling of the nations. His heart is pounding with the very heartbeat of God: *"Not willing that any perish, but that all come to repentance"* (II Peter 3:9).

And now in bold, stark contrast, he faces a church society debating between mauve or teal colored carpet, when the carpet in place is still good enough for another ten years. Or, he finds them arguing the "finer points" of doctrine: Water baptism by bending forward, backwards, or straight down!

As you read this collection of stories you will come

to understand the range of issues your returning friend could encounter. Fortunately, no one will face them all. However, the ones your friend faces need to be dealt with, using the utmost wisdom and understanding.

REENTRY BEHAVIOR PATTERNS
Entering his new culture with his new ways can result in one of five reentry behavior patterns. Four of them are dangerous. You want to be alert to their symptoms and help your friend process his feelings, working toward the expression of the fifth pattern. That is the one you want to help facilitate.

1)   *Alienation*
Your cross-cultural worker friend comes home. His attitude of "I'm *just* going home!" has left him unprepared for what he is facing. He begins feeling very negative about his home culture. Not knowing how to handle all he sees and feels, he begins to withdraw.

He makes excuses rather than meeting people. "I don't have my slides together yet" excuses him from sharing at a home group. "The crowd at the baseball game would be too noisy," he argues. Four weeks later he is *still* "suffering from jet lag." These are the types of symptoms you must be on the lookout for. They are likely shallow pretexts to hide his inner feelings.

He might internalize these feelings and sink further into this pattern of alienation. He may feel there is no one to talk to, no one who could possibly understand, no one to help him process his thoughts.

You can pull him out of that tailspin by inviting him to your house. Just the two of you—or three—is a small, safe number. Or visit some of his favorite spots together—a park, the beach, a restaurant. If he refuses such gentle encouragement, get desperate! Just show up at his doorstep and *insist* on some fellowship. Get him talking about anything, just so he begins verbalizing his thoughts.

2) *Condemnation*

This friend, also unprepared for reentry, has become negative about his home culture. The areas of challenge seem to be overwhelming. He didn't realize people would be so—unthinking! He can't understand *why* his pastor has no time for him! How could *everybody* be so—unChristian? The pressure of his judgemental attitude increases, and he becomes explosive. Everyone he sees knows within minutes how inferior and lacking in spiritual gifts they are because they are not involved in missions. He begins to criticize everything from the church pews to Mrs. Smith's hair style.

This friend also needs the gentle, understanding encouragement to talk—to process his thoughts about how things really are. But, again, if this does not divert his thoughts from condemnation, you may need to become blunt. You may need to take him to the Scripture about the root of bitterness (Hebrews 12:15).

Or, more forcefully, you may have to talk with him about the fact that our standing is in the righteousness of Christ alone. Then let him (make him) talk to you. He needs to verbalize his frustrations in a safe environment of a close friendship. Don't wait until he feels he must "unload" in the middle of your pastor's Sunday morning sermon!

3) *Reversion*

Your friend takes a hop, skip and a jump off the plane not even realizing that people aren't hopping, skipping and jumping anymore. He keeps trying to deny that any vital changes took place in him while he was gone, or in you who stayed home. He keeps trying to fit in to what was, but no longer is.

He is likely to jump right into whatever task is put before him. And his unaware friends play right into the dilemma: So glad you're back! We need a teacher for the sixth grade class! "Great! When do I start?" Usher? "Yes, I will!" Lead worship on Wednesday night? "Sure!"

He will wake up one morning doubting his sanity. He has moved into the "fast lane" of his Christian community without allowing himself to process the incredible changes his body, soul and spirit have experienced on the field.

4) *The Ultimate Escape*

Without a reentry support team to help him, the gradual deterioration of any one of the three above return behavior patterns could result in the devastating scenario of the ultimate escape of suicide—figurative or actual.

Your missionary friend went out to live and minister in a second culture. He had a good experience. Language was learned. Relationships were built and nurtured. Souls were saved. The church was strengthened.

He returns. He is not prepared for all the changes. He tries to cope. But the degenerative spiral of his thoughts could pass through all three patterns: Fearful of what he might say, he internalizes all his frustrations. *Alienation* whispers, "Nobody cares or understands. Forget them!" Fighting for survival and knowing what is right, he argues with himself: I have to get out and share the vision for the world among the church people. "But they are so ungodly!" *Condemnation* thunders. "This isn't getting me anywhere," he yells back at himself. *Reversion* reasons, "Okay, let's just forget it. I was there. You were here. We're back together. No big deal! Let's just get on with life!"

But everything *is* different! This fact cannot be denied. The whirlwind of emotions leaves him broken. He backs out of life—spiritually, mentally, emotionally, or he finds the ultimate escape of physical suicide his only alternative.

If you see your returning friend falling into any one of these four behavior patterns, your help is needed. And possibly, the help of a professional is needed. (See the Resource Section for some references.)

**5) *INTEGRATION!***

By focusing your time and energy on the Scripturally-based pattern of reentry talked about in the last chapter, you can usually avoid the struggles that accompany any of the wrong reentry behavior patterns. A music group of the '70's had as their theme song, "Don't try to drive the darkness out; Just turn on the light." Don't wait for any of the negative symptoms to express themselves. Proactively promote and facilitate the five steps of integration as your friend's reentry behavior pattern. In doing this, you will not need to be concerned about the negative.

HAS CARE BEEN GIVEN IN ALL AREAS?
How well you friend was cared for while he was preparing to go to the field and how "connected" to his support team he felt while on the field will have a great effect on his receptivity of your reentry care.

1) *Moral Support*

Paul said to the Christians at Rome, *"On my way to Spain, I want to encourage you, and be encouraged by you"* (Romans 1:12). Every missionary today needs encouragement.

2) *Logistic Support*

Paul had a host of friends who helped him. Most notably, his request for Timothy to bring his *"cloak before winter"* (II Timothy 4:13). There are a myriad details of concern that can be cared for by team members.

3) *Financial Support*

Yes, even Paul had his problems with money! Read his exchange of words with Philemon or his argument with the Christians at Corinth and his thanks to the Philippians. And today, our attitude toward "our" money makes this an extremely difficult area to deal with.

4) *Prayer Support*

Paul called on his friends to *"pray that the Gospel would go forth unhindered"* (II Thessalonians 3:1).

Books and seminars and breakfasts abound on this subject. But, Lord, just help us *to* pray!

5) *Communication Support*

We thank God today for Paul's diligence in writing his missionary letters. We read them as Holy Scripture, for that is what they are. Though our tools of communication have gone way beyond quill and parchment, it still takes effort to "keep in touch."

Each of these areas of missionary care when intertwined with the fabric of your missionary while he is preparing to go and while he is on the field, will greatly help the reentry process.

THE SOLUTION IN SUMMARY

There are nine factors in the length of time it takes for the reentry process to be complete:

- Length of time on the field,
- The degree of change at home,
- The degree of change in your missionary friend,
- The attitude of the church,
- The amount of time given to prepare for reentry,
- The length of time it takes to get home,
- The uniqueness of your friend's personality,
- The disadvantaged position of your friend to take control of his situation,
- The attitude of denial.

There are nine areas of life experience in which your missionary may face challenge:

- Physical,
- Linguistic,
- Professional,
- Educational,
- Financial,
- National/Political,
- Cultural,
- Spiritual.
- Social,

There are five reentry behavior patterns:

- Alienation,
- Suicide,
- Condemnation,
- INTEGRATION.
- Reversion,

There are six areas in which missionaries need care:
- Moral Support,
- Logistic Support,
- Financial Support,
- Prayer Support,
- Communication Support,
- Reentry Support.

The effectiveness of a missionary's care group support in the first five areas has a direct effect on his reentry support process.

There are five simple, Scripturally-based steps to the full integration of your missionary friend:
- Come home by the Holy Spirit's direction,
- Return to his sending church,
- Receive the hospitality care of his friends,
- Rehearse *all*,
- Become active again in ministry.

Allow this summary to form a grid through which you filter each of the stories in this collection. You will discover that if these issues had been addressed, each of the problems would have found a solution. Likewise, in the positive experiences recorded, you will find that there were those who applied these principles.

Again, I repeat, the solution is so simply stated in Scripture. As you read these stories, I trust you will not lose the import of the five steps for their simplicity. The reentry team is formed by people like you who can "own" one or more aspects of the reentry process and follow through until your missionary friend is fully integrated. Then, and only then, is he ready for a further assignment.

The fog of confusion is being blown away. The shroud of secrecy is being lifted. The pall of ignorance is being replaced with knowledge and understanding.

And now, with each of the following stories written by real missionaries about their real reentry experiences, I trust that you will become more aware and educated. I pray that you will be ready for your returning missionary friend—ready to help him through the minefields of adjustments to his home culture.

# Section II
## Reentry Stories

Chapter Four

# *Mission Accomplished*

*"And they returned to Antioch after the task which God had sent them to do was accomplished"* (Acts 14:26).

Barnabas and Saul had just returned from Jerusalem. Excitement was coursing through their veins. They were full of reports from the Apostles of how the Good News had spread throughout Jerusalem and Judea and Samaria. And now, they were sure, Antioch would be the launching pad for the "uttermost parts."

Five men were put forward. But the Holy Spirit selected Barnabas and Saul. Their first stop was Cypress, where Barnabas grew up. For two years they moved from city to city, from country to country, guided by the Holy Spirit. Signs and wonders! Salvation for the Jews and the Greeks! Baptisms! The adrenalin was pumping!

Then they arrived at Attalia. And God said, "Go home! You've accomplished what I sent you to do!"

Do you think ambivalent feelings might have surged through their emotions? Might Paul and Barnabas have *argued* with God? "But, Lord, we've only just begun!" Zealous missionaries, they were! That we know for sure.

But, in obedience to the One they wanted to

please—the One who had called them to be soldiers, they went home. The cargo ship docked at Seleucia. Bone tired and weary, yet anxious to get home to see *you*, they took the next boat up the Orontes River to Antioch.

Paul probably got a few jobs making tents; Barnabas might have done some farming. They *"abode...a long time* there with the disciples." And "they gathered the church together and *rehearsed all* that God had done in and through them." They got back into their church work of *"teaching and preaching* in the company of many others."

I trust you can see when I have "supposition-ized" the story and when I have recorded the exact Word of God. Nothing I suppose is anti-Word of God. What I am trying to do is "flesh out" the story with possible details. These Bible characters were *real* people! Paul even once (at least it is once recorded) lamented, *"How come I can't travel with a wife like Peter and the others?"* (I Corinthians 9:5). Not too many studies of Paul include that Scripture!

I am glad for Hebrews 11, where God records what He remembers of His servants—only good! But for our sake, we need to see the perspective of the humanness of these people. We have almost "deified" our favorite Bible saints! We need to discard—rip off—the halos with which we have crowned Bible characters. Not only must Paul be understood by us as the one who said, *"I can do all things through Christ,"* but also the one who said, *"O wretched man that I am!"*

You may ask, "What point is he trying to make?" I'm glad you asked! We are at that point: We have placed that same tainted halo on the heads of our missionaries. We have almost "deified" the ones with reports of great accomplishments. And, unfortunately, we have stopped sending money to those who can show no tangible results.

Well! Your returning missionary friend is a *real* person. He is capable of every human thought and emotion. He is susceptible to every terror of the enemy and he is responsive to the guidance of the Holy Spirit. His body knows the frailty of human limitation and his spirit can soar uninhibited to the portals of heaven. (He can even lose a part of his tooth as I just did as I am typing these words!) During the days, weeks and months of reentry, your friend will be affected by the nine factors that determine the length of time reentry will take.

Your friend will face challenges in any one or more of the nine areas of stress discussed earlier. In the first story of this chapter, *Nine Months to "Feel" American Again,* the missionary relates to all nine of the areas of challenge! Because it is impossible to know what factors may affect your returning friend at one time or another, it is imperative that you become familiar with them all! And what you can do to support your friend during each time.

But neither can reentry support be divorced from the other five areas of care. Often the stress of reentry is directly tied to the lack of care in one or more of the other areas. In her story, *One Antique Piano For Sale,* this missionary lamented her lack of logistic support and how it affected her time of reentry.

Because many—in the church, in the agency, the missionary and the caregivers—are just learning all that is involved during this significant time of adjustment, mistakes can be made. Wrong reentry behavior patterns may be overlooked or ignored. Thus, you must become alert to the symptoms of one or more of the four wrong reentry behavior patterns. And, at the same time, try to focus on helping your friend reenter using the correct pattern! (I can hardly wait for you to read the final story in this chapter titled, *Just Do It!* It is wild! But please don't until you read the others!)

In guiding your friend through the reentry process, you want to make sure that none of the five steps are being neglected. Thus, as you relate with your returning friend, you must be aware of the interplay of these *thirty-four* aspects of concern! Don't become overwhelmed! Okay! So you just did! Pick yourself up. Dust yourself off and continue reading.

From time to time throughout the stories, the following summaries will appear as sidebars.

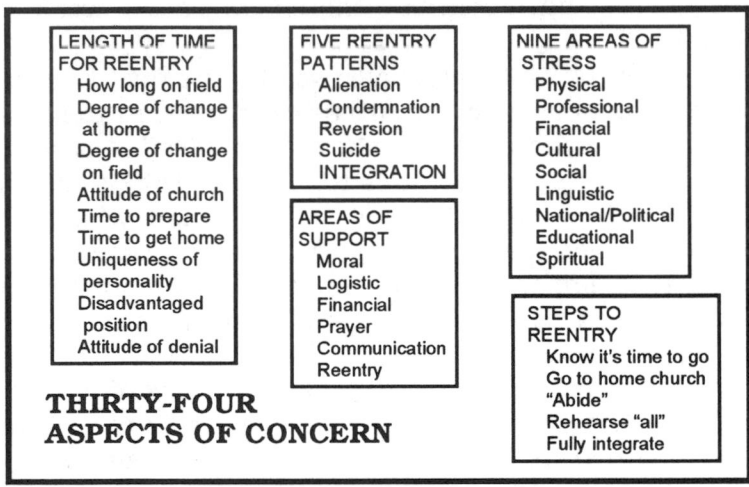

| LENGTH OF TIME FOR REENTRY | FIVE REENTRY PATTERNS | NINE AREAS OF STRESS |
|---|---|---|
| How long on field | Alienation | Physical |
| Degree of change at home | Condemnation | Professional |
| Degree of change on field | Reversion | Financial |
| Attitude of church | Suicide | Cultural |
| Time to prepare | INTEGRATION | Social |
| Time to get home | | Linguistic |
| Uniqueness of personality | AREAS OF SUPPORT | National/Political |
| Disadvantaged position | Moral | Educational |
| Attitude of denial | Logistic | Spiritual |
| | Financial | |
| **THIRTY-FOUR** | Prayer | STEPS TO REENTRY |
| **ASPECTS OF CONCERN** | Communication | Know it's time to go |
| | Reentry | Go to home church |
| | | "Abide" |
| | | Rehearse "all" |
| | | Fully integrate |

The following stories tell the tales of missionaries who heard their Master say, "You have accomplished what I sent you to do. Go home!" It doesn't take much reading-between-the-lines to discover those who were well cared for and those who floundered. The lessons you learn through these stories, of course, can apply to other reasons for coming home, also.

### NINE MONTHS TO "FEEL" AMERICAN AGAIN

I remember taking the globe from my dad's office and putting a finger on my hometown. I put my other finger on a village in Southeast Asia where I was to spend the next year of my life. The two locations were exactly opposite from one another. I would be as far away from home as I could possibly get. At the time I did not realize that, not only would I be physically far away, but I would also separate myself emotionally, psychologically and culturally from the home I had always known.

My role was to set up and run an office at a children's home. I would also teach English as a second language, and take care of infants who were too small to live at the orphanage.

To say the lifestyle was different is an understatement! There was no telephone, no mail, and no television. The pace of life was drastically slower than what I was accustomed to, but I did adapt. I was immersed in the culture. The only Americans I had daily contact with were the missionaries who ran the orphanage. English was only spoken at home. So I learned the local language. Hamburgers were not served. So I learned to eat rice and vegetables at every meal. Corn was the ice cream flavor in town. I learned to enjoy mango for dessert. I learned to not be particular about my dress or make-up. It became natural to wear my hair back every day as preventing lice was always a consideration.

But the real change in who I was came as I developed relationships with the people. I learned, after some initial adjusting, to look past our differences. I listened as they told me their personal stories of suffering. I laughed with them when I did something they found humorous. I fought the reaction to judge their ways and found myself caring deeply about the people. I found myself loving these children as if they were my own.

I did not realize how much I had changed until I returned the following year to the United States. I felt as if I had been in a time warp. All of my memories of home were a year old. My small town with one grocery store had almost doubled in size. There was a new supermarket, but I had not seen it come into being. To me it had just appeared. The post office had been relocated to a new area of town and was much more modern. My first visit to the new building was not a pleasant one. Less than twenty-four hours in the country and I had been summoned for jury duty!

I found the jet lag to be much more severe on the return to America. Nausea and dizziness plagued me the first week home. There was a fifteen-hour time difference, so I often found myself watching home videos of Southeast Asia in the middle of the night. During my third night home, an earthquake shook our house. I remember thinking that maybe I should have stayed in Asia! Since jet lag lasted about a week, I thought my adjustment back into American life would be similar in length. I had no idea that it would be nine months before I would "feel" like an American again.

My first purchase in America was not a new curling iron, but a rice cooker. My father had a bag of plain M&M's—my favorite—waiting for me, but they were too rich for me. What I really wanted was a nice, sweet slice of mango! I didn't enjoy the things that I once did. Even television seemed ridiculous. I could not sit still through a single show. As I observed the American way of life through new eyes, I decided that we were an "over-developed" nation. I missed "home." I missed speaking the language of my adopted people. At times I found myself reciting the language alone in the car. Where I had once desired someone to speak English with, I now desired a friend who could understand my new language.

I remember how much I looked forward to my first Sunday back at church. I couldn't wait to see everyone! I guess I wasn't prepared for how many things could change in just one year. The music minister was no longer there. The kids I used to babysit were so tall! I commented how much I liked someone's new car, not knowing they had owned it for more than nine months.

Everyone seemed very glad to see me. After an initial hug, I was usually met with the question, "How was your trip?" Trip? Two weeks to Chicago is a trip, not a year in Southeast Asia! Still, I tried to convey what the "trip" was like. A few seemed genuinely interested. Others politely listened, but it was obvious that they were expecting a one-word answer: "Good. It was a really good trip." Most simply did not have the time to understand what the last year of my life had been like. Instead, I had the task of understanding that their lives had gone on without me. The hole that my vacancy had left had been filled in.

This fact was made very clear to me as I began to learn about Mary. It seemed that each time I was reunited with an old friend I would be asked if I had met Mary. Who was Mary? "Oh, you have got to meet Mary!" I began to learn that Mary was a new youth sponsor. I had been a youth sponsor. Mary was on the mission board. I had been on the mission board. Mary had spent two years overseas. She had moved to town while I had been away. Everyone was sure that we would be "best friends," because we had so much in common. But the more I learned about Mary, the more defensive I began to feel. She had taken all of the positions I once held; and I felt, had taken the place I had held in people's hearts. I felt as though I had been replaced.

After a few days at home, my mother informed me that Mary was interested in renting our spare bedroom. That was the last straw. I finally told my mother how I felt. She was very understanding.

Mary and I did eventually become friends. It just took a little time for me to understand that people would need to make room in their lives for me again. But there was plenty of room for both Mary and me.

The grocery store was an overwhelming place. It had been a long time since I had seen a tile-floored market. I was used to dirt floors, fly-covered meat hanging in the open sun, and beggars following me around, hoping for a donation. The choices were tiring. Not only did I have to choose between Colgate and Crest, but there were ten different kinds of Colgate and six different kinds of Crest!

More difficult than this was walking through the baby section of a department store. My first month in Asia was the beginning of a large "baby boom" for the orphanage. Within a week we had three two-month-old infants to care for, yet we had no diapers, no baby seats, no swings, no pacifiers, hardly any supplies whatsoever. There were no diapers available in the country, as they do not use them. We used washcloths and cut zip-lock bags to use for plastic pants until proper diapers could be shipped to us.

A few months later we took in a set of ten-day-old triplets. I remember thinking what a wonderful baby shower these three-pound babies would have received in America. But there was no baby shower, no crib sets, no receiving blankets. The three shared a single crib for the first few weeks. We had none of the most basic things that preemies would need.

As I strolled through American department stores, it was hard to fight the tears. I saw so many things that I would have loved to give "my" babies. So many things we had needed but could not get. At one point during my reentry adjustment, I decided to take sewing lessons. For months I faithfully worked on matching rompers for the triplets, only to have them lost in the mail without ever being worn.

I learned much during my reentry experience. I learned that it was not wrong to have things, only to take them for granted. I learned that people wanted to hear about my experiences, but they had difficulty relating to them. Many could not imagine living on the other side of the world, let alone know how to go about understanding it. I had begun to assume that people did not want to hear my stories. For example, I was asked to share my testimony during a missions fellowship meeting. I brought my slide presentation. I quickly narrated a few of the slides. The rest I simply set to music. I raced through the pictures, "knowing" that they were all terribly bored. Later, many shared their disappointment that I had not taken more time and told them more about the people they had seen. I learned that there really are people that want to hear "all about it." I needed to give them the opportunity.

One of my biggest frustrations was with myself. I did not understand why I was sometimes unhappy in America. I had missed home so much when I was in Asia! Now that I was home, I missed Asia. Why couldn't I be happy where I was? My answer came to me during prayer. The Lord gently spoke to me that I will never be completely happy anywhere on this earth because it is not my home. My home is in Heaven. That is the place that my very soul longs for. And that is where my happiness will be complete. (See Hebrews 11:10.)

FOR FURTHER UNDERSTANDING
A more classic story of positive reentry would be difficult to write. Sally's insights on the gamut of reentry struggles forms a grid over which you can lay understanding and solutions to the problems of returning missionaries.

Note that for her being one year on the field, it took *nine months* to again feel like she was home. It is impossible to be definitive, but that ratio of time is not at all unusual.

Did you catch a very positive attitude in her story? Yes, she had a good experience abroad. But in coming home, she knew it would take some real effort to fit back in. Reread her third paragraph. This was her attitude in adapting to her Asian culture. She used this same matter-of-fact posture in her reentry adjustment.

A key sentence in this whole story is: "I finally told my mother how I *felt*." We are emotional beings. And those feelings need to be expressed. Yes, in the confidence of a close friend; not blared out as a statement of condemnation to the public at large. This is that second level of debriefing so needed.

**STEPS TO REENTRY**
Know it's time to go
Go to home church
"Abide"
Rehearse "all"
Fully integrate

An equally key sentence followed: "She (her mother) was very understanding." The confidant your missionary friend needs must be a good listener, a clear-headed evaluator of human relationships and one who can share an appropriate word at an appropriate time. *"A word fitly spoken is like apples of gold in settings of silver"* (Proverbs 25:11).

FOR FURTHER ACTION
• Following are the nine areas of reentry stress mentioned in Chapter Three in which returning missionaries face challenges. Reread her story. Jot down (or underline in the story) phrases that highlight her specific issues and/or how she dealt with them. I have given a few examples. There are many, many more!

Physical -
Professional - *I had been replaced!*
Material -
Cultural - *All my memories were a year old.*
Social -
Linguistical - *I missed speaking my new language.*
National/Political - *I was summoned for jury duty.*
Educational -
Spiritual - *Heaven is my home!*

• Let the phrases you write form a guideline for a discussion with your study group. Talk about how this missionary overcame these issues of clashing cultures.

• Think of the specific conditions in which your returning missionary has lived. Contrast those with the conditions to which he will be returning. How will you help him overcome these issues of clashing cultures?

• Is there (are *YOU*) a confidant available to listen to the heart of your returning missionary?

### ONE ANTIQUE PIANO FOR SALE

When I returned to southern Florida after two years as a missionary in the Middle East, the Lord was extremely gracious. There I was, a completely changed person with totally different perspectives, in a nation that had changed in other ways. For instance, AIDS had made the headlines in my absence, and my church had a new pastor.

I had grown closer to the Lord in my time overseas, learning to depend on Him alone. Yet people I had known at home, who had even been involved in my ministry, had changed too. I had been disappointed that my home fellowship leaders had, after only a few months, abandoned their commitment to copy and mail out my monthly prayer letter, without replacing themselves. God did raise up a dear sister whom I had never met to take over for them.

Another sister had committed to managing the rental of my house and studio. I found upon my return that the tenant still in the studio had not paid rent for five months, and it and my house were trashed. I was not only sorely disappointed, but broke as well. The account I had left in her care to pay the property bills and mortgages was depleted. But God covered the whole situation. I got my old job back and, on my dad's advice, was able to refinance the house—lowered the payments, too! I laughed for joy all the way home from the bank that day!

Still, I was brokenhearted that not only did my friend not care for the property I had been unable to sell before I had to leave, but worse that that, she backslid and divorced her husband. Also, another Christian couple to whom I had loaned my beautiful, hand-carved, antique piano, to be enjoyed and cared for, had divorced, and *sold* it! I felt angry, sorrowful, and betrayed, all at the same time. I learned that people change when you are gone. And I had changed. But how divergent were the directions of change.

Although my pre-field training had somewhat prepared me for the reentry phenomenon, the details of the actual experience were quite unforeseeable. Changes were perhaps a gradual process—like the trashing of my house, but because I missed the process, the "freeze frame" effect of seeing it upon my return was a quantum leap! It was very disorienting, even shocking. My intellect had known that these sorts of things were possible, but my emotions had not had any experience in dealing with the reality of the changes.

I also remember mourning the economic waste and spiritual nonchalance we Americans display, as compared to other countries (where Christians pray for us because of the spiritual warfare surrounding our affluence). In my adopted host country, we'd had lemon juice, olive oil, and sometimes mayonnaise for salad dressing. Upon my return, I froze in the supermarket, transfixed at the long row of salad dressings! (I quickly learned to "abound" again; I chose the fat-free Ranch.)

I had just left a war zone—complete with tanks, bomb shelters and gas masks, where one always watched for airplane overhead because death could descend unexpectedly. When I returned to Florida, I continued to notice airplanes for some time. For a while, I had to make a conscious effort to rethink the very real anxiety that would initially wash over me each time one flew over.

The international Christians I knew overseas were a close-knit community and no one seemed to notice denominational differences. Can we say that in Florida? Here, like the peevish spoiled children we can be, whole churches have split over picky, trivial matters. If someone believes that baptism should be by a particular method, there are any number of churches to choose from which do it that way. In our Middle East community, the "sprinklers" and the "dunkers" and the "speakers-in-tongues" and the"non-speakers-in-tongues" were from all the different countries and glad for each other's fellowship, as we met from house to house. I think heaven will feel something like those gatherings: *"...from every nation and all tribes and peoples and tongues, standing before the Throne"* (Revelation 7:9).

In the shell-pocked medical/dental clinic where I worked, I had seen Muslims, Christians, and tough Jewish soldiers alike reduced to simple humanity in their common fear of a visit to the dentist, as well as their common need for Jesus. We passed out tracts and Bibles in three languages, continuing to share the Gospel in the dark when the electricity failed, as it frequently did.

Not many people I knew in Miami could relate to these experiences, and words failed to explain to others much of the stress of my reentry. I had braced myself for tough conditions on the mission field, but having lived there long enough to get used to them, I thought little of my need to prepare for the tough conditions upon returning to my sending nation.

But, again, the Lord was indeed gracious. To my delight and relief, a few of my former classmates and "friends of friends" were also just returning from the worldwide mission field. These were people who could really relate! Some good friends opened their home for group meetings, rather like a returned-missionary support group. I put together a questionnaire to assess our collective experience with being sent, supported, and received back again. With variation but without exception, the consensus was that the senders/receivers had a vital, two-part role in our reentry adjustment:

1) To help meet our basic needs for transportation, shelter, food and fellowship; and

2) To give us opportunities to speak, and then really listen.

My reentry was greatly eased by caring family and friends who gathered together with me so that I could debrief, by the Lord's keeping my job available for me upon my return, and by my involvement with the re-turned-missionary group.

FOR FURTHER UNDERSTANDING

Probably the most profound statement of this story is in the middle: *"My intellect had known that these sorts of things were possible, but my emotions had not had any experience in dealing with the reality of the changes."*

This reveals a tremendously critical insight which can help you understand why your friend often struggles with reentry. The human being is a truly intricately woven fabric of body, soul and spirit...of mind, will and emotions. Bringing all of these faculties into sync sometimes requires the help of a caring, giving reentry support person—*YOU!*

The focus of her story is on *changes.* She said it in her first paragraph: *"There I was, a completely changed person, in a nation that had changed."* Change is bombarding your "changed" returning missionary on four levels of culture: World, National, Community and Personal. Note in the first paragraph how she places a national level change (AIDS) in the same breath as a very local community change (new pastor).

Reread her story, placing a W, N, C or P in the margin to indicate the level of change stated. (I found twenty-two clearly stated statements of change! You may find even more.) Some in the "personal culture" will indicate a change in her; others will indicate a change in her friends.

Now reread the story again! (YES, if we are really

going to understand the issues of a returning missionary *and* be there to help them reenter, it will take a lot of work!) Place a + or a - sign next to the letters, indicating whether that change was positive or negative. For, we want to emphasize the positive to help avert the negative.

Addressing another critical issue of reentry, note her words: *"I had braced myself for tough conditions on the mission field, but...I had thought little of my need to prepare for the tough conditions upon returning."* As has been stated elsewhere (it bears repeating), this is a common precursor to difficulty upon reentry. It's another way to say, "What's the *big deal?* I'm just going home!" But, as you are reading these stories, you are learning what a "big deal" reentry really is. Thus, days, weeks or months ahead of your missionary coming home, "force" him to take some time to think about the thirty-four issues of reentry.

Again: Is it work? YES! But the alternative to reentry preparation is the sad state of too many missionaries being lost to one or another level of suicide. (Review these thoughts again in Chapter Three.)

In stark contrast to the sadness of reentry "horror stories" is the simplicity of the Biblical solution. Note the consensus of the survey she took among returning missionaries: 1) Help us with our basic needs; 2) Allow us to debrief. The answer to the reentry process— as complicated as it may seem—is as simple as that! And it is recorded just as simply in Scripture: 1) They abode a long time; 2) They rehearsed all (Acts 14:27-28).

STEPS TO REENTRY
Know it's time to go
Go to home church
"Abide"
Rehearse "all"
Fully integrate

The insights we can learn from her story are profound. Notice another of her statements: *"People who could really relate!"* There is a beautiful Scripture in II Corinthians 1:4. God, the Holy Spirit *"comforts us in all our tribulation, that we may comfort others in their time of need by the comfort we have received of God."* When we have learned how to receive the comfort that the Holy Spirit is so willing to give, we are able to be the instruments of God to comfort others with that comfort we have received of Him.

Now, it is true that the closer our experience has been to that of the one we are trying to comfort, the easier it is to express empathy, exude warmth and show respect for what they are going through. However, life's adventures don't usually fit into such nice, neat packages of parallel experiences. Thus, we must draw heavily on God, the Giver of Wisdom in relating with our returning missionary friends.

Let me illustrate: Have you ever flown in a small float plane where, at 9,000 feet altitude, all you see from horizon to horizon is jungle following the curve of the earth—except for a narrow ribbon of muddy water? The pilot you are sitting next to says, "Keep an eye on that river. It is our guide to direction and our landing strip in an emergency." A thunderstorm directly ahead forces you to alter your course. You lose sight of the river! The raindrops pop like firecrackers on the windshield. The wind rattles your aircraft like a skeleton of dry bones. It only took five minutes to skirt the storm. The pilot resets his bearings. But where is the river?! An eon of time passes in the fifteen minutes before you again see that "beautiful" muddy river.

That little sketch of a story was easy for me to write. It happened to me! But, can *you* identify with it? Can you imagine the total bombardment to my senses that transpired in those twenty minutes?

Now I am home. You are driving me through a run-down section of a city unfamiliar to me. You make a wrong turn. After a few minutes, you admit we are lost! I react in fear—not so much to our present situation as to the memory of my flight over the jungle.

You now have the opportunity to yell at me, "You

crazy nut! Don't worry! I'll get you back on the right road." Or, you can realize that this probably involves something greater than your driving. And you are able to "comfort me."

FOR FURTHER ACTION

• Educate yourself. Listen—really listen—to your missionary friends as they tell their stories. Get them in a one-on-one situation where they will tell you the in-between-the-lines stuff—their feelings, their fears, their concerns. Pry; prod; dig out all that they want to say, but are afraid to. Let them expose all to the light of your hearing and to the Light of His Word.

• You can learn from missionaries who have just recently returned home. But you can also learn from missionaries who have been home for years! (Just now as I wrote that little sketch of my airplane ride, many of the emotions played through my system again. Yet that happened to me twenty-nine years ago!)

• Write to your missionary friend. Ask him about his current Logistics Support Team. Does he know they are doing their job? Ask him if it would be appropriate for you to contact them to make sure. Does he have a Core Team[1] leader you could check with? Is there an

---

[1] Refer to the Case Study sections of our book, *Serving As Senders,* for a complete understanding of how these liaison team leaders function. However, briefly in this context: It is our strong recommendation that every missionary (individual or family) have three to four people who take the leadership of their support team. They serve as the link between the missionary and the larger group of caregivers in the six areas of care. They also relate with the church's mission leadership, keeping all lines of communication open. (A responsible church missions leadership will relate with the mission agency, but you can check to make sure they do!)

area in which you could lend a hand to his logistics support so that when he comes home, all of his business matters will be in order?

• Keep a calendar of the reentry dates of your missionary friends. Write to them during the last several months. Begin prompting them to think about home. Ask what you can do to make their transition smooth. Make suggestions of what you would be able to do, if they want you to.

• Form (become part of) a reentry team. Preparation for reentry begins even before your friend leaves for the field by all being educated about its importance. Reentry preparation continues while your friend is on the field by your helping him keep informed about "home" and maintaining a proper bi-cultural attitude. (There is good and bad in all cultures. Help him focus on both.)

However, when a date for return is set, the reentry team must shift into high gear. For, though the two needs of a returning missionary can be so simply stated (basic life needs and a listening "ear"), the work to accomplish those goals can be quite labor-intensive.

## JOB HUNTING IN THE WORKPLACE

As we stood on the hillside, looking out over the valley to the distant villages, tears filled our eyes. We stood silently, unable to speak, wondering whenever we would return to "our hills." These had become *our* hills after I first visited the villages with some senior missionaries. And now, fifteen years later, we were preparing to leave.

It had not been a decision taken lightly. We had arrived on the mission field intending to stay a lifetime. Two of our three children had been born there, so it came as a shock to realize that God was asking us to return to our homeland. It was hard for the children to understand also—especially our daughter, who realized she would not graduate from the boarding school she had attended her whole life. What would it mean to make such a change—leaving boarding school and learning to live again as a whole family? This would be a very different lifestyle from just being together for school holidays. And what would it be like to attend public school as opposed to private Christian boarding school? It was scary to say the least. And what would we do, anyway? We had no home of our own, so where would we live? Would we seek an opening for further ministry, or go back to secular work? How would we fit into our home church again?

Praise God for people on the Church Missions Committee who did all they could to help make the adjustment easier for us. They rented a fully furnished house for our first few months, close to schools and church. Many of the different groups in the church filled our pantry. Money was made available for school uniforms. Times of sharing were organized with both the missions committee and church leadership. One of the home groups which had "adopted" us sought to include us in their activities. They also helped in practical ways, such as taking me to the wharf with a huge trailer to collect our belongings, and offering to stay with the children so we could both attend meetings.

Slowly the weeks turned into months. Sometimes it felt good to be home; other times—not! I well remember walking along the road and suddenly being overwhelmed and wondering to myself, "Why am I here? Lord, I want to go back where I belong." Initially, there were meetings to speak at. But as time went on, this became harder and harder, and we felt it right for me to look for secular work. But, I had been out of my trade for twenty years, and things had changed drastically in that time. We looked in the local paper for a position, but wondered who would want me when I felt so out of touch. It seemed too big an adjustment to make, and I shrunk from the idea. All of this made it harder to accept the fact that we were going to stay, and many an evening ended in prayers and tears as we asked God, "Why?" Surely He had something better for us to do.

One day I was prompted to make an appointment with a firm that had advertised several times in the paper. As they listened to my story of why I had no current job or reference letter, they looked at each other and laughed. "We have been praying for a Christian to come and work on the floor—and God sent us a missionary!" Instantly, I had the job.

It was scary to start work in a factory again. But at 7:30 the next morning, I was there, feeling out of place and unskilled in a trade that had progressed without me. However, the understanding and generosity of the boss overwhelmed me. I was able to regain knowledge and confidence that enabled me to eventually launch out into my own business. I had finally adjusted!

FOR FURTHER UNDERSTANDING
You may wonder why I grouped this story in the *Mission Accomplished*, rather than in the *Home, Not by Choice* section. Early on in the story, though the emotions lagged far behind the knowledge, they had heard God say—Go home! Had they stayed longer, it is impossible to even imagine the consequences. Though it took more than a year for them to be fully integrated, it was certainly a wise move to obey His direction about when to return home.

STEPS TO REENTRY
Know it's time to go
Go to home church
"Abide"
Rehearse "all"
Fully integrate

Reread the second paragraph. From your perspective, try to answer the questions he asked of himself. How did you do? Does this give you some idea of the reentry challenges your missionary faces?

Have you experienced a job change? In the same field of work? Or into another? A downsizing of your company? Being without work for a month or two? Getting back into the swing of things. Maybe you can remember the feelings of going back to work after a two-week vacation. Now feel the emotion of his struggle to reenter the secular work place after twenty years!

FOR FURTHER ACTION

• Job hunting begins in prayer. Whether ministry-related or secular, it is critical for your returning missionary friend in beginning a new career, to know that he is pursuing the work God has for him. Pray for him; pray with him. Can you do some job hunting for him even before he arrives home?

I remember being at a point of uncertainty in job selection. I even let a number of *good* opportunities pass by! Sometimes, in the days after, I did wonder "Why?" But then the phone rang! One hour into the appointment, we were accepting an emergency need in Brazil! Within ten weeks we were gone!

• Look at the details of reentry care mentioned in the early paragraphs of his story. Add them to your checklist. Verify with your returning missionary friend the areas in which he needs help. Help!

### WALKING IN GOD'S WILL

I kept thinking that I would wait until I finished my reentry to tell about it, but since I'm still trying to figure out what the Lord wants me to do, I better not wait any longer.

Obviously, since I haven't found a good job yet, that is a big concern for me. I had thought that I would get a job at the post office right away after my return to the States, but I've only been interviewed by them recently.

Conflicting with that, I now have an opportunity to go back to college to work on my Master's degree in counseling and guidance in the fall, so I'm not sure if I should take a position with the post office even if it is offered.

I have to admit that after I failed to find substantial work right after I returned in August, I was hesitant to pursue a new career vocation. I wanted to be free to go back to Eastern Europe this June to be with my former students for their graduation.

Although I grew up in Los Angeles, I haven't lived here for any length of time for over twenty-four years. I still don't feel at home here, though my parents have done everything to make me feel welcome. I keep wishing I could go back to Seattle where I lived for twenty years. The problem is that I haven't lived there for the past six years, and I don't feel too sure whether I fit in there anymore, either!

NINE AREAS OF STRESS
Physical
Professional
Financial
Cultural
Social
Linguistic
National/Political
Educational
Spiritual

Since I am still single at age fifty, I haven't felt like I belong to any particular group, but now that feeling is intensified. Because I am somewhat of a timid person in new situations, several attempts to fit into groups at churches have been unsuccessful, also. I feel like I am on the fringes of every situation and community.

Having been intensely involved in ministry opportunities in Eastern Europe and Seattle before that, I felt pretty burned out when I got back. For a while I was happy to remain on the fringes and not be involved in ministry. Sometimes it gave a fresh opportunity to grow closer to the Lord in my own way, but sometimes it tested my faith when I was so unsure of what the Lord wanted me to do.

Over time, the Holy Spirit has kept working in me, giving me the desire to serve the Lord more actively. I've been through a wilderness time of searching and uncertainty, but now the Lord is helping to draw me closer to Him in anticipation of where He will lead me next.

FOR FURTHER UNDERSTANDING
It appears that many of this returning missionary's

frustrations related to not knowing what the Lord had for his future. Though he knew it was time to come home, when plans didn't work out, and several alternatives presented themselves, it was difficult for him to find direction. The snowballing effect of this scenario can be devastating.

**STEPS TO REENTRY**
Know it's time to go
Go to home church
"Abide"
Rehearse "all"
Fully integrate

Reread his story. Note (underline) the areas of his life that he suggests were affected by his lack of knowledge. You may need to do some reading between-the-lines to see them. Of course, in relating with your own friend, you would not surmise. You would get him to verbalize his thoughts and feelings. You would pray with him for clear direction and patience.

FOR FURTHER ACTION

• A reentry caregiver has little control over most of the nine variables that seem to affect the length of time the reentry process will take. But *your* readiness to help is certainly within your control.

**LENGTH OF TIME FOR REENTRY**
How long on field
Degree of change at home
Degree of change on field
Attitude of church
Time to prepare
Time to get home
Uniqueness of personality
Disadvantaged position
Attitude of denial

As you prepare yourself for the return of your friend, you need to be diligent in the details you have learned about reentry support. Not the least being to write to him during those last three months before his return, making sure he is giving some thought to life back "home."

• In that everything seemed to work out for this missionary (He did return to the field!), is there anything you see that you could have said/done to make him feel more comfortable in the decision-making process? Hint: Which of the six areas of care seemed to be lacking?

**AREAS OF SUPPORT**
Moral
Logistic
Financial
Prayer
Communication
Reentry

• There is a clear distinction (though often difficult to observe) between *aloneness* and *loneliness*. This missionary made several statements that could be interpreted either way. Reread the story. Underscore those statements. How would you approach your missionary friend to ascertain whether he has found that godly ability to be alone, or if he needs some help in that area?

## OUR CORE GROUP COVERED US

Regarding our reentry, you know firsthand how well our home church family in Sacramento took care of us. There was only one unknown, but it was a biggie—that was a job! After a couple of months of reentry and helping at the church office, I started a job search that seemed to go nowhere. I decided to set a deadline for looking outside of the Sacramento area. Even our missions pastor was frustrated by the apparent dead ends. The same thing had happened with a previous couple. They had found a job in a neighboring county, but their leaving the support of their home church truncated their reentry process with uncomfortable consequences.

We personally knew other missionaries experiencing the same problem. One pastor, having spent sixteen years on the field, ended up as a substitute teacher for six years before he found a pastorate. Another friend, who had been on the field for four years, ended up answering phones for minimum wage! So we were particularly thankful when God did elect to keep us here by providing a job. I started work on the day I had circled on the calendar to start looking out of state. Being able to stay at our home church was vital to us.

Our core group covered us until we felt "reentered." Our special gratitude is for the family who opened up their home to the five of us without any implied time limit. Also, the core group had solicited three additional months of support from our financial supporters for the reentry period, and at a higher level to cover the greater expenses in the U.S. We were unaware that they had done that. We ended up only needing one of the additional months that had been given, but we really *needed* that one month. Not having the pressure of house or apartment expenses while unemployed eased our reentry. Another major blessing was that someone gave us a car. For Californians, that was a big help.

We were blessed in many other ways, with things that some people might consider "little things"—but they were BIG to us. Our core group enlarged a picture of us and had it on display at the church for a month before we came back. The caption went something like this: "These are our missionaries to the Philippines. They are returning next month. Please welcome them back. PLEASE don't ask them if this is their first time at our church!" Another thing that blessed Sandy was that one member of our core group worked at a grocery store. He offered to go with her to the store the first time, so that she would have someone to lean on if she got overwhelmed. (We had been forewarned in our pre-field training that the choices could send us into shock! Other missionaries on the field had confirmed this.)

After hearing stories from other returning missionaries, we realize that our prepared and dedicated core group made all the difference!

FOR FURTHER UNDERSTANDING
Their words, "Our core group covered us until we felt 'reentered,'" are music to my ears! As part of a reentry caregivers team, your work is *not* over until your missionary feels "reentered!"

We trust you are familiar with our book, *SERVING AS SENDERS: How to Care for Your Missionaries*. At the end of each chapter, we placed a segment of a Case Study of a church in Sacramento, California that was sending out their second missionary family.

Though in this book we have kept names and places

confidential, with Lou and Sandy's permission, we wanted to emphasize and recognize the work of their support team. The story you just read is the "final chapter" of their care for this missionary family.

To emphasize the point that their "smooth" (There were some bumps!) reentry was the result of teamwork that began long before they even left for the field, I am including that Case Study of their sending team:

A CASE STUDY IN REENTRY SUPPORT

One of the senders team we've been following in our case studies reports:

My wife Teri and I are the Core Group leaders of reentry support for Lou and Sandy. The only experience we have regarding our responsibility was the short time Lou and Sandy were with us between their field training in Mexico and actually going to the Philippines. Because their time in Mexico was only three months, there didn't seem to be any of the major culture shock or stress problems. Still, when they came back from Mexico, we worked to make things as normal as possible for them. This was good practice for us!

Oddly enough, the process started before they left for their field training. It began with a commitment on their part to keep those of us at home informed of what was going on in their lives in Mexico. We were kept up-to-date on prayer needs and trying situations in their training and in their "new" culture. We were told about the victories and the defeats. They kept us informed about their daughter Marlies and how she was growing and how all of them were adjusting to living with their host Mexican family. A key to this communication was that it was regular. We were "with them" as they progressed through the twelve weeks.

And that paid off. When they got back home they

didn't have to feel pressured to condense or just hit the highlights of their experiences. And we hadn't missed so many of the little things that had contributed to who they now were. There was already a group of us who had "gone through it" with them, families with whom they could feel comfortable in rehashing some of their experiences. This detailed debriefing proved as important to them as it was informative to us.

Another aspect of their reentry support was to attend to their physical needs. Before Lou and Sandy left for Mexico, they had sold most of their household things and had vacated their duplex. So there was a need for a place to stay for about seven weeks until their departure for the Philippines. Initially there was the chance they might be able to house-sit for a family that was going to be out of town. As that hope faded and eventually disappeared, Teri and I felt that we should open our home to them. There were many things that contributed to our volunteering. We already knew them well and knew that our lifestyles were compatible. The Lord had blessed us with a large enough house that eight of us could live in it comfortably (including a kitchen large enough for both wives). There was an extra room that could be just for Lou and Sandy, while Marlies could stay in our daughter's room. And, most importantly, we all prayed about it and felt that the Lord was saying, "Yes!"

We were aware that a lot of people might want to spend time with Lou and Sandy before they left for the Philippines. We planned a potluck reception after church their first Sunday home from Mexico.

Because we knew that there were quite a number of their friends that would like to share a meal or spend an evening with them, we decided to develop an appointment/social calendar so they could budget their time. We prepared a letter that was sent to the other Core Group members and all support members expressing Lou and Sandy's desire to spend time with those who wished to visit. It also explained their need for time to take care of unfinished business and to keep rested. The letter was sent out well in advance of their return. Teri acted as their appointment secretary. Lou gave us directions on how full to make their calendar and what days they already had planned for other things.

The rest was simply working with the people who called so that everyone could spend some time with them. It made things easier for us and even more enjoyable for Lou and Sandy when we could get a couple of families together at the same time. The letter proved to be successful in that Lou and Sandy were able to accomplish their three goals of visiting, doing business and resting.

The room we were able to provide for them was our den. We rearranged the furniture, brought in a bed and a chest of drawers and put a lock on the door so they could have privacy. They had their own keys to our house so they could come and go as they pleased. Even though they still had their own car, they were free to also use one of ours when they went in separate directions.

We have lived with other people at various times during our marriage, but I don't remember it ever being so tension-free. I think the major factor in this good living situation was that Lou and Sandy were doing exactly what God would have them do in preparing for the mission field and we as a reentry support team were doing exactly what God would have us do. He had prepared all of us to live together—for a while at least. And, as the widow from Zarephath who provided hospitality for Elijah found, the Spirit of God rested on our house.

Though our greater task will be when Lou and Sandy return on their furlough, we have learned a lot from this experience. Reentry support doesn't begin when the cross-cultural worker returns home. It starts before they leave. It continues while they are gone. And *accelerates* when they return. While they are in the Philippines we are keeping in close contact with them so that when they return there will be a group of us who are not "cultural strangers" to them. We will be able to relate immediately with them as they begin their debriefing.

FOR FURTHER ACTION
- Go thou and do likewise!

### A LITTLE PERSECUTION MIGHT BE USEFUL

We had never lived as a married couple in America. Our two children were born in Eastern Europe. The elder, though only four, was fluent in two languages.

NINE AREAS OF STRESS
Physical
Professional
Financial
Cultural
Social
Linguistic
National/Political
Educational
Spiritual

Before I got married I was a foreign language teacher in a public school in my European home country. Upon our return to the U.S., I was a housewife and mother of two preschoolers. We didn't have an official mission sending agency, but rather were sent out through my husband's church. It was a big help that we were able to plug right into a church upon our return, even though it was a sister church in another city. A number of the leadership were from my husband's home church.

Our first week back, we were staying with some people in a wealthy suburb of the city and one of my first trips to the grocery store caused me some shock. I spent $25 for just a few items. I knew our income had not changed, since we were still on mission support, and I knew that if I could not find a cheaper way to do things, we would be in serious financial danger.

The Lord answered before I even prayed, because in the neighborhood where we were going to be living, there was a discount grocery store very much the same as the one I shopped at in Europe! My first trip there was such a joy—putting a quarter into the grocery cart to be able to use it, seeing the items in boxes down the aisles, having to bag my own groceries (and bring my bags from home to do it). All of this was so familiar to me. I felt like I had "come home." And the prices were so low that we have been able to live on close to the same budget we had in Europe.

When we first moved into our temporary apartment, there was a dryer. What a luxury this was. I could not believe all the time I saved by simply throwing the clothes in a dryer, and not having to hang them on a clothesline. This gave me more time to talk on the telephone. In Eastern Europe, we had a telephone, but most of the people in the church didn't. It was considered a luxury, and as local calls were costly to an average family, they rarely used their telephones. Now at home, I found myself talking on the telephone many times a day, sometimes to the same person! I had a very difficult time adjusting to this social custom.

Then I saw someone driving a car and talking on a telephone! This was completely foreign to me. My first thought was, "That looks dangerous!" (Experience is now proving it is!) But then I thought, "If people can make phone calls from the car, that must give them more time in another area; for example, time with their family, time to read a good book—things like that." But I soon discovered that, for a country with so many "time-saving" devices, Americans are the busiest people in the world! Where does all that extra, saved time go? It's still a mystery to me!

### Relationships

The first year home I felt very isolated. Although we were going to a very good church, I felt that most of those relationships were rather superficial. It was easy to make friends here, but it was more like having many acquaintances, not friends. Though we lived in an apartment complex, we could go days without seeing our neighbors. Now we live in a rented house, and we have more contact with our neighbors. And yet, there is not the close, daily interacting, like meeting someone in the elevator, at the local grocery store, or walking to do errands.

I had a real struggle within my heart once we decided to stay here. I desperately missed the people and the lifestyle of our mission location. One wise missionary woman told me that until my heart becomes knit to the people here, I would continue to look back with longing. A year and a half later, I'm just beginning to sense that I have some friends, and there are some friendships I'm excited about developing. Finally, the Lord has helped me to accept where He has led us, and not argue with Him about it anymore. Friendships take time, no matter where you live. It just seems that with the busy pace of life here, it takes a bit longer than in other places.

Here is a real socio-linguistic issue! We had grown accustomed to the formality of our ministry culture. There are distinct divisions between people and your relationship to them. For instance, you would address a stranger as "Pan" or "Pani," which literally means "Lord" or "Lady." And you refer to them as such throughout the conversation. For instance, "Would (my) lord like more coffee?" You would address someone who was an older person, yet a good family friend, as "uncle" or "auntie." If it were a very good friend, you would address them as "Uncle Jack" or "Auntie Anna." And rarely, if ever, would a child address a grownup by his or her first name alone. That was considered impolite.

When we arrived home, we could not get used to the informality we found here. Everyone wanted our children to call them by their first names, even though we (let alone our children) hardly knew them! We taught our children to say "Mr." and "Mrs." because it seemed like too great a change to go from such formality, to first-name basis with every grownup! The longer we are here, the more we are recognizing how formal it is, but we want our children to continue to use the "Mr." and "Mrs." It seems to us to be a good balance between the two cultures.

**Transportation**
One difficult cultural adjustment for me was the lack of public transportation. In Eastern Europe we didn't have a car the last few years we lived there. We were used to taking a bus or walking everywhere. Once we arrived in the U.S., someone graciously gave us a car to use, for which we were very thankful. The apartment where we lived was on a city bus line, but the problem was that the bus didn't go to all the places we needed to go! And the area where we lived was not conducive to walking. The two modes of transportation I was most accustomed to—walking and riding a city bus—were basically ruled out. It was "get in the car and drive," or stay home!

Now that we live downtown, there are many more places to which we can walk, and we can take buses if we need to. The funny thing is, someone donated a second car for us to use, although neither of us saw the need for it. We were quite content with one car. Neither of us had even prayed for a second car and yet someone donated it with us in mind. So we each have a car to use, but we still do a lot of walking!

**Material goods**
We were blessed to see how the Lord provided for us

upon returning home. We came back with no furniture and no household goods. We had brought only some clothing and books and pictures. The Lord laid it on people's hearts to donate furniture and linens and lamps for our use. One missions-minded church even invited us to a mission conference. Part of the conference was a "shower" for the missionary ladies. We were given things that we had written on a wish list. What a huge encouragement this was.

I made a list of all the ways the Lord has provided for us since our return. I am in awe of His graciousness to us. When I am tempted to feel sorry for myself because we had left almost everything on the mission field, I simply pull out my list and remind myself of how much the Lord has provided for us, and how all of our needs have been met. I time and again declare that He is a faithful God!

In the abundance, there are yet little habits that remain. We were used to the mission field way of life, which meant not wasting anything. If you had left-overs from one meal, they went into the soup for the next day. When my husband started working at the church office, he became a daily curiosity. For one, he always brought his lunch from home, and usually it was last night's leftovers from dinner. He was amazed at how often Americans go out for lunch! He noticed that he was the only one who used the microwave to heat up his lunch. Other people noticed too, because his lunches were quite aromatic.

Also, he washed his Styrofoam cup and plastic silverware in order to reuse them, which was unheard of. After all, the whole reason for such things is so that you *don't* have to wash them! But he automatically thought, "What a waste!" Fortunately (or unfortunately), we are becoming more accustomed to this habit. Sometimes we even use paper plates when we have many mouths to feed!

### Christian "patriotism"

One social aspect, which surprised us upon returning to the U.S., was the Christian patriotism present in many believers. During one 10-hour car ride we searched the radio dial to find some Christian radio stations. We were dismayed to hear so much talk of politics on Christian radio, and comparatively little teaching or music. The talk seemed to equate patriotism with Christianity—in an exaggerated way. We were surprised to hear so many people talk of the "founding fathers, and the Biblical principles this country was founded on," etc. It seemed as if people considered the Constitution to be part of the Bible, or vice-versa.

What made all this hard to digest was that we had spent eleven years in several places where the government had no particularly Christian history and had for many of those eleven years been Marxist and opposed to the Gospel! Yet the Christians there had a vibrant and fruitful faith, embarrassingly richer than our own, in some respects. After all, the early church was in the same position. They faced opposition and persecution of all kinds. The "founding fathers" were 1600 years away from being born and the "principles this country was founded on" were an equal number of years away from being imagined. Yet the church did well! The church in Acts didn't need to quote Washington, Adams, Jefferson or Lincoln. They used the Bible, and so can we. What's the big deal if some president or congressman disagrees with us?

One bizarre outcome of all this is that occasionally we find ourselves almost hoping for disaster! Or rather, the return to the basics of our faith that some catastrophic event might bring. "An economic collapse might even do us some good," we find ourselves thinking. "A little persecution on the federal level might be kind of useful in emptying some seats on Sunday, occupied by the social seekers."

In short, we found that our faith had grown so used to a certain amount of adversity that we needed opposition or difficulty to feel at home. We no longer knew how to deal with prosperity, nor could we identify with a church that seemed to think extreme, continuous prosperity as the norm.

FOR FURTHER UNDERSTANDING
Is there a lesson to learn from another culture? Is there a connection between a more formal way of addressing a person and a respect for that person?

Consider: Was the giving of a second car to their advantage? Or did it contribute to the acclimation to a more affluent society? How long will it be before he doesn't wash the plastic "silverware" any more? She is using paper plates—sometimes!

Notice that she calls "Christian patriotism" a social issue. Has our Christianity become social in other ways than political?

FOR FURTHER ACTION
• Here is another story to help you learn to identify the whole gamut of cultural stress issues. Reread the story, marking with appropriate symbols (the first two letters of the word might do) the sentence or phrase that could be identified with one or another area of stress. We have copied the nine areas in the margin of the first page of this story. Begin there!

• This story is also full of positive ways people helped to make reentry more comfortable. Reread the story—again! Find the many ways people helped. Underscore them. Practice them with your returned missionary friend.

• Discuss with your whole reentry support team who can be responsible for each suggestion that you have underscored, as it would apply to your returning missionary friend.

- A wise observation: "Until our hearts become knit to the people here, we will look back with longing." Can you pass that counsel along to your missionary friend?

### SECURING OUR OWN HOME

The thought of having to take out a mortgage seemed such a big issue. We had never owned a home before and the amount of money needed seemed beyond what we could ever manage. Yet, as time moved on we realized that in order to help the whole family settle better, we needed to get into a home of our own and begin to put down some roots.

We were indeed thankful for the little bit of money we had managed to put away over the years. We were especially glad now that we had invested in a special project that the Post Office offered many years ago that matched dollar for dollar the money invested as long as it went into a first home.

We looked at the newspapers, visited open homes, went around the properties that were available and located in the vicinity of my husband's aging mother, yet still close to the schools and church. Finally we found one, a wooden house about sixty-five years old, with large bedrooms, separate living area and a good-sized lot. While very livable, it also provided us with heaps of potential to work at, doing it up to make it ours. Now we had to work through real estate agents and lawyers—something that quite frankly frightened us—an area we needed a lot more help with.

However, things went smoothly and finally we got it together. We would have to organize an initial mortgage with the Housing Corporation, as well as a second mortgage with the Bank and still make sure we had some money left for furniture!

One day the lawyer called, wanting to finalize the mortgage, so my husband had to change his lunch hour in order to go and sign papers. When explaining to his boss why he needed extra time to go out, it was revealed just what our true situation was. His boss could not believe we had no furniture. He sent his secretary up to see me and clarify the situation.

As a result, we were provided with divan beds for the three children, a bedroom suite for ourselves, and a brand new dining room set. He said that the Lord had blessed his business, so he too could bless others. What thankful recipients we were.

Yet another major miracle was about to take place. Our home group, which was comprised mostly of mature folk, got together to see what they could do for us. The spokesman rang and asked if we would be happy to share our financial position regarding the mortgages. "We would like to give you some help," he said.

But when he phoned back in a few days, we were not prepared for what he would say. They wanted to help with the second mortgage, which we graciously accepted. My husband asked how long we would have to pay the loan back. "No loan," he said. "We as a group are going to pay the money so you do not need a second mortgage." We were stunned! As we sat down and did our sums, we realized how many thousands of dollars in real terms this was saving us—ten years of interest payments saved! And no second mortgage!

And so it was on a cold winter's day at the end of July (Had you "caught on" before that this family's home country is in the southern hemisphere?), just four months after our return, we moved into our very own home. We will never forget that first evening as we all sat on the carpet in the lounge in front of a roaring fire, giving thanks to God for how He had provided for us, and would continue to do so. The children could not believe it and went around touching everything saying, "This is ours! This is our very own!"

It just amazed us, the generosity of people, and the

way God worked to put together a home for us. Even in small things, God worked. One friend rang to say she had a standard lamp, which had been her mother's, and she did not need it now. I accepted graciously, then worried myself the rest of the week about what I would do if it really looked out of place.

But it matched the room in color and style beautifully and to this day stands as a testimony to God's loving care. So much in our home has a story behind it, but above all, the lamp reminds us of Matthew 6:33, *"Seek first the Kingdom of God, and His righteousness, and all these things will be added unto you."*

FOR FURTHER UNDERSTANDING
Our Master said He didn't even have a pillow of His own! But that didn't seem to suggest that Mary, Martha and Lazarus should give up their country estate. There is a broad spectrum of Scripture from which to draw counsel on home ownership. From mobility to wise investment of finances, this issue must be considered.

A lesson well learned by this family is to receive graciously. Many missionaries struggle in this area. (In fact, the aversion to receiving money from others is a major reason many people give for *never* becoming a missionary!)

However, if your missionary could consider that they are not giving the money to him, but as he is giving of his life to the work of the Lord, the people are giving of their resources to the work of the Lord, it should help. Now, I realize that when someone slips a hundred dollar bill into your missionary's hand instead of putting it in the offering just collected for him, it is extra difficult for him to see that it is "going to the work of the Lord." But however wrong a giver's motivation might be, help your missionary friend see that it is now "the Lord's resources" entrusted to him for disbursement!

In reading the children's comment, "This is ours. This is our very own!," I am reminded of one of my experiences:

For more than two years we lived in the Group House in Brazil. Personal ownership of *everything* had long been forgotten. Just before our return home, the "new" concept of felt tip writing pens had hit the market. I was sitting next to a co-worker, watching that clear, dark, smooth flow of ink. He let me use it. I signed my name—several times. It looked great. "I like it!" I exclaimed.

The next day, he gave me one. He had gone out and purchased a pen for me. For days after, I would pause, look at that seventy-nine cent pen in my hand and think—this is mine. It's *really* mine!

FOR FURTHER ACTION

• This story centers on the housing aspect of reentry. However, the principle of your assisting your returning missionary friend can include any area of one-time major purchases.

Think of the major purchases that surround you. Realize that your friend will need to secure them all! Or at least consider the need for those items. Are you prepared to offer him wise counsel? Are there people in your church who can?

• Make a list. See if you can gather some of the needed items ahead of time. (I wonder if this missionary would have kept the lamp if it had *not* matched her lounge decor?!) Will your missionary be able to graciously receive what you give?

(I am embarrassed to admit that I just gave an old edition of a book to a missionary friend because I had just ordered the new edition!) Will what you give be the "older edition," too?

• Can you put your friend in touch with honest business people who will give them fair prices? Are these business people in your church? Is there a real estate agent? A lawyer? An insurance agent? An auto dealer?

### WE DIDN'T GO BACK TO "ANTIOCH!"

Looking back, we think several things helped with our reentry even though we did not return to our home church. First, we continued in ministry, working with the same agency as in Latin America. So we didn't have the major employment adjustment. We knew the people we were working with.

Second, we came off the field to the city of our home office...not back to our home town. We had the chance to choose a new church. It would have been harder going back to our old church, as much as we love them and they have supported us. But they and we had changed so much. We were glad we were free to be who we now are, not limited to who we would "have to be" in the eyes of the people.

Third, we were able to continue to minister here in the States and still travel in other nations. This has kept us in touch with missions.

FOR FURTHER UNDERSTANDING

You know how strongly I advocate your missionary coming back to his sending church for the reentry process. And I believe we have a good Scriptural foundation for it in Acts 14:26: *"From Attalia they sailed back to Antioch, where they had been commended to the grace of God for the work they had now completed."*

However, in this case, their continuing in ministry with the same organization (of which they had been a part for nine years) gave them the support usually received from the home church. Had they not had the three stabilizing factors they mentioned, I believe there could have been frustrations of consequence.

Sometimes relocation is mandated by completely new employment. On our return from both Peru and Brazil, though each time we moved to a new city, we were able to return to our sending church for fellowship and reentry support.

FOR FURTHER ACTION
• Are you prepared (can you prepare yourself) to offer wise counsel in the decisions of relocation?
• Discuss with the whole reentry support team the ramifications of your responsibilities if your missionary friend returns to another city! What help will you still be able to offer? Is there a sister church in that city that will help? Friends? Relatives? Someone who will assume responsibility for what you committed to do?

## OUR JOURNEY BACK INTO MINISTRY

The early months back home were a time filled with mixed emotions, very volatile and vulnerable. It would only take a small thing to happen and we would long to go back overseas, even though we knew in our heads that we were where God wanted us. Somehow it takes a lot longer for the heart (emotions) to come to terms with what we know is right.

There was a lot of grief to work through, for after all, we had left everything that was dear and important to us. We felt that we were at the height of our usefulness, involved not only in teaching in a Bible School, but getting the students involved in evangelism out in their villages. Now we seemed to have nothing. We began to realize that the changes in coming home were, in fact, harder to process than the original move to the field.

Those many years ago, we were a newly married couple with our whole life ahead of us. It was exciting, everything was new and we were determined to give it our best shot. Now we were a family with two pre-teens and a young teenager, trying our best to help them feel at home, when none of us did! Yet through it all, God would gently keep reminding us, "I know the way; My ways are not your ways."

People prayed for us, particularly those we were involved within the small group setting; but even then we often felt people really did not understand where we were coming from. After all, to most people this is home, and surely we should be glad to be home. There did not seem to be anyone around us at that time who had worked through these issues. Separated from mission personnel, we felt like orphans, often overwhelmed by our mixed emotions.

After about nine months, the elders came and asked my husband if he could act as pastor to the youth leaders of our church—purely a voluntary position, of course. It seemed like a good thing to do and would surely help in integrating us back into church life.

However, it did not take long before we felt totally inadequate and out of touch with the youth scene. Fortunately, it died a natural death as the end of the year approached and the whole of the youth work was reorganized. One thing it highlighted was that while we thought we were ready for ministry, we still needed time for reentry adjustment.

LENGTH OF TIME FOR REENTRY
How long on field
Degree of change at home
Degree of change on field
Attitude of church
Time to prepare
Time to get home
Uniqueness of personality
Disadvantaged position
Attitude of denial

The turning point in our healing came one Sunday morning at church. We had been home maybe a year or so by then. One of the elders was preaching, and to close the service off we sang the well-known and beautiful song, "Because He lives, I can face tomorrow." We not only sang this through once, but twice and then still some more. We stood, holding hands, unable to sing any more and slowly the tears came, not just a few but what seemed like bucketfuls.

As we dissolved in tears, several elders came around

to pray for us. They would ask a question or two, not quite sure what was happening, but we could not speak. We both felt like we had been struck dumb and just had to let the tears go. Something very deep and personal was happening, and it all began because that was the very song our college students had farewelled us with when we left the field.

Now, as we look back, we know that that Sunday morning was pivotal in God's working in us, preparing us for what lay ahead. Indeed, we had to let go of the past, learn to embrace the present and expectantly look to the future.

Since then we have been involved in multiple forms of ministry. We have come to realize that God's call to missions does not have as much to do with geography as with obedience. Our hearts rejoice.

FOR FURTHER UNDERSTANDING
*"And they abode a long time with the disciples there"* (Acts 14:28). It is not until Acts 15:35 that they were again *"teaching and preaching the Word of the Lord."* Because the length of time required to process reentry is different for each person (even within the same family or partnership), we need to be careful not to rush the process.

Now, it is true that Paul and Barnabas didn't just sit around waiting for some magical time to elapse. They did, after all, participate in that church council in Jerusalem, *"declaring what miracles and wonders God had done among the Gentiles"* (Acts 15:12). Look at that! They had another opportunity for debriefing!

Reversion: Trying to get back into the "swing of things" *before* the reentry process has run its course does not work. A good degree of resolve must be achieved in the nine areas of stress before missionaries can get involved in ministry again. It did probably

FIVE REENTRY PATTERNS
Alienation
Condemnation
Reversion
Suicide
INTEGRATION

seem to the elders that nine months should have been sufficient time. However, if nothing is done to help this couple process their reentry, they will remain "stuck in limbo" until the feelings are buried; until their marriage is destroyed; until they leave the church; until they commit suicide! Or, until *you* sense their need and help them readjust to their new environment!

**NINE AREAS OF STRESS**
- Physical
- Professional
- Financial
- Cultural
- Social
- Linguistic
- National/Political
- Educational
- Spiritual

Another factor: This couple had children approaching the ages of youth, but they had had no experience in youth ministry. Though it is not necessary for them to go back to exactly what they had been doing before (as did Paul and Barnabas), it is vital for the church to identify the ministry gifts of their returning missionaries and to place them in areas of service using them.

In fact, returning missionaries are under-utilized in one of the most vibrant and positive positions they could fill: Mobilizing the church in missions! See Appendix A for the number of directions this awesome ministry could go!

They admitted, "We began to realize that the changes in coming home were, in fact, harder to process than the original move out to the field." This is only too true! More missionaries "crash" on their reentry than on going to the field. Review the nine variables determining the length of time for reentry in Chapter Three.

"We had to *let go* of the past, learn to *embrace* the present and expectantly *look to the future*." What a beautiful, simple summation of the extreme ambivalent sense of time we as Christians must live in! This can bring your missionary to their final thought: "Obedience rather than sacrifice" is what God desires!

FOR FURTHER ACTION
- They had a "small group setting" that they tried to utilize as their reentry support team. However, the

group was not trained. Are you in a position to train your missionary's reentry support team? To encourage the core leaders to get you all together for more training? Are you ready for your missionary friend to come home?

• Can you talk with the church leadership about how/where they plan to utilize the ministering gifts of your returning friend after he has gone through the reentry process? Take the points of Appendix A with you!

**LET'S PLAY TELEPHONE—THE RUMOR MILL**

Our family of five returned home with $80 emergency trip money. Our phone calls to the missions committee made it clear we wouldn't be meeting with them for a long time. It was actually eight months after our return that we finally met.

Yet God's provisions are always so timely. In those early weeks home, I had stopped in to buy some things just as a girl was plopping a huge bag of corn on the counter. She asked the owner what she should do with it. He answered, "Oh, it's just dried corn; throw it out." To which I was thinking very African and said, "Are you really going to throw out that dried corn?" He replied, "Yes, you want to do something with it?" That opened the door for sharing about our just returning from Africa and how dried corn was a mainstay of our diet. So they gave me the corn. As it turned out, it was not dried corn like African dried corn. It was sweet corn. Just the tips of the husks had dried out! It ended up feeding three families!

So began a friendship with these vegetable market people. They were very helpful in letting us know that every Wednesday they would take fruit and vegetables that had bad spots or were wilting and they would throw them out. This was the Lord's blessing, indeed, as much of what they were throwing away was still very good food. So, the Lord supplied our need for fresh vegetables and fruits through these dear people.

I was so thrilled that I naturally began telling folks about God's provision for us in all these many ways. Never once did I think of ourselves as deprived, only blessed by God's timely and wonderful means. This is where the problem came in.

We had been home all of six weeks when we received a phone call that the pastor and associate pastor of our sending church wanted to see us. Because we hadn't met with the missions committee yet, we thought this was going to be their interview with us to see how our work in Africa had been. To our utter amazement and shock, this was not the case at all. It seems that several members of the church had heard my testimonies of God's faithfulness in providing for our needs. Somehow, though, the story had gotten changed around and these leaders were very much on the defensive, wondering why we were spreading rumors that "they as a church" had not been providing for us and that the missionaries were eating out of garbage piles! Not even in this situation did these godly men ask us if we needed anything, nor how our work in Africa had been, nor even if the stories the members had told them were true. They were just upset that their care for us had been challenged.

FOR FURTHER UNDERSTANDING
Though possibly harmless as a game, in real life, "Telephone" can be very hurtful. Imagine how this family felt when they found out that something they were rejoicing about had been twisted into rumors "to hurt the church."

On the other hand, if the missionaries had not been experiencing the lack of reentry support, the communication with the church leadership would have been open. There would have been clear understanding.

FOR FURTHER ACTION

- In the first two paragraphs, did you notice the quick transition from something very hurtful—no meeting for eight months—to the Lord's gracious provision? To focus on the positive is good, but you as a reentry caregiver, must "read between the lines" to learn not only how to prevent these hurtful situations from happening, but to make sure the positive focus is not just "covering up" hurt that is not being dealt with.

- To what extent can you influence the church missions leadership to make sure your returning missionary friend has an audience with them within a more appropriate time frame than eight months?

- Are policies in place (can policies be put in place) to assure clear communication on the leadership level with the church's missionaries, no matter how large the church? No matter how "busy" the leadership might be?

- Is it possible that the shock of the pastor's accusation was such that this couple did not have the presence of mind to say anything? Could you help them go back to the leadership and clarify the issue?

## JUST DO IT!

My family arrived home from a five-year mission term in Eastern Europe. Previous to this we had spent ten years in Africa. On the night of our return the following things happened:

1. Upon our arrival we were met at the airport by more than 100 members of our sending church.

It was a huge—almost overwhelming—crowd. There were balloons everywhere, a huge banner, gifts for the kids, roses for my wife (at least three dozen)! And they placed on each of our heads a home team basketball cap! (We are all basketball fans.) There was excitement in the air! We didn't understand why, but we could feel it. My wife said, "It was like we were celebrities!" We prayed together and moved on to claim our baggage.

We had had a long-term relationship with this church. For the fifteen years we served on the field, the church supported our work in a variety of ways. Financially, they became our largest single supporting congregation, but they also expressed their care through prayer, communication and field visits.

2. Upon leaving the terminal building, the church presented my wife with a five-year "new" GMC van!

Since we didn't have a car of our own, the church had bought us one. It was in immaculate condition with a red bow tied around the entire thing! It was a gift given to my wife, as they wanted to honor her and recognize that she would need a vehicle to shuttle kids and do the things that women at home are expected to do.

3. Leaving the airport we drove to a reception that was being held in our honor.

What was even more impressive in this was that again well over 100 people had come out to attend the reception. People were everywhere—sharing with us (in our jet-lagged state) just as if they had known us for years. The reception was being held at a club house of an apartment complex.

4. Before arriving at the reception, though, we made one major stop. We stopped off at *our* apartment!

The church knew that we did not have a place to stay, so they had over the past several weeks organized and rented a three-bedroom apartment in a very nice location. We had access to all sorts of amenities (sauna, weight room, pool, and the clubhouse).

What made this even "huge-er" was the fact that the apartment was furnished. But not just "furnished" as you might be tempted to think. It was FURNISHED!

And everything in it was a gift from the church to our family. This included every piece of furniture from a new sofa and love seat in the living room, a 27" television connected to a VCR, a coffee table, two end tables, a kitchen table, a beautiful bedroom suite that included a queen-size bed, a dresser, two night stands, a second dresser with a mirror, a set of bunk-beds for the boys, a dresser for their room, a bed for our daughter, another dresser, mirror and night stand.

But even this only begins to scratch the surface. Every wall was covered with ornaments and beautifully framed pictures; curtains were hung. Every closet was filled with clothing and gifts for the kids. Drawers were packed full of every conceivable item that might be needed: batteries, flashlights, tape and tools. Linens and towels—all monogrammed!—filled the closet. There was a washer and dryer, a microwave oven, a filing cabinet, a telephone and answering machine.

And again—I repeat—this only begins to tell the story. Every cabinet in the kitchen was full of food: canned goods and boxed goods; fresh cookies filled the cookie jar and frozen meat filled the freezer. Milk, orange juice, eggs, oatmeal—if you could imagine it—it was there. I want you to know that we walked around for days in awe at the incredible way that every detail had been thought through!

6. At the reception we began to understand the extent of the preparations for our reentry. Once we had overcome the shock of the apartment, we went to the reception and there during the course of the evening we were able to casually meet with several people who would be instrumental in the next few days and weeks.

I met the insurance representative who would be helping us work through all of the details of getting insurance set up. My wife met the lady who had been put in charge of "elementary schools research." She had all of the information that we needed about all five of the schools in our township and was prepared to answer just about any question we might have regarding getting the kids into the winter sessions.

We met with a lady who had been making arrangements for our boys to join the township basketball league. One interesting fact is that in less than twenty-four hours of our arriving in the country both of our boys were in their first (ever) organized basketball practice! Coaches and team members alike had been briefed and were prepared.

We also met the lady who had been involved in organizing the prayer team. We only began to realize then what all had gone on.

The night was—as you can well imagine—one that none in our family will ever forget. And it didn't end there. There was for weeks and even months to come a genuine concern for our well-being and adjustment into our home country society. Whenever there was a question or a need, it was met, up to and until the time it was determined that we were indeed established in that area. But do you know what—even after 18 months—I still occasionally have someone ask how we (or more especially, the kids) are doing.

But what did it take to make this event a reality? The process was lengthy. Some things were being planned as much as a year in advance. It included an incredibly astute senior minister who has a heart for missions and for missionaries. He has and continues to take an active role in visiting mission fields. It was on one of his teaching visits to Eastern Europe that he began to realize that our work there was coming to a close. At that time he began to ask some probing questions in terms of how we felt the Lord was leading our lives. What would be our next step? In his mind was the thought that perhaps the Lord might be leading us to serve the church that had been so instrumental in serving us. Over time and during subsequent visits to the field we discussed the possibility of our returning to serve in the area of missions under his leadership.

As the time drew closer and certain decisions were made, he then set about putting a reentry team together. This is probably the most significant thing that was done. The team was made up of ten members in the church. It was coordinated by a lady who was at that time employed by a mission organization and so was somewhat familiar with stresses to missionaries caused by reentry. Other than the coordinator, there were eight areas selected for specific attention.

The senior pastor was my mentor and a lady was selected for my wife. The role of the mentors was primarily to maintain contact and help answer any questions that we might have. They were open and available to us at any time. There was also a medical doctor, a realtor who assisted us first with the apartment and after three months—our house, a financial advisor, a children's reentry coordinator, an insurance representative, and over all of this an incredible prayer warrior heading up the prayer support team. All of these, along with the pastor's wife, successfully filled a specific role in the process of our reentry. Others drew alongside in perhaps smaller—but nonetheless—essential ways.

I am now the Minister of Missions at this church. Due to the foresight of our senior pastor and the shared work of a great team, all five of us have been fully integrated into our home culture and are active again in ministry.

FOR FURTHER UNDERSTANDING
Incredible! Utterly incredible! It has been done! It can be done again! It must be done! Our missionaries are too valuable to lose. And this is the way we can care for them on their reentry. Can you find even one of the nine areas of stress that was not addressed? And cared for?

FOR FURTHER ACTION
- Just do it!

Chapter Five

# Short-Term Missions

There was a day when missionaries carried their personal belongings into the interior of Africa in their own coffins, knowing that they would not be returning home! But today those stories are just bytes of information on some historical CD.

Possibly, short-term missions became popular to accommodate the "try it, you might like it" generation. But far from that today, short-term missions has taken its place in current mission strategy. Short-term mission agencies have exploded in number and size.

In fact, it has been found that short-term teams, targeting specific people groups, have made successful ministry inroads where long-term people have not. Yet, again, in some cases, short-term teams, with their variety of approaches, have opened the door for longer term involvement.

Of course, "short-term" has become a very broad term. To some it is dumping old clothes at an orphanage across a border on a Saturday afternoon—back home before dark, for sure! To others it is a two week "vacation for the Lord." The short-term ministry trips we lead are three weeks in duration. The additional week off work "without pay" promotes a seriousness of counting the cost. On the other hand, short-term for some mission agencies could be up to four years on the field.

Paul, the Apostle, by the way, was a career, short-term missionary! Though he gave his entire life to missions, none of his journeys was longer than two to three years!

We have found that if preparation and training for short-term missionary endeavor is serious and practical, as much benefit comes to the participant as to the field ministry. (Even as Paul said, *"...all that God has done in and through me."* Acts 14:27)

On one of my early cross-cultural short-term experiences, I was one of twenty who went to do manual labor at an orphanage just outside Quito, Ecuador. The team leader very wisely allowed time for us to visit other ministries on the way there and back. Within a year, ten of us were back on the field involved in a longer term commitment.

A major factor in reentry care for the short-term missionary is to help him see how his experience fits him into God's Master Plan of world evangelization. After the reentry process has followed its course (after he has "abided and rehearsed all"), your missionary friend is ready to pursue any one of many aspects of cross-cultural ministry. And, by the way, being able to look forward to further fruitful ministry helps speed up the reentry process.

Appendix A, *Eight Possible Next Steps*, suggests further cross-cultural ministry options.

As you read these stories that relate specifically to short-term situations, consider the care needed. Though the field time may be relatively brief, your friend has seen firsthand the realities of a sin sick world, wallowing in spiritual poverty and hopelessness.

Trying to rationalize life back home with life on the field will be difficult. It is not unusual for him to try to pass it off with a "been there, done that" attitude. *Reversion* is the wrong reentry behavior pattern most likely to grip your friend. "Let's just get on with life," he may say. That is not even a "band-aid" on the sorrowful situation that will fester in the heart of your friend. You may misinterpret his zealous desire to "awaken the Church" back home as good. It is *good*, but only after he has had some time to process his experiences. Serious reentry care is needed.

## CAPTURING MISSIONARY ZEAL

I was only gone ten weeks! I thought Mexico would be a "piece of cake!" It's just across the border! But now, socially, I wasn't part of that small, Christian family community anymore. I was back at my church. Though it too is rather small, everyone seemed quite distant! And these are my close friends, I thought.

I was only gone ten weeks! I'm back! Hello! I am missing that sense of belonging. Could that feeling of community have developed in such a short time to now miss it so?

One day, a friend asked me to look at the new video and sound equipment they had just installed in their church. It was impressive. "And it only cost $250,000," he said. "What do you think about our neat, new stuff?" Before my Mexico experience I would have been as excited as he was. But now I had new thoughts and feelings. Why, in Mexico, they aren't even concerned about remodeling their buildings. When funds do come in, they are used to build more churches in new communities.

Even before I answered—just because I hesitated, he got defensive. He gave a rapid-fire list of reasons why his church needed this equipment. I kept thinking of all the things we could have done with that money in Mexico. Where did these new thoughts come from? I was only gone ten weeks!

Now I've learned to shut my mouth and bite my tongue. I just see things differently. Let's support and care for our missionaries, I think. Man, have my priorities changed! And I was only gone ten weeks!

FOR FURTHER UNDERSTANDING
Consider the question this missionary posed at the end of his second paragraph: *Could that feeling of community have developed in such a short time to now miss it so?* The understood answer is, *YES! It could!* There are social, cultural and spiritual aspects of other people groups that are more highly developed than or just different from those of a missionary's home country. When a missionary is thrust into that arena even for such a short period of time and then hurled back into his own setting, the contrast can make the distinction of cultures seem even greater than they really are.

On the other hand, there are some widely divergent characteristics of culture. Certainly the contrast of the hyper-nuclear family of the USA (and the gross isolation even between some family members) with the extended family closeness of the Mexican culture would give this missionary reason to miss that feeling of community.

Wonder at the "danger" there would be for a church to open up to the possibility that a missionary could bring home characteristics of Christian conduct that could improve his home church!

Consider this missionary's last paragraph: *"Now I've learned to just shut my mouth and bite my tongue."* This is a "yellow flag" of caution, if not a "red flag" of danger! Missionaries who "shut their mouths and bite their tongues" often get bit by a reentry pattern called *alienation.* They want to say something; they want to share their new ideas and perspectives. Maybe the church

FIVE REENTRY PATTERNS
Alienation
Condemnation
Reversion
Suicide
INTEGRATION

in America, spending forty to fifty billion dollars a year on new buildings should rethink some of its priorities!

But faced by the defensiveness of his friend—and after "only ten weeks" (which is too short of a time for him to have become an expert on mission strategy for his church), this missionary—along with a thousand others—clams up and doesn't share his thoughts. Both he and his church are the losers.

The church loses because they have denied themselves the opportunity to look at the perspective of one of their members who has seen a bigger picture.

Far more critical, though, is my concern for the missionary. Little by little, he "shuts his mouth" on more and more ideas in more and more areas and finds himself alienated from the Body. This gradual, almost nonperceptually slow movement away can lead to the serious condition of suicide! Cultural, social, emotional, spiritual, or physical!

FOR FURTHER ACTION

- Have you learned any of the cultural or spiritual characteristics of Christian conduct that your missionary is experiencing on the field that might be good to incorporate in your life? In your church life? In your community life? How would you incorporate them?

- You are part of the missions leadership of this young man's home church. You are there to sense this youthful zeal. Now, how do you harness it into productive action? Where can his energies be directed? Do you have mobilization goals for raising up new missionaries? Are there other areas of ministry that can capture his zeal? Appendix A, *Eight Possible Next Steps*, is an attempt to give direction to the positive enthusiasm short-term people usually bring home. In fact, it would be good to share these options with them before they go, remind them of them while they are on the field and do a thorough follow through with them after the reentry process is well on its way to completion.

In a society that focuses on a "been there, done that!" perspective of activity, helping your missionary to view short-term missions as a part of the whole is very valuable.

- Incorporate into your church's missions policy methods of disseminating information about how returning short-term missionaries can get involved in other areas of mission service.

### I STILL GRIEVE FOR MY NATION

My stay in Asia was only four months, and a previous stay in the Caribbean was one month. After the Caribbean trip, I realized how much I appreciated electricity and roads.

My experience in Asia, however, was very different. I was in a modern, cosmopolitan city. I loved serving as a volunteer English teacher there. I also taught an English Bible class. But reentry was bittersweet. Not having suffered any deprivation, as in Central America, it was my realization of how much my country had lost in the past two decades that hit me hardest.

The Asians I lived with are a diligent and peace-loving people. Their young people are respectful, and their culture is relatively innocent. Family ties are very strong. The Christians I met are very committed. They worship God with their whole heart, crying out for the lost souls in Asia.

The crime and carnality in my own nation, the immorality on TV and in films, and the general depravity of my once Christian nation were more apparent than ever in coming home. It has taken some time for me to absorb. I still grieve for my nation.

FOR FURTHER UNDERSTANDING
Something very deep within an individual develops as

he grows up in his own culture. It is called *ethnocentrism*. Simply understood, my "ethnos," my people, are "central!" All others are on the periphery. Ethnocentrism says, "Anything good that has been invented or developed had to come from 'my people'! We do—everything—right! We are best!"

The baggage this carries is the implication that the way "other people" do things is not as good as ours. In fact, the way "they" do things is—wrong! They are different; therefore inferior!

Now your missionary friend enters one of those "other" cultures. Only he discovers respectful youth. He enjoys the close-knit family ties. He learns Christian commitment and passion for the lost from them.

Returning home places his own "Christian" culture in stark contrast—negatively! The crime rate, the immorality, the general depravity glare with blinding intensity on his sensitivities. All that he learned from childhood on is being challenged. We *were* a Christian nation, he concludes. The apparent helplessness to do anything about it coupled with the image of this "wonderful" culture that has exemplified these desirable characteristics can cause the most patriotic person to lose confidence in his own country. And to place a halo around the *memory* of the country just visited.

On the other hand, not in any way forgiving or minimizing the depravity of her home country, there is no doubt in my mind that her four-month stay in that Asian country did not give her the time to discover the "sins" of her host culture.

FOR FURTHER ACTION

- You have been listening to your friend share his perspective of his host culture. Have there been signs of exalting its good in comparison to home? If you see this as a potential problem for your returning friend, do some research about his host culture. Is it as good as he is saying it is?

- Develop, and help your returning missionary develop a world view that celebrates the good in all people and acknowledges the evil inherent in all mankind.
- If you find your friend disparaging his home culture after he has been home for some time, it is possible that the frustration of reentry (those negative feelings) arise from a halo he has put around the *memory* of his host culture. Help him to remember more of the reality of what was there. Gently help him break the halo he has put around his host culture.
- If, on the other hand, his evaluation of the contrast is accurate—if he has discovered a people with a greater passion for the lost, join your missionary friend in becoming a "change agent" to your own culture. It can begin with you!

### REENTRY STRESS IS *REAL*

Reentry stress is *real!* First of all, I nearly forgot how to drive after a month without a car in Mexico. Then, our first night back on this side we stayed in a motel. We registered at 9 p.m., tired to the bone! We got the last available room. When I went to pay with my Visa card, it wouldn't work! We were nearly out of cash, too, but we were able to scrape together $50 for the night. It turned out that during May the credit union changed Visa processors and issued new cards. They'd sent me a letter saying my old credit card wouldn't work after May 24, only I didn't see the letter until I picked up the mail at the post office after we got home.

Then there was the rude cashier at the service station and the search for an ATM machine! No, I won't even go there.

Much, much more difficult was when I got home and called my mother. She told me that my cousin's husband, Ted, had died. Ted's daughter and I were friends in high school and still live within a mile of each other; her parents lived out in the country. Ted was 68 years old and in good health. He had had a stroke, spent a week in a coma, died, and was cremated all while we were training in Mexico.

It was a shock. It took me by surprise. It was difficult to grieve. The process of acknowledging a friend's passing from this life to the next is supposed to happen in community. Yet, now, others had put their grieving behind them. They were going on with life. It is difficult to grieve alone. We are not meant to grieve alone. I am grieving alone.

FOR FURTHER UNDERSTANDING
Even when a missionary on the field learns of the death of a friend back home, the grieving process is difficult. It cannot be done "from a distance." As this missionary said, "Grieving is supposed to happen in community."

The time must come when your friend sits in "grandma's" chair, and with "grandpa" or *you*, he can let his heart break through in its expression of loss over her. For that is primarily what his grief relates to—*his* loss.

His relative or friend has stepped through to his eternal destiny—God knows which. If his loved one had not trusted in Christ as Savior, there could be grieving over the awfulness of an eternal hell. This would be a grieving of incomprehensible degree. If a long or agonizingly painful illness preceded death, this could add to the sorrow.

But those issues are ended. His loss—how he is going to move forward with his life without his friend—is the matter at hand.

I was eight years old when my father died. I had to be "bribed" with a fifty-cent piece to attend his funeral. My uncle was so gentle in dealing with my child emotions. I honor him to this day for his kindness to me.

FOR FURTHER ACTION

• The circumstances surrounding your missionary friend's need for grieving will be as varied as personalities are individual. Though your grieving is over, be prepared to go back with your friend through whatever steps are necessary to help him move forward.

• No matter how old your missionary friend is when he loses a loved one, the issues of dealing with the loss are serious. And they must be dwelt with. Consider all members of a family. Each grieving experience will be as individual as that person.

• Note: As we go through these stories, I trust you are learning that there are multiplied issues that can present themselves to your missionary friend. Be encouraged! They won't all happen to your friend! At least, not all at once!

NINE AREAS OF STRESS

Physical
Professional
Financial
Cultural
Social
Linguistic
National/Political
Educational
Spiritual

## ON THE LIGHTER SIDE

After a five-month stay in an underdeveloped area of Mexico, we were happy to be home. On our first Sunday back at our church, we approached one of our friends who we thought might understand our experience. Her first words to my wife were, "Well, did you enjoy your vacation?" We groaned inside at the apparent lack of understanding. And even now, on our occasional trip back to the States from our home in Central America, others have picked up on this, sharing that question in a joking manner.

We have come up with a joking response. "If you think it was such a vacation, why don't you come back with us?" For some reason, that seems to put things back into perspective for all of us.

FOR FURTHER UNDERSTANDING

On the lighter side, here is a couple who were able to

"roll with the punches." Certainly there must have been at least an edge of hurt in calling five months of difficult ministry circumstances a "vacation!" But to their credit, the best way they found to handle it was with a light humorous response.

As a matter of fact, teachers of cultural adaptation say that the very top skill needed for successful adjustment to cross-cultural living is a sense of humor!

FOR FURTHER ACTION
- Did you note that the first concern this couple had was to talk with someone "who might understand our situation?" Your returning missionary friend will be looking for someone to talk with who might understand his situation. Will that be you?

Have you made yourself aware of his circumstances? Have you been in contact with him to know how he is doing on the field? Have you done some research on the country—the people, the culture, the social, economic, political, religious climate, in addition to the physical climate? Do you know his ability to get along with teammates—the particular members on this team? What was his objective in going on this ministry trip? Will he have met it?

Let your imagination continue from these suggestions of how you can develop an understanding heart to really hear what your missionary friend has to say upon his reentry!

- A sense of humor is great! But if your friend does not go beyond a joking attitude toward his experience, it may be a sign of trouble. Joking can be a way of avoiding the serious issues of life. Are you able to not only laugh at his humor, but help him process and express the deeper considerations of his ministry trip?

This, of course, is more successfully accomplished in a one-on-one, "truth in love" confrontation rather than when he is making light of the trip in front of a large group of people.

"On the other hand...," so said Papa in *Fiddler on the Roof!* On the other hand, it was our first Bible delivery trip to Hong Kong and China. It was our first night there. We sat around a living room with the long-term workers—the ones who daily lead the teams across the border. I had expected a prayer meeting for the "Suffering Church." Or a strategy meeting for our next day's trip.

Instead, it turned into a "laugh-fest!" Everyone was telling their favorite joke. It got to the point where we were laughing even when nothing was funny!

It wasn't until days later that I realized the need for that evening. The tension of daily crossings; the pressure of schedules; the uncertainty of safety needed a release. And it was found in humor!

### FROM ECSTASY TO PASSIVITY

I went to Southeast Asia with a team of students for an outreach during summer break. Zealous and full-on for God, I was used by the Lord in powerful ways. I had been open to God working through me and now, suddenly, on the mission field, I found my calling and my gifts were released! I was ecstatic! On my return home I shared my experiences with my church and friends with great enthusiasm.

That was when I began to run into problems. My pastor, my family, and my closest friends simply responded with, "That's nice," in a welcome-back-to-the-real-world tone of voice. It was difficult if not impossible for people to appreciate or even understand my life-changing experiences. Even worse, when I prayed for people now, I didn't see the same results as I had in Asia. The power of God seemed to be absent from my prayers.

I got discouraged. I stopped sharing with people

about my experiences and vision of going back to Asia. I stopped praying for people and became a passive member of my church for the next twelve months while I finished my studies. My pastor concluded that I had gone backwards, not forwards, in my spiritual life as a result of my short-term missions trip. I did not have the energy to try to explain.

FOR FURTHER UNDERSTANDING
A summer of service in cross-cultural ministry is a good time to experience God in full measure. All the cares and responsibilities of the mundane have been laid aside. You are free to *"please the One who has called you to be a soldier"* (II Timothy 2:4).

Bringing that enthusiasm back home is the difficult part. Those who have remained home have had to deal with the daily "entanglements of the world." Furthermore, *"Is this not the carpenter's son?"* (See Matthew 13:55). Who would expect God to work through a local lad?

In this brief three-paragraph story, note how clearly (and how rapidly) the progression to alienation is written. From "I was ecstatic!" to "I didn't have the energy to try to explain."

Does your heart not cry out for the hurting missionaries who have been dumped on the rubbish heap? In knowing awareness, the mission agency does little to help. In blissful ignorance, the church stumbles on. In handicapped paralysis, the missionary languishes in pain.

May God awaken us to the tremendous needs of His servants who minister cross-culturally when they come home!

FOR FURTHER ACTION
• So that you can more easily recognize the progressive deterioration from alienation to emotional sui-

cide, *and* be able to intervene at the earliest possible time, number the sentences that speak to the downward spiral. Hint: I numbered nine of the fifteen sentences!

• Could you, like Barnabas, take this young man who found his "calling" on a short-term trip to Asia (Damascus) by the hand and introduce him (Saul) to the church leadership? Would you have the words to convince them that his ministry is valid and should be recognized here at home? (See Acts 9:26-28.)

• Assume you arrive on the scene as the last flicker of his summer flame is about to go out. What would you do—what would you say to begin his restoration? Or, would the first thing you do be to listen and listen and listen?

• Consider the six-phrase restoration of two discouraged disciples walking on the road to Emmaus as recorded in Luke 24:13-35:

—*Jesus came along side and walked with them.* You need to get on his level. Get eye-to-eye with him. Find some common ground; walk with him.

—*Jesus hid His own identity.* You, in a spirit of humility and meekness (strength of character under control), bring the focus of attention to *his* needs, *not* yours!

—*Jesus listened to their story of sorrow and disappointment.* "After all, we thought He was the Messiah!" You listen. You ask questions only to promote his continued talking. And you listen some more.

—*Jesus went to the Scriptures for the answer to their need.* You go to the Scriptures for the answer to your friend's need. Any counsel, any encouragement, any correction you give must have its foundation in the Word of God.

—*Jesus stayed with them until their hearts were again "burning within them."* You stay with your returned missionary friend until his reentry is complete—

until he has "abode" a long enough time and until he has "rehearsed all."

—*Jesus left when He wasn't needed there anymore.* You must also sense when your friend is fully integrated. You don't want him to become dependent on you. Remain friends, for sure! But now on an equal par.

### I WAS INTERROGATED LIKE A SPY

Before my final year of seminary, I was sent out by my church—alone—for a two-month summer mission. I ministered there under the leadership of a local church. My work with the church was marginally rewarding. The climatic conditions, vastly different from my hometown or my college town, were almost unbearable. I desperately missed my fiancée. I got hit by a bus. (I had made the infamous mistake of looking to the left when stepping off the curb! I was in a country that observed British-style traffic flow.) I contracted malaria. Overall, it was a tough trip.

Upon my return, the leadership of my home church (the church was sponsoring my seminary education costs as well as this summer trip) spent a whole day questioning me about "how things went." Not about how I was handling my injury. Or the malaria. Or the climate. Or my relationship with my fiancée. Rather, it was a grueling interrogation about the ministry with which I had worked. It seemed like I was being forced to be an informer—a spy! It wasn't at all a time for me to debrief.

In fact, it wasn't until I was back at the seminary, talking with a friend, that I even heard of or saw the need for the whole debriefing process. I was pretty worn out. I was still a little sick. I was "freezing cold" in August seventy-degree temperature. I was immediately plugged back into seminary work. I still had not been able to visit my fiancée. The church had decided to not cover all of my senior-year expenses. Having committed to a heavy load of student service work (all volunteer), where was the time for a job?

Fortunately, my friend, my supervisor, gave me plenty of space and time before putting demands on me. And he encouraged me to talk about the issues I was facing.

FOR FURTHER UNDERSTANDING

An accountability report of the national ministry with which a church has partnered is always appropriate. However, it should not be mixed with or confused with the missionary's need for debriefing. Certainly at another time—with the foreknowledge that a report is a part of his summer assignment—giving an accounting from his perspective on the corporate relationship of the two ministries is a legitimate request.

This missionary's story is repeated again and again: "I had never even heard of...the whole debriefing process." Mission agencies—too many in number, church leadership—too many in number, and returning missionaries—too many in number are ignorant of the impact of culture stress in reverse, the pain of coming home.

Reversion was forced on him. In his words, "I was immediately plugged back into seminary work." What care can you take so that your returning missionary friend is not "forced" back into ministry before the reentry process is complete? It will be different for one returning to stay and one home on furlough.

FIVE REENTRY PATTERNS
Alienation
Condemnation
Reversion
Suicide
INTEGRATION

There is no doubt in my mind that this scenario would have been very difficult had his supervisor not "run interference" for him and been that most needed (but lacking) part in the Body of Christ— the "listening ear." Are you that listening ear for your returning missionary friend? What can you do to develop the skill?

Can you help to identify those in your fellowship who have the empathy and compassion for this role?

FOR FURTHER ACTION

- Reread the story. Number (underline) the issues of stress this fellow faced as he reentered his final year at seminary. (I found seven. Did you?)
- Review the nine areas of challenge missionaries face on reentry. Place the seven issues this missionary faced in one or another of the categories. The three dealing with his physical, simply had to run their course. However, wise planning could have prevented the other four. What could you do to prevent these things from happening to your missionary friend?

NINE AREAS OF STRESS

- Physical
- Professional
- Financial
- Cultural
- Social
- Linguistic
- National/Political
- Educational
- Spiritual

- What could you do to make your friend more comfortable through the physical ordeals? And do you think that if there had not been the stress from the avoidable issues that his physical stress would have been lessened?

## I KEPT MY MOUTH SHUT

I went on my school's summer missions program with a group of ten other students to a country in Eastern Europe. My team leader was, in my view, very manipulative. He seemed ignorant of how to lead a missions team. Only in his second month of marriage, he was using this trip as their honeymoon!

In his leadership "power trip," he made the statement, "I hear from God; so, if you think anything different, then you aren't hearing from Him." None of the other team members seemed to notice anything wrong with that attitude. Actually, instead, they would praise him and say how this trip was the best thing ever. Because I didn't want to cause division, I kept my mouth shut for the whole two months.

Upon returning, all of the missions teams (over one hundred people) went through a major group debriefing. There wasn't really a chance to talk with anyone about problems you encountered—things one would like to talk over personally. I was glad to be home, and away from the team leader. He had graduated.

The bad thing was that these feelings affected my walk with God. I didn't blame God, but I didn't have much drive to seek His face like I did before the trip. Why? I realized that many of the phrases and concepts that were common to my relationship with God had been (in my opinion) misused by our team leader. I did not want to relate with the other team members. They would often talk about how great the leader was. I would just brush away any comments about him. I was scared, though. His favorite song, which he would often make us sing, was very popular. I refused to sing it whenever it was sung in church or chapel. It bugged me that this guy could still be affecting me.

I kept praying prayers, forgiving him and asking for forgiveness from God for my attitude. A few months later, I went on a week-long trip with a group to Mexico. It was a nice, effective trip with good, solid leaders. This acted as an ointment to my wounds. It kept my desire for missions alive. By God's grace, I've gotten over all of this and I've learned a lot about being a good leader.

FOR FURTHER UNDERSTANDING

Discovering the leader's "manipulative" nature before the trip may not have been easy. However, realizing that a couple just two-months married would not make a good leadership team could have said, "This trip isn't for me."

But he went. And quickly identified a problem. He is to be commended for "holding his tongue" during the trip. After all, the leader *is* the leader.

However, the fact that he didn't say anything upon reentry began the degenerative spiral of alienation. Fortunately, he didn't "blame God." And another short-term trip—well-organized this time—broke the downward spin and "kept his desire for missions alive."

FOR FURTHER ACTION
• Though the team leader wasn't there physically, his presence was felt in many circumstances. Reread the fourth paragraph. Underscore the phrases that indicate areas in his life being affected. Can you help your friend identify and dig out any root of bitterness before it "*troubles him and defiles many others?*" (See Hebrews 12:15.)

• As your friend announces his desire to go on a trip, help him reason through the issues and pray for God's peace in the decision. Moral and prayer support *before* your missionary friend goes on a trip generally helps to prevent tough times of reentry.

AREAS OF SUPPORT
Moral
Logistic
Financial
Prayer
Communication
Reentry

• Though the group debriefing probably helped the leadership evaluate the trip, it obviously didn't satisfy the needs of this individual. Your sensitivity would lend your "listening ear" to his need for debriefing.

As we have seen from these stories, reentry care is not only for the long-term missionary. And one of the recurring needs has been for your sensitive "listening ear." So great is this need that we devote the next chapter to specific stories where a listening ear was the loudest cry of their heart.

Chapter Six

# *Listen to Me;*
# *Please, Listen to Me!*

In an age of information overload, who wants to hear a missionary "debrief?" The out-of-focus pictures he will show we have already seen, as professional television has brought the sorrow of the world to our living rooms. Vicariously, we have "been there, done that!" We live in a terribly egocentric, *me*-focused world. Though, on one hand, debriefing of a missionary is for the good of the listeners to rejoice in what God is doing in our world (You don't get that on TV!), the primary value of debriefing is for the benefit of the missionary.

NASA will spend whatever it takes to allow a returning astronaut to speak to whomever he wants about whatever he wants whenever he wants for as long as he wants! I enjoy the breathtaking pictures of space. I read carefully for new *truly* scientific findings. And I find space exploration fascinating. However, your missionary has been on a more "far-out" adventure than any astronaut has ever experienced.

To change the analogy: Remember the ticker-tape parade given to most war heroes? Remember the lack of recognition to the heroes of a not-so-popular Vietnam War? The sum total of all wars fought for pride and prejudice pale in significance to the battle for lost souls in which your missionary has been engaged. Your missionary needs a time of debriefing to process all that God has done in and through him. *"And when they were come, they gathered the church together and rehearsed all that God had done with them, and how He had opened the door of faith to the Gentiles"* (Acts 14:27).

Can't you just picture it: Paul and Barnabas have been home for a month now. Paul is staying in a spare bedroom at the home of Manaen; Barnabas is still at Simeon Niger's house. Paul wakes up in the middle of the night shouting, "No! No! We're humans just like you!"

Manaen comes running to the room. "Paul, brother, are you okay? Was that a nightmare? Can I bring you a drink?" Paul sits up in bed and laughs! "No, thanks. But I was just dreaming again about a wild experience we had. Have I told this story yet?"

"Yes, but tell it again," replies Manaen, yawning and stretching away his sleep. "I'm sure it's important to you if you are even dreaming about it."

"We had just fled Iconium, having caught wind of a plot to stone us. We headed for Lystra, preaching the Gospel. A certain man, crippled from birth, was listening intently to the Message. I caught his eye. I sensed he had the faith to be healed and Jesus healed him— right there! He was leaping and walking around.

"Well, the people were so excited they began speaking in tongues, the Lyconiun tongue, that is! We couldn't understand a word. What an uproar! We were being rushed by the mob to the gates of the city, but their voices were not angry. I thought I heard the names Jupiter and Mercury, but we still had no idea what was going on. It was a frenzied, wild scene.

"Then we saw it! A garlanded oxen and a priest about to slaughter it! Whoa! I realized what was about to happen. They thought we were gods because of the miracle that had taken place. They were going to sacrifice that ox to us! In such a desperate moment, the only thing we thought to do was rip off our clothes to show them that we were mere humans as they. (And that was one of my favorite tunics!)" (See Acts 14:5-18.)

All right! All right! We don't know how that story got told for Luke to record it years later, but if you had been Manaen, would you have allowed Paul to interrupt your night's sleep? Of course you would! Now, would you do the same for your missionary friend? Why? Or why not?

*Listen to me! Please, listen to me!* This is the spoken or unspoken plea of every returning missionary. For *their* benefit, they need to share.

As you read their stories expressing that plea, educate yourself in the skills of sensing that need, in knowing how to get them to talk about the real issues, and in determining the best time for this conversation.

### SO MUCH TO SAY; NO ONE TO TALK TO

We had lived overseas for more than twelve years when we returned for our first six-month furlough. Having never done this, we did not know what to do or what to expect, if anything. Two memories are imbedded in our hearts. One is of a church and a town (not our own) where we were received with open arms and immediately asked to share at the first available meeting. That was followed by the pastor asking me to fill his pulpit the next weekend. This made us feel wanted and valuable—a very warm feeling.

The other memory is of a church whose pastor didn't have the time of day to talk with us. We waited two hours and then got five minutes of his time, which seemed to be a burden to him. My wife and I walked into the parking lot and cried. We felt unwanted and overwhelmed. So much to say; no one to talk to. We could write a book about our experiences of that six-month furlough, but it is too painful. We are not making any plans for a return for more than short visits. It is all our hearts can handle. We are at home on our mission assignment.

FOR FURTHER UNDERSTANDING
The ecstasy—and the agony! One pastor knows the needs of returning missionaries; another doesn't. And the results are clearly seen in this brief story. Note that though this was written years after their return to the field, their "book" of those six months' experiences could not be written, because "it is (still) too painful."

Note also that little parenthesis "not our own" referring to the town. In our effort to really understand and help our returning missionary friends, we need to be alert to even the slightest spoken, and yes, sometimes their unspoken, expressions of need. Though I don't know for sure—it is something I would have definitely pursued—there seems to be an unspoken implication that his home church (whether or not it is the one he describes negatively) was not a strong receiving church.

But all responsibility cannot be put on those pastors. Obviously, this missionary family had not received training about furlough time. In their words, "we didn't know what to do or what to expect." Then, to be so well-received by one pastor made the rejection by the second even more sorrowful. Unfortunately, it is so easy for our human nature to focus on the negative rather than the positive. More people see the glass "half empty" rather than "half full." The "agony" remains; the "ecstasy" is forgotten.

It doesn't take a long story (nor a long conversation with your missionary friend) to learn of the needs of missionaries. "So much to say; no one to listen." So briefly stated, yet it speaks volumes. We must take care that the brevity of our missionary friend's words do not go overlooked.

"So much to say...." What does a missionary want to talk about? Everything! And yet, sometimes—nothing! Confused? Yes! And that may be the exact state of your friend. At times, in the middle of his pouring out of his heart, he'll just stop. Tears may flow. Is he overwhelmed by the work yet undone? Is he remembering the national workers who could not leave after the coup? Is he overcome by the awesome privilege God has given him to minister cross-culturally? Is he lamenting the lost opportunities to minister, due to his negligence, or that of others? Is he grieved by the apparent apathy of the church at home?

"...and no one to talk to!" Paul Tournier, in his book, *To Understand Each Other* said, "Most of the conversations of the world are *dialogues of the deaf!*" Each person is only waiting for the other one to stop so that "I" can have my say! What a pitiful state of affairs. Even Jesus, on the road to Emmaus—though He knew exactly what was going on in the hearts and minds and emotions of those two discouraged disciples, took the time to listen to their story of sadness and woe.

In our sound-bite, commitment-measured-in-microseconds society, we find it difficult to really listen. But that is exactly what is needed by our missionary friends.

FOR FURTHER ACTION
- If you have a missionary friend on the field who was not given training on reentry, you can make it your business to help him. Do you know if he is prepared for reentry? Write to him and find out. Your letter has to say more than just, "Are you ready for reentry?" If he has not had good training (which is most likely the

case), he won't know what you are asking. Ask him some probing questions that speak to the issues you are learning about in this book.

- Though a reentry time may include many aspects, such as retraining in a skill, encouraging and building up the support team, meeting new family members (by birth or marriage) or paying respects to those who have passed on, there are at least three major areas in which you can help:

STEPS TO REENTRY
- Know it's time to go
- Go to home church
- "Abide"
- Rehearse "all"
- Fully integrate

—Some initial time for rest and relaxation (R&R). In generations past, this was accomplished by the five to ten weeks it took the ship to get your missionary home. There was nothing he could do but relax and unwind and meet new and interesting people.

With travel today making no place in the world more than twenty-four flight hours away (and those hours in themselves add to the stress of reentry), a missionary needs some initial time for R&R—possibly a regrouping for a family. For a single missionary, it may be a holiday with family or a close friend—or even a solitary retreat may be his desire.

You can help with the plans. Do you know of a family going on vacation who would let your missionary friend stay in their home for a week? Can you (the church, home fellowship, a group of families, or YOU!) afford the cost of a beach house or mountain cabin? Let your creativity run wild! There are many ideas God can bring to your mind. Be sure to check those ideas out with your missionary friend *before* you rent the place!

—Some time for public debriefing. Whether your friend is going back to the field or staying home, for *his* sake, you can schedule some meetings for him to share his field experiences. I repeat, for *his* sake, he needs to share with the Sunday School—the kindergartners, primary, middle and upper graders, high schoolers, young adults, middle adults and senior adults! With the public and private schools. With the Rotary and Kiwanis Clubs. A newspaper article. A radio talk show. An interview with the governor!

Do you get the idea?! Set a schedule of meetings with as broad a spectrum of society as possible. Why? This forces him to rethink his experiences through the minds of each of the groups he is addressing. And that is good. He is processing and reprocessing. He is remembering details in one talk that he didn't think of in another. He is clarifying in his mind his accomplishments done in Jesus' Name. He is able to admit his failures. He can thank the Lord for his successes. He is giving an honest report. People now see him as he really is—an ordinary human being, called by God to minister cross-culturally.

—Some time for private debriefing. It is a rare and cherished friend who has learned the skill of active listening—one who can listen *from* his heart and listen *to* the heart of the speaker. An active listener can sense the pathos—the entire gamut of human experience—trying to be expressed by his returning missionary friend. You are available to cry with him when, in the middle of the night, he calls. Out of your sleep you say, "Hello." Nothing! Again, "Hello!" Nothing! As you are about to hang up, you hear a slight whimper. You ask, "Is that you, (your friend's name)? I'll be right over."

This aspect of reentry care has been so neglected that nobody seems to be ready for it. It is *time*-consuming! Even your missionary friend may say, "Hey! It's cool! I'm OK!" And leave you wondering why I am making such an issue of it. Do you remember the last story in Chapter One? That missionary was hurting to the core! Yet, he had to maintain the image that "everything was great!"

Get in your friend's face, as I did, and say, "You don't need to fool me. Let's talk!" And then *listen* with your whole being!

## A LADY REACHED OUT TO US

Through wise counsel and arrangements by a friend, a beautiful "hide-away" was provided for us for our first two weeks just to relax. That was good. But the time came when we had to start adjusting to living here! I was exhausted from the pressure of working so many roles at the mission. Suddenly that responsibility was completely gone.

Initially, there was great relief, but a feeling of worthlessness quickly followed as people asked, "And what do you do?" There did not seem to be the respect or even interest in what I had done; only what I was doing presently. Presently? Presently, I needed to rest! Spiritually I felt drained. Some days, I would just sit and look out at the beautiful trees and sky and cry. I had not driven for almost five years. It was traumatic just to take a driver's test and exhibit my parallel parking skills. I didn't feel that people were friendly or caring. When I was out anywhere, even church, I felt ignored. People seemed to talk about acquiring "things" all the time.

NINE AREAS OF STRESS
Physical
Professional
Financial
Cultural
Social
Linguistic
National/Political
Educational
Spiritual

When I went shopping for groceries, I was appalled at how much food they bought, when it was obvious that they didn't need that much because they were already overweight. (Remember that I'd come from an Asian country where almost all the people were very slim.) I was ashamed of the sloppy dress and careless and rude manners. And I felt that the way people spent money was sinful. All the women were getting their fingernails done to the tune of $40 and up. I thought of the sacrifices that some of the missionaries had suffered, like eating celery and onion soup for four days because they couldn't afford anything better. All of this made me very angry. I withdrew and didn't even want to go anywhere—even to see our family.

There was, though, excellent teaching on Christian

radio, and our church had such good praise and worship. This began the healing process. Also, there was a lady who reached out to us. When she heard that we had been missionaries, she was ecstatic. This was a novel but welcome reaction for us. She also had been a missionary and knew what we were going through. Not only did her interest in us bring the comfort and healing we needed, but also it gave us a clearer perspective of others' apparent disinterest. Initially, I felt terribly let down by Christian people who I thought would be very interested in what the Lord was doing through His children around the world. I had to come to grips with the fact that people were not and still are not interested in learning about either our struggles or our ministry.

But why? I came to realize that they didn't have a point of identification with what we had been and were now experiencing to really help us. The news here in the States is very limited regarding the world perspective. It seemed centered on trivial and gossipy, rather than newsworthy, items. The information we knew about the situation in China was not even mentioned, or was downplayed. They just didn't know what it was really like out there. Also, most of them had never had any experience travelling or living outside of the States or in any type of mission work. This does not distress me now like it did at first. People cannot understand what they have not experienced personally or in their spirit through prayer.

FOR FURTHER UNDERSTANDING

This missionary covered a number of aspects that presented reentry challenge. In fact, it sounds to me like her writing this story probably helped make the catharsis more complete.

But there was one theme that was repeated often. Did you catch it? She finally came to "grips with the disinterest of the people back home."

I do not believe that her final resolve, "People cannot understand what they have not experienced personally," helped her reentry. Possibly, it provided a surface excuse for them, which helped her avoid the pitfall of condemnation. However, several times she did indicate her alienation: "I withdrew and didn't even want to go anywhere." Condemnation or alienation? One is as dangerous as the other.

FIVE REENTRY PATTERNS
Alienation
Condemnation
Reversion
Suicide
INTEGRATION

FOR FURTHER ACTION

- Inserted in the margin of this story are the nine areas of challenge a missionary faces upon reentry. Highlight and somehow relate her words to one or another of the categories of challenge.

For example, her statement, "...people asked, 'What do you do?',", challenged her professional standing and worth. The world places a high value on our position in life. For one who had been about her Father's business, lowering herself to address that question brought stress. Paul, the Apostle said, *"God is not impressed with a man's position"* (Galatians 2:6b). Should we be?

You will find at least twelve more statements that relate directly with one of the nine areas of challenge. In fact, almost every sentence in her first three paragraphs could be highlighted!

- I do agree that one who has "not been there" will have a more difficult time relating to the experiences of a missionary. However, a doctor can offer a cure for a disease without having experienced the illness. And a pastor can warn against sin without having experienced it. Likewise, you as a caregiver can be available to your friend upon reentry to listen and understand and help him move forward to full integration.

- Don't let the excuse "they just don't know" hold you back. Become knowledgeable. Begin your preparation to become a good reentry caregiver long before your missionary arrives home. Read his letters carefully. Ask him to explain things you don't understand. Keep current on *real* world affairs, especially as they affect the region in which your friend is working. Read books and articles about other missionaries' experiences surrounding reentry. Relate with internationals living in your community. What are they experiencing? What are the issues they are confronting? Those could very well be the reentry stress points your returning missionary friend will have to face.

• Can you find the key sentence in her story? The focal point of her recovery? Yes, the Christian radio teaching and the praise and worship at her church and the beautiful creation around her certainly "began the healing process."

And not to discredit those, there is yet another sentence that is key: "There was a lady who reached out to us." The reentry process needs to take place in community. It needs the heart of God clothed in "flesh and blood." It needs a listening ear. Develop your listening skills. Read Paul Tournier's book, *To Understand Each Other* or David Augsburger's, *Caring Enough to Hear.* Then—*listen!* Practice on your friends here—now! Don't wait until your missionary friend comes home!

### IN A PERFECT WORLD

Isolation, confusion, anger, frustration, failure, condemnation—all of these feelings were present on my reentry. I don't think they came totally from my relationship with the church. Because my status on the field was pretty low profile, and because I didn't make much "noise" when I came home, I remember a lot of confusion about what I was supposed to do next. Obviously, I had some insecurity problems, so I never approached the leadership with any confidence. Oh yes, feelings of failure and jealousy were present when others got to share their stories before the congregation, but that only compounded my inability to talk with my missions pastor. When I did try to describe my journeys to some of the elders, I felt patronized and dismissed. I was an outcast; I had no place to call my home church.

I felt so honored that God had chosen me to go. I felt—Huge! Something had happened so intensely personal, like a journey of healing for me (and a few other lives along the way). We had fun and people around us thought God was fun too. The folks I was with loved and gave from their hearts. We learned that from each other. It seemed pretty easy to do over there. Of course, in the tough times we would lay hands on each other and pray. I guess being so close to a group of people gave me that luxury of community. There was a connection with God that I haven't had since—either spiritually or emotionally.

Initially on my return, there was a small cluster of friends who were interested in hearing about my experiences. We stayed in touch, but I found it difficult trying to communicate something that intense, that personal, to friends who could not relate. Fortunately, they stuck with me. They helped me get back on my feet. My feelings of isolation and frustration did keep going back to my church. I had no valid point of reference without the backing of the leadership. I had no foothold in the church that I called home.

After several Sundays back, I decided to re-introduce myself to a few people I recognized. At one point, I ran into one administrator who recognized my name! Finally, I thought, I was not totally forgotten. He requested me to follow him to his office because he had something there for me. He disappeared and came out with a bill for my insurance that had not been paid the three years I had been away! I could have been knocked over by a feather! My heart sank! I was totally blown away! At this point, I was emotionally broken down and this was the last straw! Spiritually, I was at an all-time low. My ego had come home wanting a ticker tape parade and a slap on the back in front of our large congregation, but the best I could be acknowledged with was an unpaid bill.

It has been fifteen years since my return. Looking back has opened some old wounds. Some wounds, no doubt, were self-inflicted. But still, if the truth were told, in a perfect world, I would like to have been accepted back by the church leadership.

FOR FURTHER UNDERSTANDING
Buried! Buried in isolation for fifteen years were the gut-wrenching feelings expressed by this returning missionary in his opening statement. Had he had a good cross-cultural experience? Yes, it was "a journey of healing for me and a few others. I was connected with God."

There is another connection we must experience in life, for we are the Body of Christ—all members "fitly joined together." When this man came home, he was looking for that connection with his church leadership.

Unfortunately, that connection was never made. Maturity softened his final statement: "...in a perfect world." If it were a perfect world, we could have been connected! Give me a break! It is because we live in an imperfect world that we all the more need connectiveness in the Body of Christ!

I began this paragraph with the words, "In defense of a *large* church...." I stopped and scratched them out! There is no defense for a large, or any-sized church to not provide proper care for their returning missionaries. (I have said it before; it bears repeating.) If a church is going to claim the responsibility for sending missionaries out from their Body, they *must* carve out the time and the energy and the personnel to bring them home safely. Missionaries are too valuable to lose.

Unfortunately, to this day, this man admits that spiritually and emotionally he remains in isolation. And his church remains oblivious to his need. God, forgive us all!

FOR FURTHER ACTION
• Did you note the persistence of his friends? Though they "could not relate," they "stuck with me." Even if you sense that you cannot relate "perfectly," stick with your returning friend. You may bungle through a few conversations, but persistence, in time, will have your friend "back on his feet again."

• When he tried to have an audience with the church leadership, he felt "patronized and dismissed." If you became friends with this man today and heard his story, what would you do? Would you tell him to just find another church? Would you help him confront the current leadership? (The senior pastor is still there; the missions pastor has moved on.) Would you suggest he write to the administrator who "welcomed him home" with an unpaid insurance bill? Which area of support was grossly missing? Does your friend have a good network of caregivers?

AREAS OF SUPPORT
Moral
Logistic
Financial
Prayer
Communication
Reentry

Do you see why the wisest man on earth told us to "Cry out for wisdom and understanding and knowledge?" (See Proverbs 2:1-5.) The answers to these questions—and others that would come to your concerned mind—are not easily found. But through wisdom and counsel, you will hear His solutions.

• How more clearly could he have expressed his need to relate with his home church? To the degree you have influence with your church missions leadership, make sure your returning missionary friend receives the proper "reconnecting" with the Body of Christ back home. It may be a "simply-stated" five

STEPS TO REENTRY
Know it's time to go
Go to home church
"Abide"
Rehearse "all"
Fully integrate

step process given to us in Scripture, but make sure it isn't *simply* forgotten in the excitement of your friend's return.

### ALL THE GRIEF CAME FLOODING BACK

While we were living overseas, a very important person in my life died. She was one of the people that walked me through those horrible teenage years that can be so devastating. Before we left, we knew we would never see her again, but that didn't make the loss any easier when the news finally came. It hurt! As we were preparing to return home, I kept reminding myself that she would not be there when we arrived.

Even just recently, while attending the funeral of a young cousin of mine, all of the grief from the loss of my mentor came flooding back, and it still seems strange that I can't go and see her.

FOR FURTHER UNDERSTANDING

There isn't one of us who hasn't been touched by the loss of a friend or relative. We have felt the loss and suffered the grief. Family and friends have gathered. Comfort has been offered. And received. It may have been a gentle touch; it may have been shared tears. But it was done in community. There was closure. And we all moved on.

We can identify with the pain of a mother awaiting the discovery of her daughter's kidnapped and murdered body. The wrist bands worn by those who have not found their sons or brothers lost in battle speak to the same need for closure.

For the missionary who receives news of a loved one having died while he is on the field, there is no opportunity for the shared grieving. It is impossible to bring a closure to this loss. He will have to face that scenario when he returns home.

FOR FURTHER ACTION

• Though you experienced your personal grieving, closure and moving on in community with family and friends, in order to help your missionary friend, you are going to have to go back to that point in time with him. You may want to talk about who was at the funeral. You may want to go to the cemetery. You may even need to relive the events leading up to the death.

Closure is part of our human experience. It will take an extremely sensitive spirit to understand to what degree of remembrance your friend needs to go to find his.

• On the other hand, you will need to take care that the process does not become morbid! Death is the most inevitable fact of life! And it only announces the end of Act III in God's Great Drama. The good news for the believer is the awesome Script describing the beginning of Act IV: *"To be absent from the body is to be present with the Lord!"* (II Corinthians 5:8).

Unfortunately, Act IV has another Scene, running simultaneously. If the one who died was without Christ, the grieving is of another sort! It is unthinkably grievous! It can only drive us back to the sovereign wisdom of God. And our strong confidence in Him!

(Act I began in John 1; Act II in Isaiah 14; Act III in Genesis 1; and Act IV at death or in Revelation 21.)

### THEY NEVER ASKED ME TO SHARE

Three things stand out in my memory of reentry:

1) My home culture is so selfish. From pushing to the front of a line to cutting others off on the freeway, consideration and manners are conspicuous by their absence.

2) My home culture is so fast-paced. I found that I could hardly think in English, making my response time very slow. Yet, the best part of coming home was also related to the language. I was able to read things in English and also understand everything that was said

to me if others spoke slowly enough!

3) But the biggest thing that hurt me was that my home church never asked me to share what I had learned, what I had done, where I had been, what I had seen, what personal growth had taken place in my life. Had I led others to Christ? They never let me unleash all of the things that I had learned through an active prayer life and devotions; and the biggest thing of all, dependence daily on Christ for all of my needs.

FOR FURTHER UNDERSTANDING

Listen to me! Please, listen to me! It is being said in many ways—in many contexts. But it always comes back to the simple need for a listening ear. Yes, the selfishness was there. And the fast-paced lifestyle had her dizzy at times, making it hard for her to get back in the "swing of things." But "Why wouldn't they listen to me?" was her real question.

Consider this: If the church leadership had allowed her to share, there are eight areas of Christian growth to which she could have given personal testimony. The church is often the major "loser" in not listening to returned missionaries.

FOR FURTHER ACTION

• Reread this brief story. Underscore the eight areas of spiritual growth this church would have benefitted hearing about.

• When your friend comes home, you can help him formulate and organize his thoughts for sharing. And remember, it is *not* those "ten minutes on Sunday morning" that you or he should be looking for. Rather, a diverse array of venues and a wide range of ages is to be desired.

Appendix D, *Guidelines for Sharing*, gives you and your missionary friend some suggestions for making his time of sharing vibrant, informative and challenging.

### DEBRIEF ME, PLEASE

In addition to being very active on our church missions committee in a church where our mission budget is $12,000 a month (and where I have talked repeatedly about giving returning missionaries more attention...with no response), I am also a missionary. But I live in comfortable North America with a decent house and lifestyle. This kind of missionary has a difficult time getting any support—financial, prayer or encouragement, as it does not look like we are out there "suffering for the Lord."

I travel cross-culturally for perhaps two to three weeks every second month. I go into new territory each time and work with the local pastors.

Let me give you a recent example. I took two other team members and went into a new country, Suriname. I did not know the two other team members so there were a lot of personality adjustments, but that is not unusual. We had arranged transportation with a local brother who had a van. In addition to the usual repairs, expenses and lateness, we were going down a busy highway and had to stop for some construction. "No brakes!" We narrowly avoided a head-on collision, but did collide with three cars in front of us. We were shook up, with bruises and cuts. For five hours we stood on the side of the road in one hundred-degree temperatures. Police who wanted a payoff threatened us, and put us under tremendous pressure. I have a heart condition and suffered severe angina, and my diabetes kicked in. I came close to blacking out.

We were then offered accommodation in what was supposed to be a hotel! For the duration of our stay, there was no air conditioning, no screens and overwhelmingly high temperatures. There were lots of good adventures too, of course.

The day of departure I was sick from a stomach bug. We arrived at the airport and it was hotter inside the building than outside. After more than an hour in line with my stomach really acting up, we were told that our flight, and all flights had been cancelled! 25,000 fires were burning and the smoke was destroying the visibility. No planes were landing; thus no planes were taking off! The next day the city was covered with black ash. Four days later, by running, rushing and cajoling, we managed to get on the first flight out. By this time our budget for accommodations and food was shot and we were in debt.

I got home on Saturday. The next morning the pastor noticed that I was home and gave a quick, humorous welcome: "Looks like Bill is back from Suriname." That was it! No one seemed aware that I had even been away. My wife had called many people for prayer for me, but there seemed to be no awareness.

I just feel the need for a chance to talk about our experiences (good and bad) when we get back. The most I get is about a minute of, "How was your trip? Where did you go? Oh, yes. That's nice."

I love what I am doing. It is a blessing and a thrill. However, I need to debrief! And at this time, my wife is the only one who will listen. Even my board forgets where I have been. I can't imagine how hard it must be on single missionaries with no one to listen.

FOR FURTHER UNDERSTANDING
This is a unique story. Unique for the fact that the reentry part is only the last three paragraphs. I included the whole (though somewhat edited) story to point out that this missionary, so in need of someone to listen to him, used this opportunity to debrief!

When missionaries return home—from two weeks or two years—they need to debrief! How else can it be said?

From his Board that seems unaware of his goings and comings to a church missions committee that will not receive his counsel, it seems to me that he needs help in building a full team of support personnel.

AREAS OF SUPPORT
Moral
Logistic
Financial
Prayer
Communication
Reentry

FOR FURTHER ACTION

• Six trips a year! That requires a lot of debriefing! Can you set up a rotating debriefing team? One that might be able to handle two or three stories each?

• For his personal debriefing, he has his wife. However, there too, you might want to be available.

• Can you help this man establish a better foundation for a full support team of caregivers? Can you be the coordinating liaison person? Can you gather around yourself two or three others who will "own the vision" with this missionary? Can you divide up the responsibilities of the six areas of care among this core team? Can you now build beyond that core a committed group of people whose love for the lost and vision for this man's mission compels them to serve as caregivers for this missionary?

(For a fuller consideration of this need and process, refer to the book, *Serving As Senders*, available through Emmaus Road International.)

Though we have set these three "For Further Action" ideas in the context of the missionary who told the story, I trust you can make the parallel application to the needs of your missionary friend.

## ONE PERSON WAS ENOUGH

With each succeeding reentry experience, I am becoming more aware of how extreme cultural differences can be. But let me go back to the first time I reentered after being away just two years. I was single then, and believed that I'd had a positive two years, had grown a lot, and had learned a lot of language. I had just returned from South America, but I was anything but ready for the changes that faced me that first day.

On leaving the airport, I looked around in amazement at the wealth displayed in the beautiful homes and swimming pools. Having just left some awfully squalid areas in South America, an emotion welled up in me that was very difficult to explain. I cried for about half an hour. It was all so beautiful and yet the contrast of where I had been with this—my world—seemed so terribly unfair. Somehow, deep inside of me it hurt. This world was wrong and it hurt.

It hurts less now after years have passed. I'm not sure if I've become hardened, or if I've just become realistic.

When I arrived in front of our old home and saw my widowed mum standing there waiting to welcome me back, I spontaneously rushed up and threw my arms around her. (Looking back, this was probably more appropriate in a Latin context than our rural Australian context.) In that next second or two, so much confusion took place that it's all so difficult to explain.

I'm sure my mother was dumbfounded by this affectionate behavior. It was anything but typical for our family, and she involuntarily recoiled. As she pulled back, I felt everything within me accuse me of being a klutz. She was probably asking herself, "Who is this man?" And I was certainly asking myself, "Who am I?" I had changed and I didn't fit the old familiar pattern.

Then, in walked my young brother. He was thirteen when I left home; now he was sixteen. He was a boy when I said good-bye to him; now he was a man. I honestly wouldn't have known him if I'd met him on the street, but the affection I had for him was still there.

Over a meal we sat and talked—well, the rest of the family did—he just sat and watched, quietly observing. At one point when the meal was finished, we were left alone. The first words my dear little brother spoke to me were filled with venom: "You're back home now. You can just cut out that foreign accent here." I was cut to the core! This was honestly the first time that I'd even realized that, yes, my accent probably *had* changed as a result of my contact with English speakers of other countries. I was shattered, but managed to keep it together—at least outwardly.

Later that evening, absolutely exhausted from the flight and my first day back home, I was preparing for bed when in walked my older brother. He'd been drinking. He came to me, threw his arms around me and put his head on my shoulder. He smelled so bad. I was afraid he was going to vomit down my back, but his hug was such a relief and a comfort that it seemed like a fitting end to the evening, until he stood back, and in his unsteady stance, looked me squarely in the face and said, "So you think you're smart with all this religion and languages and stuff now, do you? Well, you can just keep it all to yourself here."

I went to bed and cried for three hours. I thought, there is no understanding from my family. Will there be any help from my church? Unfortunately, they were no more prepared to help me than I would have been able to help Bell invent the telephone. Our worlds were so far removed from each other, that I gave up almost any hope of ever having any real understanding from them.

But there was one spark of hope and ray of sunshine! She was just one old lady in the church who had spent some years overseas herself in mission work. One day she invited me to have a chat. She asked me intelligent question after intelligent question. Suddenly I felt like I was *worth* something! My contribution to the world had been *recognized* by someone. I hadn't just dreamed the previous two years of my life. Someone *asked* and *listened* and *cared*. That was enough. One person was enough. We prayed together and it was wonderful.

FOR FURTHER UNDERSTANDING
Could it be said more clearly? More simply? One person asked and listened and cared! It is true. When all is said and done, the greatest single need of a reentering missionary is that one person will commit to listen—to listen, not at their own convenience, but at the time of need of the missionary.

FOR FURTHER ACTION
- She also asked "intelligent question after intelligent question." In order to do this, you must be current on what God is doing in 21st Century world evangelism. And more specifically, what part your missionary friend was playing in God's Plan. When he talks about his ministry in Mozambique, don't go looking for it on a map of Asia! When he talks about redemptive analogies, don't ask him what kind of coupons they are?
- Read current missions books. Become knowledgeable of world current events. (By the way, you will not get that on network TV!) If your missionary is serving in Indonesia, subscribe (via Internet) to an English-language edition of a Jakarta newspaper! At your local colleges and universities, meet and relate with international students from the country in which your missionary friend is working.
- Develop the skill of asking open questions—ones that cannot be answered with a "yes" or "no." Develop the skill of reflecting your understanding and acceptance of what he is saying. He will feel it is safe to say more. Getting him to express his full gamut of thoughts and feelings is your goal. He needs to process them all. And that is done best by saying them out loud.
- "You shouldn't feel that way!" does *not* encourage him to say more. As you give of yourself to being a good listener, there will be plenty of time for him to sort through attitudes appropriate to a godly life in his new culture.

Chapter Seven

# Silly Little Things

In this group of brief stories we find the returning missionaries relating incidents that we would categorize as reentry *shock* (as opposed to reentry *stress*). Reentry shock could be likened to the shock of electricity: Briefly there is an uncomfortable tingling or biting sensation. But it soon dissipates.

Likewise, in reentry culture shock situations, there is usually just a brief moment of embarrassment—a little tingling sensation or hair rising on the back of the neck or a blushed face that soon gives way to laughter as understanding of the situation comes.

But let's go back to the electric shock: In that instant of shock there is also the fearful realization that had that electric charge been of a higher voltage or had it lasted for a longer period of time, more severe consequences than a "tingling sensation" would have resulted. As a precaution from further danger, we look for the broken wire or damaged piece of equipment and lay it aside or fix it.

With reentry culture shock, however, your returning missionary doesn't know when the next "broken wire" will bite him! Nor does he know how high the voltage will be. Nor does he know how long it will last! And bit by bit the reservoir of resistance to the biting of these experiences is drained and more serious consequences can result. The "silly little thing" can become "the final straw!"

After each story are specific suggestions relating to that episode. However, in general, on a regular basis, ask your friend to share—to talk about—those "silly little things" that are happening in his life. "Any crazy thing happen to you today?" would be a good question to ask. And get him to laugh with you about it. It is being able to laugh at these culture shock situations that can help to salve the pain of the more serious issues he will face.

Now, we don't want you to *laugh yourself silly* over these stories. Thus, we have established a scale to gauge the degree of laughter each of these silly, little stories deserves. We have given them our mark. Will you agree? Here is the scale, from the slightest to the greatest:

*Glint in the eye, smile, grin, titter, giggle, chuckle, chortle, snicker, snort, guffaw, cachinnate* (Laugh yourself silly at that one, will you!), *roar, split a gut, laugh yourself silly, die laughing!* This is certainly the ultimate laugh!

Happy reading!

### FOREWARNED AND FOREARMED—MAYBE

To be forewarned is to be forearmed! I had been forewarned and now I was forearmed. In what battle was I about to be engaged? My first trip to the supermarket.

I had been on the field for two years. Grocery shopping was a daily activity. It was a time for friendship (and chatter)! If a certain item could not be found today, it might be available the next day or the next week or the next month.

But as I said, I had heard story after dismal story

about how the multiplied choices of a supermarket can shatter the strongest of character. I was determined it wouldn't happen to me. From the newspaper ad, I carefully prepared my list. I knew what I needed and I wouldn't be distracted from it.

With single-minded determination I firmly placed my hands on the shopping cart handle and began. There was no looking around, no chances of a smile at anyone, no exchanged greetings, and no shared tidbits of community news.

I started up the first aisle. Yes, put the peanut butter jar in the basket; check it off the list. The next aisle finished and the next. The blinking blue light announcing a special sale on a certain brand of peas did not deter me from purchasing the predetermined brand on my list. Another item checked off. Aisle by aisle my cart filled and my list got checked off.

I swung down the last aisle and was on the home stretch. I rolled my cart up to the checkout counter. In my mind's eye I saw the winner's ribbon draped across the cart. The crowds were cheering! The sound was deafening in my ears. I had won!

Suddenly, a pimple-faced half-boy, half-man standing at the end of the counter asked, "Paper or plastic, ma'am?" I lost it! This wasn't in the script. Nobody had prepared me for this. What do you say? How do you answer such a profound question? I stared at him, perplexed. He smiled at me. "That's okay, ma'am, I'll make that decision for you!"

FOR FURTHER UNDERSTANDING

If you don't give this story a full *die laughing* rating, something is wrong with your sense of humor! This missionary, no doubt, at least *split a gut!* It cannot be overemphasized, a good sense of humor will help your missionary friend over—or through—many an awkward situation.

In our pre-field training, we tell a missionary to take a good sense of humor with him to the field. You remind him to bring it home!

Think back—even before you got to the bagger's question, *paper or plastic?*, you knew what was coming! Right? Of course! We lived here when that little bit of supermarket sales technique was introduced. In fact, the first time we were asked that question, it might have taken us off-guard. What?! But for us it was not one of a "hundred" issues bombarding us all at once. So with ease we were able to file it as another gimmick in the highly competitive marketing world.

Now—enter your missionary friend. *Everything* is "new and different!" All of his senses are being challenged by media promotion. The unlimited array of choices can be mind-boggling. And add to that a *final straw*, "paper or plastic?"

(Just this morning I enjoyed a last minute breakfast with a missionary friend of ours returning to the field after a year's furlough. We went to the International House of Pancakes. On our table were *only* four choices of syrup. As he read the labels, he groaned: "Always, always, so *many* choices!" It is a good thing we didn't go to the Baskin-Robbin's 31 Flavors ice cream parlor down the street!)

FOR FURTHER ACTION

• This grocery store issue is so common, who hasn't heard it told at least once? Go with your friend on that first (and maybe, second) trip to the store. Third?! Well, there has to come a time when he should be able to do it on his own.

• Help educate your returned missionary on wise selection of the multiplied choices in the marketplace. An item twice as expensive, yet guaranteed to last three or four times as long, might be worth the greater initial investment.

## LINGUISTICALLY SPEAKING

My main problem was with music. When I was asked to lead a choir in one of our supporting churches in the Midwest, I accepted because I do love to work with choral music in either Spanish or English.

I could not understand why the men were staring at me. After a pregnant pause, my wife whispered to me from the soprano section that I was asking the basses to sing the "black notes" with greater emphasis. They were stymied. All notes are printed in black ink. In Spanish, however, quarter notes are called "negras" and I had somehow done a transliteration in my mind. I turned red, and quickly asked them to sing the "quarter notes" with greater emphasis—which they did!

FOR FURTHER UNDERSTANDING
This is just another one of those "silly little things" that probably rolled off his back with not more than a *chortle!* (Note from the scale that that's less than a full laugh!) On the other hand, linguistic difficulties can mount up to heights of embarrassment and frustration. Certainly the more fluent your missionary friend has become in the language of his host culture, the more difficult it will be for him to again express himself in his mother tongue.

Likewise, if he has found the host culture language to have a greater variety of descriptive words (The typical American English conversation uses fewer than 700 different words!), trying to express himself with such a limited vocabulary could be a source of frustration.

FOR FURTHER ACTION
• You may want to subscribe to an English language news magazine for your friend, either in hard copy or through the Internet. Not only will that keep him up to date on world news, but will allow him time to think in his mother tongue.

## THREE STRAWS IN THE SADDLE BAGS

There is no doubt in my mind that there really are weird things—stupid, little things—that happen to folks on reentry. I believe the enemy has planned to try and discourage us, taking advantage of our already compromised mental energies. Wanting to give a small, token gift of appreciation to my faithful support team, I bought coffee cups from our mission. They were very nice coffee mugs and had the mission's emblem and motto on them. However, the first three friends I tried to give them to refused them, all stating in different ways and separate setting that "We already have enough cups. Thank you." Weird? Anyway, it was like a slap in my face. It discouraged me so much that a gift that I could afford was rejected, I never tried again.

Another time, I was invited to a singles' gathering for a home get-together. I brought a small pocket photo album that had about ten pictures in it. When the conversation turned to what I was doing, I thought it would be appropriate to bring the pictures out and share them. I'm sorry, but the hostess was such a "jerk!" She flat out told me, "Oh, we don't want to see those" and literally grabbed them out of my hands and made me put them away. I was just humiliated!

I waited a whole two months to have an audience with the pastor of my largest sending church. While the pastor was kind enough to sit and listen to my 30-minutes of conversation, his closing remarks were, "Well, now that you've gone there and done that, have you gotten it out of your system? Are you ready to stay home and find a ministry here?" He was serious. All I could do was mumble, "I'm not sure about anything!"

FOR FURTHER UNDERSTANDING
The "silly, little things" are often the "big things" of reentry. We have all said (or heard said), "That's the final straw!" Or, "That was the straw that broke the camel's

back!" For a time there was even a game around called, The Last Straw. A multi-hinged plastic camel had two saddlebags across his back. One by one participants put little plastic "straws" in the bags—ever so carefully. Finally the weight would be too much! And the whole thing would collapse! It's those "silly, little things" that keep piling up and piling up. The time comes when the weight of them is too much—emotionally, psychological-ly or spiritually! And ker-bang! The back breaks!

FOR FURTHER ACTION

- Not being a coffee drinker, I also have a difficult time graciously receiving coffee cups as gifts. However, not being able to avoid them, I now display my collection of mission agency coffee mugs! You could do the same.

- On the other hand, possibly you could advise your friend on more appropriate gifts. A capsule of sand from the foot of the great Egyptian pyramids sits on my shelf as a prized gift from one who had been there.

- Though this certainly seemed to be an appropriate time to show her pictures, knowing ahead of time what freedom she has in sharing might have avoided this embarrassment. You can help by setting times and arranging meetings in which your friend can share. You can also help your friend by reviewing with him the *Guidelines For Sharing*, Appendix D.

- (One editorial comment to this story said, "I don't think these situations are funny at all.") A point well-taken. To one person, situations like these could be "sil-ly, little things;" to another, the "final straws."

- Help "lift the straws out of the saddle bags" by getting your friend to talk about the situations. Help him try to find some humor, or at least some way to lighten the load.

For example, to the pastor's hurtful (she took it as *hurtful*) comment, she could have replied, "I'm not sure, but if I do stay at home, I would like to help you educate the church in how to care for returning missionaries." Even just thinking about the fact that she could have said that could bring—*a smile!*

And she still could go back and say, "Pastor, I have been doing some thinking about your last question and my answer. Yes, before I go back to the field, I would like to help you educate the church in how to care for returning missionaries."

• One missionary was able to do just that. Neither she nor her church had a clue about missionary care. After she read the book, *SERVING AS SENDERS: How to Care For Your Missionaries*, she was given permission to go to each of the 30+ Home Fellowship groups and introduce them to the concepts of the book. Now it is "required reading" in that church!

• Help to educate your church friends in how to heap *"apples of gold "* (Proverbs 25:11) on your returning missionary instead of "straws of destruction." Role play. Actually practice! Read your friend's last newsletter, have someone representing him walk into the room, and let's hear what is said!

### A LITTLE TAB WILL DO YOU—IN

It is amazing what we remember about reentry years and years later! I think it was around 1976. We had just come back on furlough and the very next day we were invited to a Little League game with family. We were trying to not look out of place, but it felt so strange to see so many Americans all in one place. I noticed I was the only guy with long pants on. My brother-in-law asked if I wanted a soft drink. I said, "Sure." He handed me a cold can of Pepsi.

Now the last time we had been in the U.S., canned drinks weren't that popular. And the ones I remembered were opened by hooking a finger in the loop at the center of the can and pulling outward. This would tear off a tab that would then be loose from the can.

Well, on the can I now held in my hand, I saw that the loophole was much too small to get a finger into, and it didn't lift up easily as I thought it should. I noticed that it swiveled, so I tried that. In the wrong position, I tried pulling on it, all to no avail.

I remember the embarrassment I felt having to ask a lady next to me how to open it! She helped me, but had this look on her face like, "Where have you been!?" It was my first day back, and I knew it would be a long adjustment to my own culture.

FOR FURTHER UNDERSTANDING
Probably this is worth no more than a *chuckle*. But a chuckle will do! Obviously, this returning missionary had a good perspective on the "silly little things" that could cause such great consternation. He was not going to let that happen. So much of a returning missionary's reentry is dependent on his attitude. He realized it would be a long time in adjusting to all the ways of his home country.

FOR FURTHER ACTION
• No action needed! Well, you might want to give lessons in soda can opening. Or, make sure your friend can laugh at such things if/when they happen to him.

### INS, IRS and the SSA in the USA
While living as missionary evangelists in Mexico, my wife became pregnant with our third child. Having been trained in cross-cultural ministry, it was a simple and obvious decision to stay in Mexico for the birth. We weren't concerned about citizenship issues since we are both U.S. citizens and I "knew" that our child would automatically be the same regardless of country of birth.

Arriving at the U.S. consulate armed with certified copies of my own and my two older children's birth certificates, as well as my wife's hospital birth certificate, I was told they couldn't help me until I produced a "certified" birth certificate for my wife. We were surprised since we "knew" that even if just one parent is a U.S. citizen, the child obtains citizenship through them. The official agreed that was true but since my wife was indeed a U.S. citizen they could not proceed without a certified birth certificate to prove she was a citizen.

I said: "Fine, then, she's Polish—but I'm a citizen. Here's proof. Now let's proceed."

He said: "We can't do that."

I said: "Why not?"

He said: "Because we know she's a U.S. citizen."

I said: "So you're telling me that if she were not a U.S. citizen and had absolutely no rights as a citizen, you would process my son's certificate of citizenship right now, but because she is a U.S. citizen, and you know she's a U.S. citizen, you won't process it because she can't satisfactorily prove she's a U.S. citizen."

He said: "That's correct."

After a few more minutes of this "twilight zone" conversation, I felt as though I would soon lose my temper so we gave up and left.

It took a couple of months to obtain the required birth certificate for my wife. By that time we'd moved hundreds of miles further south. This made it very inconvenient to follow up, but since we'd been told that we could only complete the process at that consulate, I made an appointment to coincide with a solo trip I had planned to the States.

Now armed with all required proof, I was confident of victory. Wrong again!

He said: "We're sorry, there's nothing we can do."

I said: "Why?"

He said: "Because your wife isn't here."

I said: "But you've already seen my wife—here's her paperwork."

He said: "We're sorry, but blah blah blah etc. etc."

I explained how we no longer lived in the area and how difficult it would be to drag my wife there for yet another appointment. No response. What doubled the frustration was the fact that we were acquainted with the man who was second-in-charge at that consulate. He attended the church of a friend. He knew who we were and what we were doing. He had even been at a service where I had been a guest speaker! And yet, no help!

We later discovered we could pursue the matter through the I.N.S. office in Los Angeles. Several long distance calls produced the necessary forms, which we returned with the $90 filing fee. Still nothing! Oh, they managed to cash the check, but lost everything else. More calls. More frustration. I gave up.

Seven years later! Now you must have a social security number for each child claimed on your tax return. A trip to the Social Security office produced a similar conversation as at the consulate. Desperate, I called the office of my congressman. "You have what it takes to get the child a U.S. passport, and with that you can get the Social Security number."

So after an anxious period of hanging by my toes between the I.N.S., the I.R.S., and the Social Security Administration, the paperwork went through and it was done...and so am I. The passport works as good as a birth certificate, and God have mercy on anyone dealing with the I.N.S.

FOR FURTHER UNDERSTANDING

Paperwork hassles for a returning missionary are not limited to birth certificates and social security numbers. Permits and driver's licenses. Credential renewals and credit checks. Even our "Paperwork Reduction Act" now requires extra paper to explain the reduction! Have you ever (as I have) received a sheath of papers to review. On one of them—with no other writing—it says: "This page is intentionally blank!" Give me a break!

However, I don't think this missionary even *tittered* over this issue. "It was done...and so was I!" suggests at least a *groan*, if not a *lament!* But those words are on a different scale!

FOR FURTHER ACTION

• If all else fails to get your returned missionary friend to see some humor in life, advance the videotape to the scene of Uncle Albert *laughing himself silly* in the classic, *Mary Poppins*. And see if he can keep from laughing. If he can, there is serious trouble!

• You can help your returning missionary friend through the maze of paperwork hassles by keeping licenses and credentials current for him while he is on the field.

While we were in South America, my California Administrative Credential was due for renewal. I was not allowed to do it beforehand. (I didn't ask why; it's just the law!) And if I had waited until I arrived home, the time for renewal would have been expired. Thus, a faithful logistics support member of our team submitted the form, properly filled out, in a timely manner.

• Gathering the correct forms for your missionary friend is another way that you can help. For example, if your friend has been out of the country for eighteen months or longer (by current law), other than the normal Income Tax Forms are advantageous to use. I said "by current law" because this is another way to help. Make sure the correct laws apply to the new status of your missionary friend.

One single lady had been advised that since she was out of the country, she didn't need to file *any* tax papers. She came home to a huge penalty from the IRS!

## MY MOTHER'S MAIDEN NAME

I remember how frustrated I was trying to order phone service. When the salesperson asked what long distance company we wanted to use, I said that we'd just use the one you're supposed to use. Her silence suggested she didn't think that was too humorous. I had to choose one, she clarified. Once that was clear, I asked what was available. Well, you can imagine her response! There are hundreds!

Finally, I got so flustered that I said I'd have to call back later. I asked around, chose one and tried again. Naming a specific carrier, I thought all would be smooth sailing.

However, since we hadn't had any service here, they had no record of us. Nor any previous history since we had been out of the country for nine years! "Sorry! No credit," she said. They wanted a deposit, references, mother's maiden name, etc. It just let me know how out of touch we were.

FOR FURTHER UNDERSTANDING

I'd give that a *snicker*, or a *snort*, depending on your political persuasion over the breakup of Ma Bell. Those were sure the good ol' days, weren't they?

Again, the choices that a returning missionary faces can be an overwhelming issue. We, who live with them day by day, have a hard time believing that. Think of it, how many TV channels are now available? How many web sites are there on the Internet? (I dare not even suggest a number. By the time you read this, the current number could be doubled! Tripled?!) Models of cars? Brands of toothpaste? We become immune to the enormity of choices!

FOR FURTHER ACTION

• Part of the logistics opportunity for the reentry team is to hook up the phone for your returning missionary. That is, if you have also provided housing for him!

I remember well the "cared-for" look of a friend who stopped at our house on his way home on furlough. That broad smile came across his face when he told me his new telephone number. His reentry team had handled that detail (among many others) for him.

### PETS

I flew from the Orient to a city on the East Coast, expecting to stay in an apartment owned by one of my supporting churches. I had my cat with me (they knew about her). When I arrived, I found there was some "problem" with using the apartment, although I was to have it for at least two weeks. So, instead of letting me go directly to the apartment, I had to talk with the administrator.

He started out by saying something like; "You must be tired!" I'm screaming inside, "I'm exhausted and what is more, my cat has neither eaten, drunk or peed for about 20 hours, so could I get her settled before we do this?" But I didn't say anything. Eventually, we did get settled (she peed for what seemed like ten solid minutes!). I'm not sure if people in America don't travel much, or what! I can't imagine doing that to someone who has just arrived in the Orient to visit me!

FOR FURTHER UNDERSTANDING

Not particularly being an "animal lover," I was going to reject this story. However, in fairness to the gamut of situations that face returning missionaries, we need to be aware of their pets as well.

After all, we did bring a monkey home from Peru! He flew home in my wife's plastic-lined straw purse. The only problem we had was halfway through the flight, the sedative our dentist had given us to give him wore off. He almost got loose in that plane. What a sight that would have been! Fortunately, the flight attendant just smiled and said, "Oh, how cute."

(I would give this one a *grin.*)

FOR FURTHER ACTION
- Be sensitive to a cat's urinary needs!
- You ask, "Why didn't she say anything?" I don't know. Probably too much was going on in her life to have that presence of mind. She was probably doing all she could to cope with the kaleidoscope of changing sights and colors and sounds rushing past her jet-lagged eyes.

I hold all missionaries "guiltless" upon reentry. Yes, *They should have...they could have...it might have been, if only...!* And we do train missionaries in preparation for reentry.

However, the fact of the matter is—now, they are whatever they are! And they are too valuable to lose. They are here, and they need our help. Therefore, we need to be available to them. Even to pick up the "thousand" pieces they may have broken into.

## LINES THAT DIVIDE AND SEPARATE

It was August and the Lord had made it clear that I was to go back to the States for a season before returning to Central America. I took the long train ride to the border. I had been gone for two years. My brother and sister were excited to see me, and I was looking forward to spending some time with them, also.

The first thing that was a surprise (shock) to me happened just as we crossed the border. There were actually lines dividing the lanes on the highway. Even more of a shock was the fact that cars were staying within the lanes. And the drivers used their signal lights to let others know they were changing lanes or turning. Yes, I was back in the USA!

FOR FURTHER UNDERSTANDING
The differences in the environment that will surprise one returning missionary may go completely unnoticed by another. In this situation it was the literal lines that divided the highways and streets. However, there will be "hundreds" of differences that will be noticed.

We cross the San Ysidro border between San Diego and Tijuana no less than one hundred days a year. Though there is just a narrow stripe of paint letting us know that we have "crossed over," the stark contrast that that narrow line of division represents continues to amaze me.

Let's see, where would you place her situation on our Humor Scale? To me, it could at least bring a *grin*. However, some of the other "lines of division" could be more serious and not even bring a *glint in the eye*.

FOR FURTHER ACTION
•  A skill your friend needs to develop for the initial crossing of cultures is to look for the commonalities of the cultures, rather than the differences. You can help him identify them.

•  On further investigation, however, it becomes clear that these are mostly surface similarities. Though they help your returning missionary through the initial phase of reentry, the time comes for dealing with the deeper, more basic issues.

At this time, you help your friend to recognize his strong identity in Jesus Christ. He is the Anchor in the storms of changing cultures.

•  Read Appendix B, *Who I Am; What I Do*. Even before your friend returns, begin a dialogue with him on the valuable points contained in that article.

Chapter Eight

# Mks, Third World Kids

I open this chapter with a story written by Josiah Thiessen. It is not particularly about reentry. But it gives us a valuable perspective into the mind of our missionary youth.

### EXHIBIT A: MK

"I say we see if we can get Joe's bike off the ground," put in Tom.

"OK, let's go." I kicked her into gear and headed for the sand pit, channel surfing rapidly with the gearshift. Crashing his Suzuki 185 in all the most unique variety of places and ways was Tom's idea of fun in the village, and since trying to crash my dad's motorbike as successfully as Tom crashed his without actually damaging anything my Dad would notice was my own private recreational preference. We had a great time.

My buddy Zach and I were carrying out a brilliant scheme we had hatched for Easter vacation entertainment: driving our dads' motorbikes cross-country in search of the village where Tom's family worked, some 200 kilometers away.

We knew Tom from school but had never been to his

village before, so he was thrilled when we showed up. Of course, we and our motorbikes found plenty to occupy ourselves: honing clutch control in the sand pit, exploring local trails and hacking our way up and down dry riverbeds.

Back at Tom's we employed the services of some loitering African kids to wash the mud off our bikes on the promise that we'd shoot a bunch of bats for them the next morning. They immediately fell to contesting vigorously amongst themselves for the job opening.

So what does this brief glimpse of MK life tell you about MKs? Nothing in particular. No, it does not represent the experience of the typical MK. If you have interest in the experiences of a typical MK, I would be happy to refer you to your local TMK. TMK, for the unenlightened, stands for Typical Missionary Kid: a well-balanced individual who, having spent a significant part of his life in a culture different from that of his parents, has developed an implicit understanding of both cultures and is on exhibit as an example for those less fortunate. He may be located in the phone book between Elvis and the Tooth Fairy.

"Tell me about your cross-cultural experiences," you insist.

What cross-cultural experiences? A brief autobiography, perhaps?

"Oh, just tell us about what it's like growing up on the *mission field.* You have such opportunity—such a unique experience growing up there!"

Oh, I see. Shall I repel you with vivid descriptions of the cultural food I've eaten?

"You can't be serious!"

Or wax eloquent on the mind-numbing grammatical complexities of the language I can proudly claim to speak fluently?

"Say something... anything. No way... that's so cool! How do you say...?"

Allow me to share with you the *anthropological aspect, the transitional experiences of reentry, my rich multi-cultural background,* or lay on your heart the burden of overcoming the *language barrier,* and *dealing with culture shock.* (Words in italics can be defined by your standard missionary handbook, or they may be determined from the context of your church's next missionary slide presentation.)

Perhaps I might describe how effectively I have learned to understand and adapt to this culture—only after a fierce struggle with my unquenchable *western mindset* (another great term).

Actually, I am not an acculturated African, nor a naively intrigued tourist, but neither am I an MK on display waiting to be analyzed.

So what, you demand, is the purpose of this fragmented piece of literature? Naturally it is another analysis of MKs, or more precisely, an analysis of our dislike for analyzation!

Speaking for myself, I'm a person, not an MK!

Children of career missionaries—MKs, Third World Kids, Third Culture Kids. Or, as Josiah said, *"Typical Missionary Kid."* They may be given any one of these titles. Many have been born on the field, have "visited" their *parents'* homeland for three, at the most, four times before they are now young adults, taking their place as "normal" citizens in a strange land! If it were only that easy!

On the one hand, youth are more flexible and adaptable. On the other hand, they are less experienced in communicating the issues of uncertainty and verbalizing the frustrations that accompany reentry. They also are under greater peer pressure to conform than are their parents.

Following are a number of stories of young people's

experiences on reentry. How thrilling it would be if all youthful reentry stories were as this next one. Unfortunately, the statistics do not bear such a positive report. Thus, on reentry, as much emphasis must be placed on care for children and youth as for their parents—possibly more!

### HAUNTING DEJA VU

It was as if I had never left. Things were different yet still the same. As I stepped out of the airplane door my lungs drank in the winter Ecuadorian air, a mixture of smog, jet fuel and more smog. Above, bulbous gray clouds fled from the brilliance of a freshly formed rainbow. All around me stood the mountains I grew up with, their pure white caps shining through the blanket of exhaust that coiled itself around me like a constricting boa, cutting off my breath.

Directly before me loomed a loud building, an airport fashioned out of glass and foreign investments. My mind played back memories of an airport floor constructed entirely of tiny squares of ceramic. My eyes shifted their view off to the left. There in the shadow, like an old discarded box, lay the airport I remembered. Ten years, one month and a few days before, my goodbye tears had formed a stream in the cracks between its little ceramic tiles. For a moment I thought I saw something there. I thought I heard laughter. I glanced at my wife beside me. She seemed oblivious to the laughter, to the taunt that echoed off the glass and shattered my soul.

My heart began pounding as we boarded a bus that would take us to the terminal building. A few minutes later, as our car sped under the rainbow and into the city, I realized that this trip was going to be one of haunting deja vu. From the first instant at the airport, that spooky feeling persisted. Like a race, like a game, someone or something was following me. Its heart bled fear and its mouth dripped mocking. This confused me and somewhat angered me. Returning to one's homeland, I assumed, was supposed to be pleasant. This was not pleasant.

My mission in coming back was twofold: to fulfill my school requirements for a cross-cultural internship was one; to just remember fulfilled the second. I never expected the remembering part to be so grueling. The first day the host missionaries took us to the house where I grew up. The car pulled into the familiar cul-de-sac and I slowly got out. Rooted to the pavement, I just stared at that house. The walls of winter ivy like emerald waves crashed over me, drenching me in emotional claustrophobia. My entire being was gripped in a concoction of amazement and terror. The amazement came because before me lay an exact replica of my childhood home, a treasure chest filled with golden memories. The terror tied me in a helpless, hopeless rope of confusion and sorrow.

The few minutes we stayed there were too many. We left and visited place after place with the same result. Sometimes the laughter was a silent snicker. At other times, my pursuer's anger caused me to weep like a baby.

I visited the church I grew up in. One Sunday night they asked me to preach. So, confidently, I strutted to the wooden pulpit and turned to face my waiting audience. My eyes surveyed the faces of old friends and new strangers alike. In that crowd were my spiritual fathers. I couldn't hold it in. My body shook with convulsive sobs so strong that all I could do was cling to the podium and stare. Tears came frequently all throughout the sermon making my now sparse Spanish even choppier.

A train passed behind the church that evening just like it had every night ten years before. Even its fierce click-clacks and whistles added to the mocking I received that night of embarrassment.

All summer long I tried to visualize this ghost. That is what it was, a shadowy specter that haunted me. But why? As I thought and pondered, the picture my mind painted was of a boy. A boy who was forgotten and discarded like a toy sold at a yard sale into the eager hands of strangers. The boy was faceless like the ghost that warned Scrooge of his gloomy future. Why me? I wondered. But then I began to see a pattern.

Once we took a trip to visit friends in the South. We visited villages serenely placed by lakes under the shadows of snowcapped volcanoes. He followed me there. We visited old friends, now grown men and women and he followed me there. When I walked along familiar streets downtown or through favorite parks, I could hear his obnoxious giggles and accusations. But when I explored new parts of the city I couldn't hear him. At the movie theater, he was nowhere to be found. Why did I feel and hear him only when I remembered my past?

My wife and I were invited to a dinner in the home of my parents' friends. Upon our arrival we found a surprise party thrown in our honor. Around the table we shared the best of Ecuadorian food, laughter and memories. I sat next to the owner of the house. Juan was one of my spiritual fathers.

My heart broke that night as he poured his out and shared with me the events that transformed him from a dynamic church leader he once was to the embittered husk of a man he was now. I looked at this man and fought back the stinging in my eyes and throat. Juan's eyes remained free of expression; his tear ducts dried out long ago.

Before I left his home, I found an old black and white picture they had of our family. I took the photo with me. Somehow I knew it was the key to my struggle. That night the laughter was fierce. I decided then that I would confront my enemy in a battle to the end. I made up my mind to return to where I had felt his presence the strongest. To where I had the most memories. I went back to my childhood home.

With permission from the current resident, I entered the house. With video camera in hand, I bolstered myself as I walked into a place so jammed with memories my senses were spinning out of control. The smells of the waxed floor, the lemon tree and the kitchen cabinets mixed with the sight of the Smurf wallpaper in the office, the blond-finished closet in my bedroom, and the same balding brown carpet I played on with my brothers. I continued my tour de force through the rest of the house somewhat surprised that I hadn't been assaulted or laughed at.

After I shut off my camera I thanked the owner for his kindness. Motionless, I stood in the alley staring at the small, one-story, German-style home. And then I saw it. I saw the rock, nestled beside the gnarled plum tree I used to abuse. In front of the wobbly black metal gate, the rock stood firm. I crouched down slowly for a better look. Like a giant's only tooth, it jutted out of the ground, independent and razor sharp. Memories of matchbox cars and little green soldiers falling from its steep precipice to a "toyish" death flooded me as I reached my hand out toward its rusty orange surface. The feel of the rough, chill stone against my trembling fingers soothed me.

It was then that everything made sense. I could now see the boy. He was next to me. His face, once shrouded by a mask of fear now became crystal clear. I almost expected what I saw. His face was identical to the face of the twelve-year-old boy in that black and white photo I took from Juan's house. It was the face of a scared, confused and heartbroken little boy.

The entire world stood still while the jigsaw puzzle pieces of my life were snapped together. The picture now complete, I stepped back and saw my life as a whole. I was haunting myself. I had been terrified at the prospect of seeing myself.

When I boarded the black and white plane in the background of the picture, I left behind twelve years of childhood memories; memories tied to this house and to this city. I left a part of me behind that could not grow up. Ten years of absence had left a gulf that separated me into two beings.

The rock that stood before me was the only bridge stone to close the gap between the two images. That sunny winter day, I reached for the boy and held him in a timid embrace. As I held him, the warmth from my arms melted his icy heart and he no longer hated me.

At the end of the summer, my wife and I boarded the airplane that would take us home. I leaned back in my seat and exhaled deeply. A few moments later, our plane passed over the majestic Andes peaks and headed north. I said farewell to a land that I loved, knowing this time that I hadn't left anything behind. My wife let go her death grip on my hand and tried to pop her ears. A smile crept across my lips as she mentioned something about a feeling of deja vu.

FOR FURTHER UNDERSTANDING

What can be said?! The poetry to which this story is set encapsulates the feelings of an adult looking back on the childhood he lost by being taken by his parents to another country. Don't let the flowery language disguise the depth of feeling sensed by this man as he saw the changed and unchanged environment of his young childhood.

This is an account that must be read and reread a number of times to catch the breadth of insight he gives. He remembered the "toyish" death of his little green soldiers, but he also remembered the stream of tears in the ceramic tiles of the airport. He stood in awe before his home church congregation preaching the

Word, yet he sat in unbelief next to Juan, as he told of his bitterness. He trembled at the illusive taunter, but determined to face this yet unknown ghost of his past. He saw the face of a scared, confused and heartbroken boy; then he held him in a warm embrace. He was terrified at the prospect of seeing himself, yet he bridged the ten-year gulf that had separated him into two beings. He was whole again!

The variables involved in the reentry stress for children are as numberless as each one's thought and interpretations of everything that happened to them before they left, while they were gone and now on their return. Their frame of reference—how they look out at life, people, the world, God, even themselves—has been formed in the daily repetition of life experiences.

NINE AREAS OF STRESS

Physical
Professional
Financial
Cultural
Social
Linguistic
National/Political
Educational
Spiritual

FOR FURTHER ACTION

• Reread this most interesting story. Identify (underscore) the phrases that indicate one or another area of stress that this missionary experienced.

• In preparation for your friends' children coming home, find out what their attitude was about going *to* the field. Many are initially reluctant, but as the adventure of it becomes a reality, they change their attitude before leaving their home country. This is good, for a good attitude toward leaving indicates the likelihood of a good attitude for returning.

• Keep in touch. Does their attitude change (for better or worse) once they are on the field? As a teacher of missionary children on one field, I had to deal with a reverse loyalty attitude. Many were hailing the host country as "paradise" while "putting down" everything about their home country. Needless to say, had this not been dealt with there, those going home would have had a more difficult time adjusting.

- As they are preparing to come home, what is their attitude now? They are leaving friends. They are leaving a relatively protected life, yet full of adventures they will not find an equal to at home. Friends? Where? Who? When? Why? How? The ambiguities of changing cultures allows for little security. Review the last story of Chapter Four. You can provide a measure of stability by planning ahead of time for their needs to be met.

### BAD IS GOOD

When our family moved back to the States, we knew there would be a reentry problem. We had been out of the country for six years and much had changed. And we had changed. Our children were now teenagers! To give us an opportunity to "regroup as a family," we were able to stop over in Honolulu for about ten days.

A good pastor friend of mine, who had visited us in the Philippines several times, made the arrangements for us. He was God's gift to us in this time. He met us at the airport with our tons of luggage and our dog. The dog went to quarantine (animal culture shock!) and we were driven to a beautiful home right on the beach.

The owners of the home were away for a month and they had left us notes just to make us feel at home. The refrigerator was full of food, and money was left on the kitchen table to buy anything we needed. We were overwhelmed with the generosity of this pastor and his church. They even had a vehicle for us to drive around the island. It was just a wonderful ten days.

After settling back in our home, our children had some difficult adjustments. They often found that they did not know the language. Though English was our language (and had been in the Philippines), their peers now were talking a different dialect! "Man, that is really bad!" The word "bad" had taken on the connotation of "good." How confusing can you get?

Their peers were all talking about dating and finding the right guy or gal. There was a big pressure to date. Our kids had been growing up in a culture that put no such pressure on them. They always did everything in groups. It was unthinkable to go out alone with the opposite sex. That almost constituted engagement!

Youth clothing was also very different. Peer pressure to wear the "in" clothing was great. Unfortunately, we could not afford new wardrobes. This only increased the reentry pressures on our children.

FOR FURTHER UNDERSTANDING
Probably one of the wisest moves a missionary can make in returning home is to take the time to *regroup as a family.* Roles will change; responsibilities will be different. It is a time to reestablish home country rules and procedures. Yet, even this will present some problems, for the children are (in this case) six years older! Expectations on them now are not what they were when they went to the field.

FOR FURTHER ACTION
• Reread the first three paragraphs. Underline or in some way note the details of this most generous gift of hospitality. Pay particular attention to the action words: pastor *made* the arrangements, *met* us, *drove* us, *left* notes. There are more! It is the action words that make a difference in your friend's experiences. Make a list of the *action* words that you and/or your church can provide for your next returning missionary.

• No single dating! "Bad" means "good!" Clothes styles. Make a list of changes that have taken place in your society over the past two years. Are your missionary friends aware of them? Have you prepared them for the radical changes in cultural values or even the not so radical material conveniences they will face on reentry? Are they prepared for how casually our society talks about partial-birth abortion? Violence in our youth? "Malling" on the Internet? Do they even know what "malling" is?! Or the Internet, for that matter?

## TELEPHONES...

My wife and I and our two children went off to serve the Lord in Latin America. Our older daughter was only four years old when we went there. All of her formal education was comparable to what she would have received if she had been in the United States. However, culturally, her experiences were very different. I did not realize how different until I accompanied her to the States when she started college.

I helped her get her things situated in her dormitory and, after making sure she had some quarters, instructed her to call me at my parents' house if she needed anything. I would stay in town for a week, and my parents lived only a twenty-five minute drive from the college.

Later that afternoon I got a call from a telephone operator asking if I would accept the charges for a collect call from my daughter. I did, of course. When she came on the line she was almost in tears as she explained how frustrated she was, trying to figure out how to make a local call on the pay phone. It seems that the directions explained in detail everything about collect calls, credit card calls, and everything else that has complicated the U.S. phone system in the previous years, but had neglected to explain something that surely "every American knows"—how to make a local call! Of course, you just put the money in the slot and dial the number!

## ...AND DRINKING FOUNTAINS

I had graduated from a mission high school where my parents served in Latin America. I had worked hard. I had a 4.0 GPA. I had done well on my SAT tests and was on my way to the States—a single "adult"—to attend college.

I stepped off the plane into a huge, modern airport terminal building. I was thirsty. I walked over to what I was sure was a drinking fountain. Yes, there was the familiar spout, but I couldn't find a way to turn it on! I looked all over for a button or knob. Nothing!

I walked away—embarrassed and thirsty. It was even more devastating when I realized I could have stepped aside to watch how another person got the machine to produce water! Later I found out it was operated by a foot pedal!

FOR FURTHER UNDERSTANDING
There are some issues of reentry that cannot be anticipated—coins in a pay phone, water fountain handles, etc! But the returning missionary can be aware that likely there will be many new and strange experiences to face.

How could a child, having grown up in a close, Christian missionary community, face a greater challenge than to be thrust into the public college scene in America? Note the wisdom of this parent (and daughter) to attend a college near a close relative.

FOR FURTHER ACTION
• As they have been encouraged to take a good sense of humor with them into their ministry culture, you can write to them, reminding them to be sure to bring it home with them!

• If your missionary friend's son or daughter is coming to your city for college or work, and there is no close relative, can your family "stand in the wings" as this youth enters this stage of life?

• If you are not available, or if the young person is going to another city, can you help this family make some kind of personal connection where an accountability relationship can form?

### THE REST OF YOUR LIFE

Funny, when asked about reentry, how you just seem to think about the first couple of years; but in actual fact, it doesn't stop there but carries on and affects the rest of your life.

I was at a church the other day and someone asked if I was American! I was rather shocked, as that question hadn't been asked of me for about a decade. The voice is the hardest thing to change and the biggest giveaway when trying to assimilate back into a society where you don't know much. *(Editor's note: His "society" and church are not American!)*

Another long-term effect I have had was the self-esteem problem. Now I know that everyone has these sorts of problems, but I guess with everyone being insecure at boarding school, someone has to be the scapegoat...and I was it! That has followed me all my life and has not helped me in merging into my own "strange" society.

But time brings healing and perspective. Even though I seemed to hate it at the time, the lessons I have learned and the strength I have from a good foundation in Christ makes for a good adulthood. God has guided me into a ministry that I love, and my past has helped as I have a broader love for people from diverse backgrounds. Believe me, as much as my past was not easy, I wouldn't give it up for the world.

FOR FURTHER UNDERSTANDING

At least he acknowledged that reentry may take "up to a couple of years." Most (both missionaries and the people back home) expect (hope) it will be "over, and things will be back to normal" within days or weeks, at the most. This is a myth which must be dispelled.

In many arenas of life experience we acknowledge that events change—forever—the course of the lives affected. Psychologists use the Holmes Stress Assessment Scale to register the effect of various changes. A move, a change of employment, the death of a spouse, or even a traffic ticket is given a number equivalent. All add up to a stress factor. A total above 150 signals major danger! But *all* of life's experiences change a person's life. How tragic an expression of shallowness for one to say about a person who has experienced any of life's stressful events, "Oh, they'll get over it."

We don't "get over it!" We change. We adjust. We compensate. We accommodate the change. But we *don't* get over it. It becomes a building block in our life experience. It becomes a part of who we are becoming.

In looking over the Scale, I jotted down the life events which would happen *just* at the time of reentry for any missionary. The number adds up to over 300! According to Dr. Holmes, this gives your missionary friend a ninety percent chance of developing an illness. In addition, there may be other specific issues that they will face, making the number even higher.

The experience of being a missionary, whether on a three-week ministry trip or a four year term, is *not* something to "get over."

His conclusion is a pearl of wisdom. Whether life experiences appear good or evil (from our perspective), from God's—*"All things work together for the good to those who love God and are called according to His purposes; That we may be conformed to the image of Christ"* (Romans 8:28 *and* 29).

Job, an ancient Biblical sage believed—and lived by—this perspective: *"The Lord has given and the Lord has taken away; blessed be the Name of the Lord"* (Job 1:21).

Once your friend (and you) have assimilated that attitude into your lifestyle, the wisdom of God through Paul allows you to *"comfort others with the comfort you have received of the Holy Spirit"* (II Corinthians 1:4).

FOR FURTHER ACTION

• How can you help your returning missionary friend develop a positive attitude toward *all* of life's situations?

• How can you help your church friends accept that your returning missionary friend has changed? And that they must relate to him as a changed person?

• Don't try to "remake" him into the image of the person you remember that he was before going to the field.

• Accept him in his new personality, acknowledging that he needs to relate to the "new" you, also!

### LOST IN A TIDAL WAVE

The sun shone brightly that terrifying morning. Slowly Tom and I trudged out to the road. Through my mind raced questions: Where am I going? What should I do? How will I feel? As I looked toward the woods, memories came back to me. If I were in that tree I had found yesterday, I wouldn't have a worry about this dreaded day. Better yet, if I were back home again, I'd like that first day and I'd know everybody. Why, why, Oh! Why did this have to happen?

Then I saw it—that bright orange bus. My heart started thumping. With each beat the bus loomed larger and larger. It came like a tremendous ocean comber to drown me in a wave of meaningless faces. Unwillingly I stepped into the bus and sat down beside Tom. They all knew each other—but what about me? On my right was Tom, but his face was expressionless. I found no refuge in him from this giant chamber of steel.

How unlike the usual calm stroll I used to know

walking to school. Just the birds singing and an occasional comment from a neighboring house. Now it was different; changed completely. A squeaky rattling old bus that seemed like it would fall apart any moment. At every stop the noise would rise until it was like the buzz of a huge bee close to my ear.

As with a splash of water on the window these thoughts were washed away. I focused my attention on the rolling countryside that was just turning to fall. Bright yellows and oranges scattered among the evergreens and birch. Then the wide open corn fields just ready for harvest.

In what seemed like only minutes I could see the town ahead drawing closer—every moment pulling me into a world of...I didn't know what! I saw other buses like our own as we drove onward. Then—there it was, looming ahead of us, its windows flashing the reflection of the early sun. We circled the monstrous wood and brick building. We stopped at its gaping doors.

We were squeezed out the bus's door like sausage out of its skin. We surged forward, carried irresistibly toward its mouth. I turned to get one last glance at the bus as it departed. The orange mass of metal that had so recently been the object of my despair now seemed like the only hope I had of getting home. It was gone.

I was in the monster's throat. I felt a downward pull—a sinking feeling. I was being swallowed! The noise was like thunder crashing outside my bedroom window in the middle of the night. I stayed close to Tom, who was now my only island in this sea, but once I turned my head and Tom was gone!

Then in the jostling someone tapped my shoulder and asked, "Are you Tina?" Surprised to hear my name, I turned around. "Yes," I replied, "but how did you know me?"

"I know your cousin Heidi—there's a striking resemblance between you two." I paused a second trying to picture my cousin. (I never thought I looked like her.) Then I remembered Heidi having told me about somebody she had known here.

"Oh ya," I exclaimed, "Heidi did mention you. What's your name?"

"Trisha," she answered. "I live about a mile up the road from you." I was relieved to know someone at last. But Trisha was busy and was carried away in an undertow of current that almost knocked us off our feet. I was alone again.

As I looked around to see if Tom was in sight, I noticed that the whole hall had filled up and more students were coming in. On the bus the new faces had seemed but as an ocean whitecap. Now those faces had turned into a tidal wave. I was like a tiny grain of sand—lost and being carried along in a mountain of water. I felt as though I were drowning. I struggled up as the turbulence pulled me with it towards the stomach of this monster.

As I entered a room I saw Trisha! My heart began to hammer. I must reach her before I am lost again. I walked forward, my eyes never leaving her. I sat down behind her. Feeling a little less afraid, I began to look around me to see where I was. In every direction were new faces, and more new faces! Never before had I seen so many kids together.

Undecided as to what I should do, I asked Trisha. "Tina," she exclaimed, "what are you doing here? The seventh graders sit up in front." Then she turned and continued talking to her friends. So I focused my attention on the front. It was empty. No one my age seemed to be in this auditorium. There has to be another room some place in this...in this mysterious monster. Reluctantly I walked out a door.

Suddenly I realized that I had come out into a different hallway. My heart skipped a beat as I edged closer to the wall trying to figure out how I got into this nightmare. No, I couldn't even remember the general direction. I was totally lost. I couldn't return to the place I had just come from because I knew I didn't belong there (as if I belonged *anywhere* in this monster). My mind was spinning. It was impossible to think straight.

Now I could see the other side of the hall. How could all of those people have fit into this small passageway? Well, that's not what needs worrying about now, I reminded myself. Knowing that I couldn't go home, I walked forward to find the other room that must be hidden somewhere along these long, now almost deserted hallways.

Somehow (I don't know how) I came to a door that had just closed. I ran to it. This might lead me outside. I needed a breath of air. As I opened the door, noise drummed upon my ears like the crashing of waves over a grounded ship, tearing it to pieces, until only the broken hull remains. As I leaned against the door, I knew I was that deserted ship being torn apart and my frame was still being beat upon by each new wave.

Suddenly my mind was jostled back to reality. My legs were shaking as I looked around the new room trying to find where to sit. This was the right place, but all the seats were taken. I felt like turning around and going out to wander through the halls, but I decided against it. I stood as far to the corner as I could so no one would notice me. The principal was talking now. I'd better listen. He mentioned something about lockers. What were the lockers for? Aren't we having desks to put our books in? But now he'd switched to another subject. I need to concentrate, I reminded myself.

What did he say? We change rooms every hour! Oh no! I'm really going to be lost. "You are now going to get your schedules," he yelled over the mounting roar of voices. The noise grew so loud that I could hardly hear the names. My head was spinning. I didn't have the slightest notion about how this school worked. My name was mentioned. I looked up. It was my turn to get a schedule. No chance! I'm not walking in front of that mob of faces just for a schedule! Again my name was called. I'd better go up, something told me or I'd be even worse off. But I just couldn't go. My feet wouldn't move!

The drone of many names continued but I wasn't listening. I was trying as hard as I could to get this straight in my mind. I was to change classes. How is a new student supposed to see any number on a room with a flow of human momentum pushing you around? If you stopped, you'd get trampled. If you turned, you'd knock everyone over. The best way would probably be just to wait until the long narrow hallways cleared out, but first I needed that schedule.

Turning my attention back, I saw some of the kids passing out the schedules that hadn't been picked up. I heard one of them call my name. Again I was against going to get it, but I pushed myself forward. I felt a hand on my shoulder and turned. "Sit down," a teacher told me, in a very annoyed voice.

I was relieved but I had sure made a fool of myself. And was even more confused than ever. Now I was worse off! I'd have to go up to the front to get my schedule. I sure dreaded the time when my name would be called. "Tina!! Will you come and get your card, please?" He sure sounded disturbed. I turned red as a beet and my legs were shaking. I walked up to the front and got my yellow form. I thought for sure he'd give me a big lecture, but I was lucky. Glancing over the schedule, I noticed a place for a bus number. Maybe I'll be able to find the bus, but no, the blank was empty!

There was my locker number. People started leaving to go to their lockers, each group was going with a different teacher. I didn't know which one to go with, so I just went with the first group, to get out of there.

I was off into the intestines of the monster again. For the next hour I was in one class, lost and to the office again and into the halls just to become lost once more. All through that morning I was dazed, almost unconscious.

At lunch break I looked back into my mind to find what I had done, but my thoughts were muddled. Every class had been only half an hour instead of 50 minutes. I could just vaguely remember the last period. Now one thing streaked through my mind that I remembered in every class: everyone was with someone. A dense fog had prevented me from thinking, but now in the lunch room that one thought became clear. I had seen another girl who seemed to be just as lost as I was, but I couldn't remember what she looked like, or her name.

The nightmare was replaying itself in my mind. I sat at the end of a table and closed my ears to the roaring as I recalled how it used to be at home. For but a moment (the first since I entered the school) I was unaware of anything else around me. Calm. Then, suddenly the bell blurted out a warning. The stampede began again.

The afternoon went by surprisingly fast. I think it was because I was dazed; not alive mentally. I just followed a girl who seemed to know her way around. She never knew I was following her.

When the bell rang, ending the last period, I started thinking, "How will I get home?" Somehow I had gotten through the day, but now how was I to get home? Suddenly I heard the loud thumping that told me the other classes were leaving. "Excused!" our teacher hollered over the tramping that was now coming from the halls even louder than it had been all day. It seemed I became more scared than even the moment I walked in the door, because now I had to figure out how to get home and didn't know where to start.

As I stepped into the hall, I was swept into the tidal wave again for the last time that day. I searched worriedly over the hundreds of faces to find one I knew, but there was still none. I didn't try any longer to resist being pulled along by the crowd. It was a dark inky water, rushing on and on and on—just follow the rope. No time to think. I had to get out of this monster's belly! I had to find my bus! I felt a spark of sunlight hit me and I looked up. Ahead I saw a faint stream of light. It's real sunlight! All day long I hadn't seen anything but artificial light. I rushed forward not wanting to lose this chance. Out into the world of trees and grass again, I felt like I was waking up to a new day.

Every way I looked there were busses, busses and more busses! I walked around the building twice before I decided who to look for—Tom! He'd figure out something. Every step I took became faster until I was running. One by one the busses slowly departed. I became so desperate and frantic that I probably wouldn't know if I did see my bus. Finally, in utter despair, I gave up.

When the last bus pulled away I was sure all hope was gone. I sat down on the curb to think up another way to get home. There seemed to be no way. Why couldn't I be back home at my old school where I didn't have a single care? My mother is probably worrying like mad. I've got to do something!

Turning around I saw the mouth of the monster was still open. There might be help inside. How could I walk back in there after my day of dread? In one frantic second all that had happened swirled through my head. I'd almost rather be shot into space, but it was the only way. Slowly I advanced. I paused as I had earlier. The same feeling of fear came over me as my mind again focused on this day's experience. I forced myself with every ounce of will power.

The light vanished and the giant halls loomed in front of me. How could I find help in this deserted hall of horror?

Many teachers passed by me but I didn't have the courage to ask for help. Finally I could stand it no longer and blurted out, "How can I get home?" The teacher walking by didn't realize my distress and murmured, "Go to the office." What a help. I felt like I could no more walk into an office full of adults than jump into a whirlpool. I just walked around some more. Slowly and nervously I paced in front of the office. Finally someone came out and told me I'd better go home now. "I can't," I blurted out. "My bus is gone."

"Come on in," she said as she walked back into the office. Everyone looked up. I melted in fear, but they were friendly. I was shocked.

In no time I was buzzing away from that monstrous prison. I looked back. As it got smaller and smaller in the distance, the dread of this nightmare also diminished. The bright yellows and oranges scattered among the evergreen and birch began to fade in the evening twilight. I was sleepy.

## FOR FURTHER UNDERSTANDING

Can you believe it? The colorful, vivid language of a seventh grader, telling of her first day at junior high school. Her last stateside schooling was in second grade. The four intervening years were in a K-12 jungle mission school with no more than one hundred students.

What more needs to be said? She has expressed the real thoughts and feelings of multiplied hundreds of MKs beginning a furlough year of school in this "foreign" land.

Note also, though, that in the midst of this agonizing experience, she is always thinking—looking for solutions. Jungle-wise, but city-ignorant!

## FOR FURTHER ACTION

• It's rather lengthy, but reread this story. Underscore the variety of ways she describes her fears and uncertainties. Also highlight how often she is searching for solutions to each dilemma she perceives.

A good way to build commitment to help the children of your missionary friends is to relive with this girl the terror of that day. Reread it several times!

• Seventh graders probably wouldn't want their mothers accompanying them to school. But what could this girl's mother—what could you have done to ease this first-day-at-school trauma? Could Mom or older brother have pointed out the bus number as they boarded it? Could big brother have set a place to meet after school?

• There are radical differences of educational systems and standards from one location to anther. This demands that attention be given to ease MKs into their new environment with as much orientation as possible. Identify from this story at least five ways orientation would have made this a more pleasant day for this girl. Hint: One way would have been to bring her to the school days in advance to become familiar with the building.

### YOUTH LEADERS WERE AFRAID OF OUR KIDS

As we sat on the carpeted floor of our newly acquired home—there were no chairs to sit on—a new stage in life was beginning. The children were settling into their new schools, but did find it hard to cope with many of the things their fellow students did. The lies, cheating and language were a world away from the missionary boarding schools they had left.

While our daughter, in senior high school, found some good Christian friends, it seemed to be much harder for the boys in middle school. During break times it was easier for them to escape into the world of books than try to seek out friends that might try to understand them.

One might expect that entering the public schooling

system would be hard, as the children were not "in touch" with the trends of music, nor were they highly skilled at or have an understanding of many of the sports that were played. But we did not expect entering the church youth groups to be just as difficult. Even there it was hard to make friends. Yes, there too, they felt alienated and "different" as their accents and their lack of local knowledge made them stand out. These were not easy days and many a time my mother-heart ached as we tried to talk about and pray through the issues with them. I felt so helpless in really being able to do anything.

During our second year back home, there was a large evangelistic event with Luis Palau held in our city. Both my husband and I were involved in some of the organization, so we knew how things should work. Our youngest son, then a 13-year-old, made an open profession of faith and was duly assigned someone within our church to follow him up. A number of months passed.

Upon enquiry we discovered that the person who was given his card was scared stiff to have to counsel an "MK." Was he afraid that our son might know more than he might? Or ask some awkward questions? Or that we may interfere? Whatever the reason, what our son needed more than anything else at that time was someone to come alongside, encourage and teach him, reinforcing the things he was learning at home.

It was several years later that we were talking with one of the leaders of the church youth group. She openly admitted that as leaders they were all afraid of our kids; for in her words, "What can we offer these MKs who have grown up in Christian schools and who have missionary parents to teach them?" I do not believe she came to this conclusion because the children exhibited any sense of superiority or showed they "knew it all." I sense more, it was a fear in the leaders, not knowing how to deal with kids whose backgrounds were a little "different" and who took more effort for them to understand.

FOR FURTHER UNDERSTANDING
Would you expect youth adapting to church life to be as difficult as fitting into the public schooling system? Yet, for these children it was. Each new environment has its own "culture" and each child has his own—different—identity.

A mother who "felt so helpless" suggests that their agency may not have provided adequate (if any) training on parental involvement in youth reentry. Though more and more attention is being drawn to reentry care, it is still a little known area of need. Or, more likely, one so difficult, few want to approach it!

Further, why did she wait "several years" before she confronted the youth leadership? Possibly because parents themselves are caught in their own reentry adjustments. Thus, they are often times not able to give adequate help to their own children.

FOR FURTHER ACTION
• Is it possible for you to establish a "reentry forum" for returning MKs? A place where they could share with the youth who stayed home, and a place where they could learn from them about the new culture they have entered.

• There is a growing number of agencies which are establishing effort toward returning MKs—especially on the college level. Refer to the MK section of the Resources for organizations willing to share their ideas and experience.

• These are *your* returning young people—a part of your Body. Months before they are scheduled to come home, check with their agency to learn what is being done to prepare them for reentry. Is there a class offered in their school on reentry preparation? Is what they are doing accomplishing the goal?

- With communication systems linking our world into a global village, are they able to learn about the climate and the culture and the people of the city or town where they will be returning?
- But most crucial to this story, make sure the youth leaders in your church are given some training in relating with returning MKs. His mom knew exactly what he needed: "Someone to come alongside, and to encourage and teach him."

### I'M REALLY *NOT* AMERICAN

Coming home for me was much the same as moving *to* the United States. I experienced the same problems that I had had as a 12-year-old. Man...was I different! My clothes, accent, slang, hairstyle, even the way I walked told them that I was different! This time it was made worse by the fact that it was happening to me in what was supposed to be my "home country."

I suffered the hurt of isolation, but I was also a curiosity to the other kids. They were somewhat careful not to ridicule me too much because they did not know me and what I might be like because I was from "America!" This was one of the hardest things for me, because I could not convince them that I was actually from "their home town." I guess I had done such a great job of adapting to my host culture for three years that my own culture could not or did not want to recognize me as one of their own!

For a long time my nickname was "American." I did not have any bad feelings toward Americans, but it sure hurt to be thought of as one. I expected to "come home" and be accepted for what I had always thought myself to be. Kids my age were not concerned about such things, and so I was on my own with these thoughts. This is what caused the feelings of isolation.

But the positive side of being a curiosity is that it gets you a lot of attention. That helped to break down some of the barriers. Also, if I say so myself, I'm kind of outgoing, so I can adapt when I want to!

FOR FURTHER UNDERSTANDING
Kids are as individual in temperament as is their DNA! "Isolation—ya, I had to deal with being called *American.* But I can adapt when I want to." For some (very few), reentry is "no big deal!" This is great!

It should be noted that his three-year experience was at an age and long enough to have a good stay in his host culture. Yet short enough to get him back home for those important senior years of school.

Our own children, now grown, still comment how they wouldn't "trade for anything" their two two-year experiences (during their teens) in South America for anything—how their time in a second culture broadened their perspective of the world.

FOR FURTHER ACTION
• It does not *seem to be* the case with this youth, but care must be given to make sure a casual—"Hey! It's cool!"—attitude is not covering up any underlying unresolved issue. We don't want to fear that some ill-omened glitch is lurking in his mind or emotions. But we also need to be aware of the subtleties of his intricately woven human nature.
• It seems like this young man could be a facilitator at your "youth forum!"

**BUT FOR THE GRACE OF GOD**

August 24
Dear Mom,
Hi! This is Tuesday night after dinner. What I want-

ed to tell you is that I'm sorry I got so upset about the gifts that you gave me. I *did* think they were okay, but it's just that they were *you* and not *me*. I'm sure you remember how it felt when you first went to college. You just want to be yourself and make your own decisions including what you put in your room. Please don't take it personally. It's just that my emotions were running strong!

Jo

August 26

Dear Mom,

I just found your letters this morning. Today hasn't been good. It started last night when I couldn't get to sleep. I was feeling sorry for myself and bought a few candy bars. Dumb idea! I know I can't turn to that for comfort.

Today, I ended up sitting out and just watching most of basketball practice. That was good for me because I can learn some of the "ways" that are still very foreign to me. On the other side, I need to get in there and practice. It is just so hard on my ego to be the one who is slow at everything because it is all so new to me. Also, I'm not like them. I try to be nice to everyone and helpful, whereas they are brash and rude.

Most of the time when I say something at practice or when I'm with them after practice, they hardly pay any attention. Sometimes it seems like they just don't care about me. But I know a lot of it is that I just don't do things the "cool" way.

I guess I just have to go to practice with a tough mental attitude. Gone is the emotional and compassionate person I want to be!

My RA just came in and she is about the nicest person I've met here. So I'm sure there are nice people around.

Jo

August 29

Mom,

It's hard for me to open up, and they say hardly anything to me. I guess because most of the basketball girls already have friends (not to mention boyfriends)! They talk about them a lot. Jill Smith even has one. Rachelle has a boyfriend too. You remember them. Beth is from a town about an hour and a half from here. She also has a boyfriend. One thing that really bugged me about her was that she and Angela are really into soap operas! They watch them every afternoon.

It is a very educating, though disgusting experience to see how they have been totally warped by those stupid shows where everyone is having an affair. It's so sad to see them so wrapped up in them and to know about every single character's life—on the show and off, and to relive practically every episode. Just pray, because I don't see how they can live such a double life. On the way to church they play secular rock music. They know most of the words. They seem comfortable singing about loose sex and out-of-control lust. Then they get out of the car and go to church. They sing about the Lord, but then turn back around and conform to the world!

Now Angela is really wild about guys. She has a boyfriend but says she can't wait 'til all the guys get here and she can get to know them and hang out with them.

Jo

September 6

Dear Mom,

Joel Wilson called me. It was awesome to talk to him. He wouldn't tell me who he was at first and made me guess. I had no idea. He sounded so mature and old. He promised to write to me. It was so good to hear from someone I know.

I don't know if I'll make the team. I didn't do too well—maybe okay—at practice today. I was comparing myself too much and not just concentrating on doing my best.

Pray for me as I try to be friends with the other freshmen players. It is really hard, particularly because I was so shocked at the way they were in the beginning and I was so in culture shock that I was really out of it. So as long as I wasn't like them, I was on the outside. A lot of it is my fault, too. I wouldn't make an effort to meet them in their room before practice or walk with them.

I've decided to keep my door open a lot. Like now, when I'm typing this, it is open. I think that will help a lot so they don't think I'm some secretive person who is impossible to understand.

It is cool to go through this one notebook I keep and read through things that God has placed in my life. For example, do you remember the time in China when we had gone to the service and the guest preacher called us up front? Well, during that time I just started pouring out all my burdens to God and released them all to Him. After doing that I started seeing the multitudes of Chinese just walking down the streets in China. I really felt called then.

I was going over these things and then I started looking at my guidebook with all the courses. I circled everything that I thought I might have some interest in, like graphic arts and education. I kept reading about all these subjects I would like to study, and I really think that I should work with my counselor in developing an interdisciplinary major where I can study a mixture of my interests. I know that this is a pretty rash decision, but I just don't think one particular major is what God has for me. I'm pretty sure that decision was just my own idea.

Jo

September 12

Dear Mom and Dad,

It is almost midnight here and I am waiting to hear from you. You probably think I went to bed but I can't sleep. I am just so miserable here. I didn't mention it before, but suicide has even come to my thoughts several times this week and last. I know satan wants to put thoughts like this in my mind but I also know that this college stuff isn't for me now. Tonight I've wolfed down three candy bars and a Dr. Pepper just from being so depressed. Please help me get out of here! I have a sore throat and a fever. Tomorrow I'm going to the nurse and not to class.

Jo

September 13

Dear Mom and Dad,

It is about 1:20 and I am going crazy. I am supposed to make this decision about the team. I'm trying to call the coach and read her my decision. I wrote it out because I wouldn't know what to tell her if I hadn't. She isn't there though. So I tried to study PSYCH for a quiz today but that was no use. All I can think about is how confused and messed up I am.

When I got up this morning I didn't know what I was going to do. Yesterday a million people talked to me about it. First I talked to you guys, then Sarah Wells. That was good, but then when I talked to the coach, I got confused and couldn't think straight. Then one of the captains talked to me and I couldn't communicate with her because I couldn't express my reasons. Then a lot of people in my hall talked to me and they all wanted to be helpful but my thoughts were just so confused.

At lunch, I was totally socially inept. I could have faced it had I been in a world by myself or at Harbor High School where everything was routine and familiar. After lunch, I came back with Rachelle and I knew that

I had to call Coach and then study for PSYCH. Rachelle said to me that they are studying now and asked if I wanted to join them. That was too much for me. I want to—to go over there right now and be a part of something—life! But I can't. Why? WHY? Jo, you want to so badly so why can't you? You're not stupid!

In speech this morning, we had to write five roles we have. Who am I? Well, the person I've been isn't a person—it's been a robot. I'm a student, yet I can't concentrate and it all seems so little and unimportant now. I'm a daughter. I do feel that love and connection. I couldn't put that I was a basketball player. I didn't want to be, either! What's the use of a ball just being bounced all over the gym? I put that I was a roommate, yet I barely communicate with Tia. I put that I am a sister and I can say that because I feel very close to all my siblings. Yet, basically, I am an island!

So, that was speech class—learning about the "real" me.

And then Bible: I got there five minutes early and just sat there and stared straight ahead for that time while there were others around me; yet, I didn't know what to do with them.

I need out. I can't handle this. Why can't I function? I'll call the coach now and read her my "decision."

Jo

January, the following year

Dear Joel and Christa,

Hi! I decided to write you all this evening as I am bubbling over with joy over what God has done in my life. You may find that hard to believe but it's true. I thought that you could pass the message. Hopefully this one will move as quickly as the other one did along the Harbor High/mission field news chain. Actually, I hope it will move many times quicker and more widespread than the other did.

Starting a few weeks after I left for college, satan began to attack me. He attacked in every possible way. It's hard to explain the extent of his attack, but it was in every possible area of life. It got to the point that I could hardly function. Many mornings I just couldn't get out of bed and face life. He made everything (I mean everything!) about life seem totally hard, overwhelming, impossible, and unbearable—even the little things. He distorted everything about life to me and lied to me all the time. It got so bad—and it continued for so long—I thought it could never get better. Everything was totally hopeless. I tried to fight in every area, but it was just too much.

What made it even worse was that satan made it so I couldn't express myself or talk about what I was feeling or going through with my family or friends. When people tried to talk to me I could hardly stand it and just wanted to get away from them because I was experiencing such torment.

Actually, there were even more times when I tried to take my life than the one that you all heard about. It just seemed that that was the only way to be with Jesus and get out of my pain. I know now that this was a lie from satan but it seemed the only way.

I was so miserable every second of the day. My life was like a nightmare. I couldn't think straight at all. Obviously, is anyone thinking straight when they take approximately 70 extra strength Tylenol, 30 Anacin and 5 Prozac to end the nightmare and be with Jesus in heaven?

Well, the nightmare increased tenfold when I began throwing up in the middle of the night and my parents found out the truth. It about killed them! They took me to the hospital where the staff began pumping my stomach and inserting tubes down my nose and into my arms. I was still throwing up when they told me that they were going to have to airlift me to a major city for a possible liver transplant. It was the worst nightmare any 18-year-old could have, especially me, who seemed to have it all together—top of my class, plus awards.

In that hospital room, I was totally miserable thinking how the whole world probably knew by now. I remember being in my bed just kicking because satan was tormenting me, especially with thoughts of how, for sure, you will not be able to face life and all the people now. I remember the liver specialist coming in and telling me that I would probably get really sick, go into total confusion and pain and that I might not make it through. They said that they might even have to put a hole in my brain to ease the pain.

But by then my "whole world" did know and they were praying for me. Within 24 hours God completely healed my liver and my mind became clearer than it had been for three months. The doctors were amazed. After God intervened, they were ready to release me to the care of a Christian-based counseling program.

I was there for eight days. God continued to work in my life and defeat the lies and distortions of satan. My mom and I traveled across country to see friends and family. My grandparents invited a ton of people over one night and satan began to attack me again. That night was bad and I ended up doing what I had done before with people—escaping to bed because I couldn't handle it.

The next day we continued our journey and satan continued to torment me. This lasted all the way home. It was just as bad as before and even worse. Awful!

The second night home I believe God completed His work in this season of my life. My dad was talking to me, asking me how I was doing. I was in the same state as before, not being able to describe what was going on. Now it was even more intense as I felt so bad after everything—everything I had already put them through. Life again seemed hopeless.

Dad told me to come and sit on his lap and that started the completion of the healing. There was a spiritual victory when I could finally make sense of my thoughts and what was happening inside me. I began to cry and Dad did too. I described the lies. They sounded so stupid when I could get them out and talk about them. So dad listened and then spoke Truth, the same Truth that has been there all along—and satan was defeated!

Jo

September, one year later

Dear Joel and staff,

I don't know if you remember communicating with my husband and myself last year at just about this time. We had been missionaries in China for nine years. Our second child, Jo went to college last year for about six weeks. After about a month there, she started sending us e-mail messages that she did not fit in at all. The one from a year ago Sunday night was desperate. She mentioned suicide in it, which she had never in her life mentioned before. She had just graduated from Harbor High School in the top of her class with many honors.

Jo's life always seemed so together. Our son, James, had come home the year before to attend college and seemed to do just fine. So we were quite shocked to see all the troubles that Jo was having. The word *suicide* scared me to death and we called you for advice. You recommended letting her come home if that's what she wanted to do. I thought your voice kind of broke as you said you were thinking of some other missionary parents who wished that they had let their kids do that, but it was too late.

Jo did come home and for the first few weeks she was elated. But then came the black periods, and she seemed depressed. Kids from Harbor High would write and try to be encouraging, but just the slightest mention that they were surprised that she had dropped out of school would upset her. It was all new to us, and we prayed and sought the Lord and all the help that we could find.

In December, Jo tried to take her life. She took about 70 Tylenol and also Prozac, which the doctor had just recently put her on. The doctors in the emergency room gave us little hope for a recovery. She had taken too much. And we were too late discovering it. She had taken them in the afternoon, thinking she would just instantly die, but she had no ill effects. So, that night after the service, she took more, but then began vomiting. That was when we discovered it, and rushed her to the hospital.

Many doctors and specialists told us the terrible things that would most likely happen including a coma or terrible pressure on the brain. But the Lord sovereignly moved in. Many people were praying and Jo had no side effects! The Lord healed her body. Her mind also seemed much clearer after a couple of days.

She was then released after eight days of counseling at a Christian-based counseling program. The guilt and grief for us as parents was tremendous. I, personally, had always tried to be the best parent that I knew how to be. My own family had had their problems and a big goal I had was to provide a loving, secure environment for the kids. The enemy condemned me with Jo's suicide attempt, which, but for the grace of God, would have been successful.

Amy, the lady working with Jo, stopped me in the hall of the counseling center one day and said she wanted to talk to me. She proceeded to tell me that my husband and I had been excellent parents to all of our kids. I said, "Oh, sure!" But she said, "I mean it. I have spent hours with Jo and know all about your family, and you have!" Amy's words did minister to me. I felt the Lord knew how much we were hurting and kindly let us know.

Jo had one relapse and they diagnosed her as bipolar and put her on Lithium. That was last February. Ever since, she has seemed to do well.

As I mentioned, this is the one-year anniversary since we got that fateful e-mail. It has been a hard day for me. I get to go visit her this week and am looking forward to that. But today I pulled out her old e-mail messages of a year ago. The last two I had never been able to bring myself to read again. The prior ones still seem like she was doing okay, though struggling with "normal" reentry issues.

Anyway, even a year later, the pain is tremendous when remembering the struggles of this past year. I had to call my sister to pray with me this morning to be able to get through the day. We are traveling this week and there was lots that I wanted to get done. Then this afternoon the mail came. A friend from our church sent me a big newspaper article about reentry, depression, and suicide in MKs. They quoted you a lot in the article. The tears started flowing again, and I had to call my husband at work. He understands the deep pain that such an experience brings.

Well, Joel, I don't know if you really wanted an update, but I felt like I needed to rehash this all. We would love to hear from you with any perspectives that you might have. The article mentioned two college MKs dying of suicide. That just breaks my heart. I so feel for the parents through it all. If I had not been living with Jo and watching her so closely, I would not have believed how fast she could go from being seemingly okay to the lowest pits! She had never in her life exhibited behavior like that. My heart just breaks for the parents whose kids have succeeded in their suicide attempts.

We are just thankful that Jo is alive and seemingly well now.

FOR FURTHER UNDERSTANDING
Go ahead and cry! I do even after having reread this story many times. If you are reading these stories to just "have a better understanding" of the nature of reentry problems, I trust that is being accomplished. But if it is in your heart to learn how to be a good (better) reentry caregiver, I trust you realize the emotional effort and mental energy it will take. Not forgetting, of course, that wisdom and understanding  come from God!

As described earlier, there are basically three wrong reentry behavior patterns exhibited in slight variation by returning missionaries: Alienation, Condemnation and Reversion. Each of them, left unchecked, can lead to the ultimate escape of suicide, whether mental, emotional, spiritual, or the irreversible—physical suicide.

FIVE REENTRY PATTERNS
Alienation
Condemnation
Reversion
Suicide
INTEGRATION

Though her mother thought everything was "normal" until the last two e-mails, I believe the downward spiral was already expressed on August 26 in phrases like, "It is hard on my ego" and "I'm not like them." Admittedly, these are not "suicidal" thoughts, but the beginning of the trail doesn't start at the jumping off place.  But step by step, she walked through the maze of uncertainty and confusion. She walked close to the edge several times: "There were even more times when I tried to take my life." She eventually arrived at her point of no return: "It was the only way out of my pain."

And that is how satan works: Lies that come out as half-truths; frustration that leads to confusion; isolation that results in loneliness. His tactics form the slippery slide described in James 1:14-15.

Now, for the Lord's part! How could you, the recipient of these e-mails, make a difference? Remember, she was top of her class, had graduated with honors, had never displayed such erratic indecision before and had a good family life. And her brother had made a safe, successful reentry the year before. Were there any warning signs? What about her statement, "It was so good to hear from someone I know?"

FOR FURTHER ACTION

• What were the compounding factors that caused her to withdraw—to alienate herself from her college culture? Following are some thoughts that came to my mind. Read them. Then, go back into the story and highlight the statements she made that underscore each of these issues:

—Her frustration over whether she was good enough for the team.

—Her indecision regarding joining the team.

—Her concern about how loud and brash the other players were.

—Her frustration about her teammate's preoccupation with boys.

—Her frustration over changing a major.

—Her concern for the apparent casual lifestyle of her teammates.

• In rereading this story, did you see any other symptoms of alienation that degenerated into the September 12 admission of contemplating suicide? It may take several rereadings! It may take securing a number of the resources in the Resource Section, and studying them. And it might even take talking with some suicide survivors, and parents of ones who did not survive! May God be your wisdom and strength!

• We have focused on one of the most serious issues resulting from a lack of reentry care, physical suicide. But we can remind ourselves that we don't need to "drive the darkness out," if we will pro-

> STEPS TO REENTRY
> Know it's time to go
> Go to home church
> "Abide"
> Rehearse "all"
> Fully integrate

actively "turn on the light!" (This is not to say that casualties won't happen even with the best of preparation.)

• The five steps to a successful reentry are so simply and succinctly stated in Acts 14 and 15. It might be good at this point to again read Chapter Two, the Scriptural foundation for the reentry process.

### HAPPY BIRTHDAY

Our middle son's birthday was August 9, just three weeks after our arrival back home. Because we had to make up for two months' mortgage, we had no money to even have a birthday party or any kind of gifts for him. Sometimes, in such situations, it's hard as a parent to really feel good about the choices one has made to be a missionary, but God was faithful and on time.

The second Sunday we were home and a week before his birthday, a dear sister in Christ slipped $10 into my hand after the church service. I knew it was our boy's birthday in my hand.

Our neighborhood had just gotten a new supermarket that had a cake and deli department. All of our children had gone in several times already and had oohed and aahed over the cakes with all their wonderful decorations. Missionary children are so neat that way. They don't take things for granted. They really appreciate the grandest of things that are so simple.

When this dear saint of God gave me the gift, I walked out of church and told my son in a very excited voice that he could choose any one of those fancy cakes in the supermarket and we would go to the Thrift store. Whatever the remaining change was, he could have it to buy his birthday gift. He found his cake—a deep, rich chocolate one with chocolate frosting. And at the Thrift store, he found his gift—a 4-foot blue stuffed Cheetah. We were thrilled; his birthday really was a fun time.

FOR FURTHER UNDERSTANDING
How deeply Mother feels what she said about the "choices one has made about being a missionary" will

determine the seriousness of its effects on her children. If it was just a "passing emotion," no problem. (Two paragraphs following, she did acknowledge how "neat" MKs are!) But if this attitude is a recurring lament, it is a danger sign of giant proportions!

From our field experience of teaching in and administrating mission schools, the one factor that stands above all others in a child's success cross-culturally (including reentry) relates to parental attitude! And the main deprivation of missionary children is the attitude of a parent feeling sorry for what the children are missing in life. The things they are "missing" pale in significance when compared with the advantages of cross-cultural living!

(I have actually heard parents say that it wasn't *fair* of God to call them to the field and not call their children! Give me a break! We don't serve a god of such cruelty. The Giver of life doesn't make mistakes. Missions is a family affair for families!)

FOR FURTHER ACTION

• Oftentimes your concern for child and youth re-entry is best served by addressing the attitudes of the parents. Pray with them to make sure their calling is of God. Reason with them that God calls families to the mission field.

• Because you have committed yourself to as frugal a lifestyle as you have asked your missionary friends to live on the field, when they come to visit you, their children won't see all the "trinkets" of materialism to entice them! I am glad he got his birthday party. But a *blue* Cheetah?!

## ON THE STREET

We were home on furlough, my mom and dad, my three-year-old brother and me (the baby). The church had made arrangements for us to stay with a family for a few weeks. We were there only a few days when we were informed that friends of theirs were arriving and we would have to leave—today! So Mother and Dad quickly packed up our things and, with suitcases and two kids, they started walking and praying, not knowing where we would stay for the night.

The Lord provided a place through another member of the church who "happened" to be driving by and saw us walking. He offered us a ride to wherever we were going. When he heard what had happened, he invited us to stay with them until we could find our own place.

FOR FURTHER UNDERSTANDING

Though this child was possibly an infant-in-arms or at the most a toddler, impressions of "other people" are making their mark. The faithfulness of her parents to God overruled any negative she might have sensed from this most inhospitable host.

It is difficult to understand the thinking of some people. Though changes had to be made (When they offered their home to the missionaries, they did not know their friends would be coming.), could there not have been a more gentle approach?

FOR FURTHER ACTION

• If your friends called that they were coming, how would you have handled your missionary guests? Rented a motel for them? Pulled out some sleeping bags? Given them your room? What other alternatives to "sending them out on the street" can you think of?

• As you think about your own missionary friend, realize that the best laid plans can go awry. Are the people who have committed themselves to an aspect of reentry care reliable? Were they coerced into doing something? (Danger sign!) Have you thought of contingency plans?

## GIVE IT TO THE MISSIONARIES

I was a teenager, on furlough with my parents, and getting ready to start college. I was invited to the women's missionary meeting at the home of a young couple who had recently married. When we arrived, she happily showed us through her new home. It was a lovely home and they had furnished it tastefully, complete with a formal dining room set in the dining room, table and chairs in the breakfast nook, and another table and chairs in the downstairs, where we were meeting.

During the meeting, an appeal was made for another missionary family who had just arrived on furlough. They had been given a table but only one chair. The six family members were taking turns enjoying the luxury of sitting while eating.

The leader asked if anyone had any chairs they could give or loan to this couple for one year. The women looked around at each other, and finally the hostess responded. I thought she might offer to loan one of her three sets of chairs to the family. To my shock, she said, "I think we might have a broken chair in the attic that they could fix." Others chimed in with more broken chairs. And so the needs of another missionary had been met!

FOR FURTHER UNDERSTANDING

Truth is wilder than fiction! Unbelievable, you say? Unfortunately, not. There is a mythical mindset in the Christian community that missionaries can (should) live on a lower level than we who are "working for our hard-earned money."

On a short-term trip to Ecuador, my wife and other ladies were sorting through barrels of clothing and school supplies that had been given for orphanage use. Clothes were torn and worn out. Zippers and buttons had been taken off. And yes, the used tea bags were there! But the ultimate had to be the pencils that had been sharpened down to the metal eraser holder. And, of course, there was no eraser!

FOR FURTHER ACTION
- What will be the immediate needs of your missionary friend upon reentry? Have you asked *him* what housing, transportation, or clothing needs he will have? Are you able to begin meeting those needs?

## COLLEGE BOUND

We moved to Australia when I was 16. Though the thought of moving right before your senior year may sound like it should be upsetting, the Lord softened my heart and I was really okay with it. The good-bye process was hard, but I had my family. This time away from everything and everyone we knew was great for our relationship as a family. I can honestly say we are all now best friends because of this chance we had to lean on each other in hard times.

Three years later, I left Australia for Bible college in the States. Not only was I moving out of the house, I was moving to another country! My family was to stay. The actual reentering to the USA was fine. My dad flew with me and dropped me off at school. I knew the Lord had called me to the Bible college and I definitely wanted to be back in the States. I connected with a wonderful group of lifelong friends right away.

Two years later, I graduated with an associate's degree in theology. After that, I kind of felt like I was pushed out into the open and wasn't sure which way I was supposed to go. Going on to college was such a natural progression, I didn't really seem to notice until after that, that I had missed some things. I had missed the "rite of passage" from youth to adult—the whole process of leaving my teens.

I guess the final word is that it's okay to feel a little

lost in certain areas. I connected with old friends from high school who had changed (for the worse) and I saw God's providence in removing me from that crowd. I also caught up with old friends that have continued to grow in the Lord as I did. We enjoy fellowship, reminiscing and discussing how exciting it is that we have so much in common because we kept our eyes set on the Lord. The Lord has been faithful.

FOR FURTHER UNDERSTANDING
You can almost "hear" a person's view on life in their writing! Do you hear the solid family relationships that strengthened and sustained them all in the "hard times?" College—yes! Friends—many! Calling—clear! And then—"I'm on my own!?" But even then, whatever "softened" her heart to go, strengthened her heart to being out on her own.

FOR FURTHER ACTION
• Here is another candidate for facilitator for your "youth forum!" She is certainly living out the Scripture, *"Don't let the keynote of your lifestyle be nastiness, silliness or flippancy, but a sense of all that we owe to God"* (Ephesians 5:4).
• Is the structure of your college and career (young adult) activities focused on the eternal? Can your returned single missionary friend challenge them to a life of greater devotion and commitment to the heartbeat of God: *"Not willing that any perish, but that all come to repentance"* (II Peter 3:9)?
• Does the structure of your church's children's ministry incorporate mission awareness? Does it allow participation in local cross-cultural ministry? Are songs regularly sung (not just at the missions conference) that give the church a missions challenge? It is still true that the majority of career missionaries make that commitment before they are out of high school.

### FEELINGS BURIED FOR TEN YEARS

Our plane left Asia and headed for our new home—America! Culture shock can be terrifying to a missionary child—even a teenage child! The differences I experienced were exhilarating at first. However, when the novelty wore off, the constant strangeness tore my heart from its happy, secure moorings.

We had flown to "Mars" and there was no ticket home. The irony of the situation was that Dad and Mom, who could have helped me find myself in all the confusion, didn't understand what I was experiencing. How could they? They were Americans *coming* home. I was an "Asian" child *leaving* my home. Oh, yes, I was a U.S. citizen. But I had been raised in Asia.

High school was a nightmare. In every way I felt a misfit: From the dress styles to the cursing to the necking in the halls to...! I wanted no part of this American teenage lifestyle, but neither did I want to be ignored. I wanted to belong; I needed friends.

In college I fell in love with a European classmate whose future plans included a specialized ministry. The Lord used this relationship to force me to confront my own bitter feelings towards America. No, I wasn't proud of my country, I hadn't accepted it nor even tried to understand it. And everybody knew it!

I wanted to marry Lars and escape to another land, but Lars was proud of his heritage. Nationalism was strong in his veins. My attitude puzzled and angered him. Lars stopped seeing me and I was heartbroken.

Much soul-searching followed. I realized that for ten years I had buried my agony deep inside—confusion, fear, and hatred for this country. I hadn't even known my true feelings, but God brought all the ugliness to the surface. There followed confession of my sin, and the healing began. I can truly say that from that point on I began to love this country with as much intensity as I had once hated it.

FOR FURTHER UNDERSTANDING
Condemnation: "...bitter feelings towards America! And everybody knew it!" Where were Mom and Dad? Lost in their own readjustment? Oblivious to their daughter's needs? Did they not have the tools to help her? Had she hidden these feelings from them?

Alienation: She did not withdraw. "I want to belong; I need friends." But she "withdrew" in this one aspect of her life. Buried feelings. But as with all unresolved conflicts, if buried in one area or relationship, they will "resurrect" in another. And Lars, proud of his own heritage, saw the poison this would bring to their relationship, and broke it off.

Wake-up call! Out of the depth of her loss of Lars came the confession of sin and healing.

FOR FURTHER ACTION
• You are Lars! There was something in her character that attracted you to her. When this ugliness raised its head, having a good sense of national pride, is there something else you could have done besides "dump her?" As grievous as some aspects of America have become, there is still a lot of good in her. Could you have helped her see the "glass half full?"

• She was talking about it. "Everybody knew it!" she said. Could your college group initiate an intervention? In whatever country we live, scripturally, there is some pretty strong teaching on respect for country.

• Could you do a study on the Kingdom of God with your friend? For there is a *city we long for, whose builder and maker is God*" (Hebrews 11:10).

**WHAT I'D LIKE TO TELL THE PEOPLE BACK HOME**
I want to answer a few questions I have been asked: No! We don't live in mud huts. No! We don't eat "foreign" food. It is very natural. MKs are not perfect. We're

human and have faults and virtues like everybody else. When you subconsciously or otherwise treat us like we should be perfect, we get chewed out by you (who have *no right*) and then by our parents (who know better).

No! All MKs are not super brats. Those few who might act like it on furlough are probably trying to hide the culture shock they are going through.

No! Just because you're an MK doesn't mean you know your Bible any better than anyone else. All the time when we were on furlough, I was asked to quote Scripture or find something in the Bible I had never heard of. People were shocked, and whispered behind their hands.

No! MKs don't go around barefoot and in rags. Mrs. X (I can't remember her name.) had seen a picture of me in a paint-spotted tee-shirt and cutoffs and assumed I didn't have anything better to wear. Please send money! The money sent to missionaries is never enough! Even though it often appears my folks aren't doing anything, they are! And our national friends will tell you so!

FOR FURTHER UNDERSTANDING

This was written by a young man just after returning to the field with his parents. They had been on a one-year furlough. His previous time in his "home" country had been four years before when he was nine years old. Now, for the next four years this will be the memory of where he will spend his adult life.

Can you hear the defensiveness? Reread his story and underline the phrases that suggest the sadness of a boy not treated well while on furlough. I underlined ten! Maybe you can find even more.

To understand the special needs of a missionary child requires an understanding of that child's parents. In no area of life does a child emulate more the attitude of parents than in a cross-cultural setting. Parents who announce to their children that God has called them (the parents) to the mission field and they (the kids) will just have to come along, are setting them up for failure. If not failure, at least a most difficult time of reentry.

On the other hand, parents who excitedly express the great privilege that God has given to us *as a family* to serve Him cross-culturally will find the children more easily adjusting to their position as Third Culture Kids.

FOR FURTHER ACTION

• Discover the attitude of the parents of your returning missionary children. This is a very delicate issue in that the parents are also going through their reentry stress. This might be better done through an ongoing relationship while they are on the field. Or, even as a prerequisite, test their attitude to whether or not you will send them to the field! Wow! Yes! In the study, *TOO VALUABLE TO LOSE*, it was determined that the high rate of preventable attrition was caused, in part, by many being sent to the field who should never have gone!

• This young man, having returned to the field with such a negative attitude, still needs care. Can you develop a correspondence relationship with him to help him express and deal with his feelings? Appendix C will give you some ideas to get started.

• Are there young people in your church who have had some cross-cultural exposure who could relate to the youth of your reentering families?

Chapter Nine

# On Furlough

On furlough! What a term. To some it may sound a bit like "Gone fishin'!" To others it may bring ideas of that well-deserved, year-long "vacation" the missionary has spent four years working toward. Still others may see it as the time for the missionary to "repay" the church for their financial support over the past four years. Again, others may wonder, "What's he doing here? I thought we sent him to serve the Lord over there!"

Furlough. A leave of absence. Home stay. Home leave. Home assignment! Call it what you will, it is that time when the missionary "closes up shop" in one culture and arena of ministry and makes (tries to make) the adjustment into an entirely different setting. In the one environment, he has adjusted to the climate, the food, the living conditions. Most of all, though, he has become *"unencumbered with the affairs of this life that he might please the One who has called him to be a soldier"* (II Timothy 2:4). Thus, his total (at least, primary) focus has been on the things of the Lord in ministry.

Then, usually without adequate time for mental or physical transition, he is plunged into a marathon of meetings and meals that make him wish he could be back "home" on the field—just to rest! This rapid change in his environment has been described as "a time warp" or "a quantum leap" into the unknown.

Do you remember the quantum leap in cultural change we mentioned earlier? Our British friend reflecting on her last "bath" in the river with her village women in South America. This "reflection" is occurring less than forty-eight hours later as she is sitting "at tea" with a friend of hers in Buckingham Palace!

It might do us well to remember the days of slow transit! The days when it took a missionary a month or two to travel home. I wonder if that "slow boat *from* China" helped the missionary make a more reasonable transition.

The missionary on home assignment faces some unique challenges. First is the matter of logistics. Trying to set up a home to give the family some sense of stability in another country presents several major difficulties! Yet, once they are established, the necessity of extensive travel often takes the missionary away for long periods of time. Or, the whole family travels.

A converted Detroit city bus with its low-geared transmission just "wallowed" out of our court a few days ago. It had been converted by a zealous and dedicated missionary family. Mom and Dad, plus two boys and two girls, ages ranging from eleven to five, had spent an evening with us. This bus will be home, transportation and classroom for a year as they crisscross the country, building a team of caregivers to join them in the vision given to them by God.

Depending on the nature of their work on the field, home assignment can also involve additional training: a course to keep a license current; a class to improve needed skills.

Because educational standards and methods vary greatly from country to country, missionaries on home assignment must deal with the best overall option for their children's schooling, which might just be the least "bad" option! Then, the children must cope with that decision. And the parents must cope with the children! (Reread MK story, *Lost in a Tidal Wave*, for a youth's perspective on furlough schooling.)

Did anyone say, "Money?" Yes, finances become another major issue. Living costs are generally higher in a missionary's home country. Then some financial supporters, thinking "Oh, they're home now," drop their commitment until the missionary returns to the field and "the work of the Lord!"

There is yet another aspect to the financial strain. Over the course of time that the missionary has been on the field, some supporters have dropped their commitment. New ones have to be found to replace them. Or, possibly the monetary exchange rate has changed, giving the missionary less buying power with the same number of dollars.

Oftentimes, spiritually drained from the constant "giving out" on the field, a missionary comes home to the new demand of having to tell all the "glorious stories of the great things" that happened through their ministry.

In the following stories are some of the real reentry issues from the lips of missionaries on furlough. As best as possible, try to relate to their situation. Try to put yourself in their place. Try to see "furlough" through their eyes and mind and emotions and heart!

The next part is more difficult. Try to relate their perspective to your own missionary friend. Could any of the experiences of these missionaries fit the profile of your friend?

### TO WORK OR NOT TO WORK

For every Christian there comes a day when God becomes undeniably real. For some it may be at salvation. For others it may come through a dramatic healing. For me, it happened this way:

We are a family of four. I had been in the field for a little over a year when I found myself struggling over the issue of working while on our two-month furlough. Through our church and support team, the Lord had provided for our day-to-day living expenses, but I had planned to work to cover some other expenses.

Before leaving for the field we had tried to become debt-free. We'd paid off our car and personal loans, but we could not pay off one major credit card. This furlough, however, found me with additional expenses: A $1500 hospital bill for minor surgery, home schooling registration and tuition fees for our two high schoolers, and that ever-haunting $5000 credit card balance. All of this led me to only one understandable solution: I would work while on furlough and raise the money for the hospital and schooling expenses and hopefully put a dent in the credit card balance.

Upon our arrival, employment by two different Christian brothers was offered. A good solid plan and provision from the Lord, right?

Still, there was the struggle. The struggle in my heart was about how God provides for those who trust in Him. I had heard the miraculous stories of provision from other missionaries, knew the miraculous stories of provision in His Word, and read the stories of miraculous provision for "great men of God" like Hudson Taylor and John and Charles Wesley. As for me, however, God provided not one job, but two. That's miraculous, right?

Still, there was the struggle. A struggle that found me in prayer crying out to God for His guidance over which job I should take. A prayer that soon summoned the reply, "What have I called you to be?"

"Well, Lord," I replied, "You've called me to be a missionary."

"And what makes you think that stops when you

leave the field?" He asked.

"Well, I guess it doesn't," I said.

"Those things I have shown you, those things that I've taught you, those things continue to do. Continue the work I have given you," He said.

I questioned, "Yes, Lord, but what about the jobs? What about the bills?"

He responded, "Your work is with Me now. Only be obedient, trust in Me and I will do the rest." Indeed, God had already been working. Just one week earlier we found out that there was a mistake made on my hospital bill and that the balance was $1000 less than we thought. Also in meeting with the home schooling directors they said that they had been praying and felt led of the Lord to support us and waived the registration and tuition fees. Still, as I shared all of this with my wife, we couldn't help but wonder about the $5000 balance on our credit card account.

That evening I shared with my wife's parents the answer I believed I had received from the Lord. Their looks gave me a mixed message. I didn't know what they were thinking. After a brief discussion they informed us that the pastors from their church wanted to speak with us and that we should set up a meeting for the next day. The following morning found my wife and me sitting in a living room with two pastors who were eager to hear what I had received from the Lord in prayer. Not knowing quite what to expect, I shared the story.

The pastors settled back in their seats and, with a quick exchange of glances, began to share that they felt the answer the Lord had given me was a confirmation on a direction that they had received from the Lord. They explained that there was some money the church had accumulated and that they had been praying for months on a direction for its use. Knowing about our situation with the credit card bill, they shared with us that the Lord had directed them to handle the balance and that they would issue a check to pay off the account in full. A few days later we received a check in the amount of $5000. We paid off the account, leaving us debt-free! God had done the impossible.

With David I say, *"What is man that You are mindful of him"* (Psalm 8:4). And indeed, who am I that You are mindful of me? Who I am is a child of God! Through His Son is demonstrated His grace towards me, a grace that I stand in even now and a grace that without I would surely be lost.

## FOR FURTHER UNDERSTANDING

*"'My ways are higher than your ways, and My thoughts than your thoughts,' says the Lord"* (Isaiah 55:9). That is probably the best understanding we can receive from this story!

In his last paragraph, he states the theme of Appendix B, *Who I Am/What I Do*—a very good perspective.

## FOR FURTHER ACTION

• I can imagine the diversity of counsel this missionary received as he "struggled" through to God's solution. As you are available to be a "sounding board" for your missionary friend, be very sensitive to the Spirit of God in the counsel you give. Oftentimes, His ways are not the "logical" solutions we so easily see from our human perspective.

• Does your church have a policy on financial support for furloughing missionaries? Some mission agencies, knowing that the cost of living in one's home country is generally higher and that many people drop their commitment while the missionary isn't "working for the Lord full-time," require a forced savings plan each month their missionary is on the field. These funds are used, then, to help during furlough.

• Does your church have a policy on financial support for those who are coming home to a career change?  The agency we were with required—before we went to the field—two month's living costs in reserve for our return, or one month's reserve with a promise of employment.

### LOGISTIC DETAILS

My husband had to return six weeks prior to the three children and me. He had received notice that he needed to be enrolled in classes by June 6 or be dropped from his Ph.D. program, yet our furlough cycle was not complete until July 15. So, the children and I stayed on for the remaining weeks. Because it was not on our regular furlough cycle, we had to pay for his ticket out of our own pocket. This was a huge amount of money, but we were trusting God to provide for us. We knew this is what He wanted.

We had acquired a repossession home the previous furlough, so we did have a house to come home to, but we had the unfortunate circumstance of having several dishonest renters and in mid-April, before our return, we received a note saying only, "There has been a fire— more later." So for April and May there was no one in the house and no one to pay the rent. My husband came home to an unfurnished house. They had left behind one single mattress, which he had in our master bedroom, one cooking pot, and one chair. He had no vehicle so he had ridden the bus to and from school.

The day the children and I arrived at the airport, my husband tried to brace me for the awful situation he had been living with. To help ease the shock, just that morning a doctor friend had given us a double bed, a couch and two very fancy living room chairs. Another doctor friend had just given us a ten-year-old vehicle that we could all fit into. Every time it started, we gave God praise for the miracle!

So, on the way home from the airport, we stopped

by the local Prison Ministry Thrift Store and the owner, a friend, told us to go through his store and find whatever we needed. I had less than $100 that I had carried all the way home from Africa, in case we needed anything in the airports. As I went through the store I was trying to be very careful not to go over that amount, as it was all we had. I had no idea then how we would even buy groceries, once I had all the household things.

But when we got all through and up to the counter with the dishes, silverware, cups, glasses, pots and pans, lamps, children's beds, dressers, and one iron, Zeb asked, "Have you got it all?" To which I said, "Yes, I think we can survive on these things." His reply, "Okay, then take it all away!" He refused to charge us anything! He refused to take my money! Now we could use that money for groceries for our first week home. I'll never forget the total feeling of dependence on God during those days.

Although our sending church prided itself on thinking they were the ideal caring and sending church, they had no clue of our need nor how the Lord amazingly provided. They never once asked us how we were doing, nor if we needed anything.

AREAS OF SUPPORT
- Moral
- Logistic
- Financial
- Prayer
- Communication
- Reentry

## FOR FURTHER UNDERSTANDING

All members of a team are responsible to take action to reduce reentry stress! In this story, the returning missionary family could have taken several steps of action. Likewise, a supportive church could have helped to make the transition less traumatic. (I say "less traumatic" rather than "easy" because reentry is never easy. There are always—even in the "best of them"—some feelings of discomfort as adjustments are made.)

## FOR FURTHER ACTION

- Reread the story. Think of some things friends

could have done to help this family. Here are a few:

—Have someone to meet the husband at the airport.

—Repair the house after the fire.

—Furnish the house.

—Stock the refrigerator. (Purchase or loan one first!)

—Send someone over to accompany Mom and three children home! Does this sound like a "wild" idea? It is! But the question always arises, "How valuable are our missionaries?" If the children were little, what a help it would have been to have another adult on that long journey home!

• There are also many things the missionaries could have done to pave the way, making their reentry less "bumpy!" Here are a few ideas. Are there more?

—Had a reliable property manager to prevent or minimize damage to house.

—Informed the missions committee of the awkward situation (and financial drain) of the husband coming home first. Or, the even more difficult situation of Mom and three little children travelling alone.

—Had a greater emergency fund saved.

—Worked out with the agency an exception to the rule of "furlough cycle."

—Had established a core team leadership of their support team to act as a liaison, particularly at this time in the details of logistic support.

• When your missionary friend comes home on furlough, are you (your church) prepared to assist with the logistics of their immediate needs? Are you aware of what his needs might be? You certainly don't want to provide a furnished apartment only to find out he plans to live with his brother's family!

## CULTURAL IDENTITY

I myself am Australian and have been married for ten years to my French wife. I consider that we have an above average marriage, although on a day-to-day level it is often hard work. Maybe I should explain that: I think that if our marriage was anything less than above average we would have probably sunk (whatever that means) before now. We spend time in three different countries—mine, hers and on the field (an African country). Without any doubt, our marital relationship is much easier when we are in neither her country nor mine (although we speak each other's language with ease, and even communicate to each other in either language, and enjoy living in each other's country). There is much more solidarity when we are both the foreigners in a country.

When we are in France, it becomes so obvious that I am a foreigner. She has all her close friendships that leave me a little out in the cold. I can't say that I have a single close friend there. Then when we come back to Australia, I know *she* feels excluded. I'm left trying to juggle between the joy of catching up and wanting to spend time with friends, and not wanting to leave my wife "on her own." This can be very tricky!

This last time returning from Africa, first to France and then to Australia, both my wife and I noticed a change in our perception of our individual identities. It almost seems that in direct proportion to our success in adapting to each other's country, language and family, our own cultural identity is reinforced and we feel less and less comfortable in the other's culture. In other words, the more I outwardly fit into French culture, the less Australian I feel, but the more Australian I *want* to be. It is so ironic, but we have both observed this. I think it must have something to do with the fact that, being mobile and culturally "unplugged" for many years, creates an enormous desire in each of us to belong somewhere, and that pull is obviously to our own cultural roots. So instead of becoming bi-culturally mobile between the two cultures (although outwardly that certainly is the case), we actually find it harder to face living in each other's country as the years go by.

FOR FURTHER UNDERSTANDING
Wow! With the depth of cultural perception in this brief story, their marriage will "weather many-a-storm!" Understanding brings togetherness: "We both have observed this."

Cultural roots *are* important. Remember David? It is late at night. The adrenalin is pumping. He and his warriors are in the heat of battle. But what comes to his mind? "Oh, for a drink of 'home town' water!" His hometown is in the hands of the enemy. But his parched throat—No! Rather the roots that establish him as a citizen of Bethlehem—have him longing for a drink from Jacob's Well. (Read about this culturally motivated adventure in II Samuel 23:13-17.)

The missionary who travels beyond his own culture must deal with this issue. This missionary indicated their lack of becoming "bi-culturally mobile." He pinpointed the problem. That is Step One toward the solution. To enjoy—really appreciate the good and accept the bad of another culture—is the goal. But it takes work to break the ethnocentric thinking that fights against *multi*-culturalism.

FOR FURTHER ACTION
* Do you have any counsel for this couple? Do you think they should just stay in Africa? He said their marriage is more stable there.
* He concludes, "It seems to be getting more and more difficult to live in each other's country." Are you a student of culture? Have you tried to relate with the internationals who live in your hometown to better understand your missionary friend's need for cultural identity? Are there other sources for cultural understanding? The Internet? The library? The Bible! Yes, the Bible is

crammed full of cultural issues! How about a short-term ministry trip to get you beyond the comfort zones of your world and increase your understanding?!

- What are the "roots" issues that are important to your missionary friend? Do they center on family? On locations? On events? On church? Think of ways you can help provide the stability he needs through his cultural roots.

- On the other hand, don't be surprised if he is not "taken up" by roots! It is possible that he has learned, and is living in the ultimate solution, "This world is not my home...!"

### CONTRAST OF TWO FURLOUGHS

My first furlough began just days after Mt. Pinatubo erupted. It was a very frightening experience. It was hard to believe all the devastation that it brought into the city where I lived, which gave me great conflict about leaving at that time. I could see that there was so much work to do and so many people needing help. It broke my heart to leave.

My flight was one of the first flights out of Manila after the eruption. I was very thankful that I had bought this ticket five months before. Friends on the West Coast were taking time off work, so even though I had a very tight schedule, I stopped to visit them. The Lord put everything together.

I was glad for the week I had with my friends before heading home to New England. They took good care of me and gave me some time to rest. They took great interest in everything I shared about my time in the Philippines, especially the big news about Mt. Pinatubo.

When I flew home, there was a group from my church, including my mother, to greet me. There was not a dry eye at the gate. How good it was to be there.

My home church had changed quite a bit in the

two-plus years that I had been gone. It was much larger. It was meeting in the town hall instead of the house where the church had started. There was a lot of excitement about all the Lord was doing. It took a while to get used to the changes. All the new faces—I could not keep track of all the names. I was made to feel at home, though. I had ample opportunity to share with the church what the Lord was doing. Everyone seemed to be really interested. All this, but it still did not feel like the church that I had left.

One great blessing was that the singles group had grown and was more active. I enjoyed the fellowship with this group while I was around.

During this furlough I did a lot of travelling. Since my family lived some distance from my home church, I had to keep a balance between the two places. Besides that, I was visiting other churches on the East Coast and the Caribbean. The five months that I was in the States went very quickly.

My second furlough was quite difficult. My only anticipation of that was a note from my pastor saying that my church wanted me to join a mission group before they would let me return to the field. I had no idea what would be next.

I spent nearly a month in California visiting friends first. It was the best thing for me, as I received a lot of encouragement. I visited one church where I was given an opportunity to share about the Philippines. The pastor gave a message that morning about missions. Through it the Lord reminded me of how He had provided for me in the past to go out. I remembered the confidence I had, knowing that all my needs would be met. The message spoke to me, saying that He would do it again. I just had to wait on Him.

As I continued on home I had a great peace. I did not know what to expect, but I knew that He would make the way for me to return to the Philippines.

Upon my arrival at the airport, again there was a group to meet me. We went to get ice cream together so that we would have a chance to visit.

This time was harder though. I was expecting to stay with a family from church, but no one had opened their doors. I felt like the pastor had not made the need known to the church, but a family who used to attend the church did open their home for me. This was only for a month, though. Someone pointed out that since the wife was working in the home, it did not look good for me stay with them.

The church had gone through a split and was meeting in the house again. There was someone new that was leading worship with a guitar. After service, I sat at the piano and we played a couple of songs together. The pastor came to me saying that he did not want any changes to the worship. His wife would play one hymn each week, otherwise it was just to be the guitar. I was very surprised, because I was hopeful to be part of the worship team again. What made it harder was when people would ask me why I didn't play the piano as I had in the past. Even when the pastor and his wife were on vacation, I was not asked to play the piano.

What had been a strong singles group no longer existed. Many of my friends from that group had gotten married and were attending different churches. Others had just left.

My pastor did have me come up front to share a few words and said that I would have more opportunities to share in the future, but that day never came. I had been quite close to the pastor before going to the Philippines. Now he seemed very distant. It was hard to plan for times to get together. We did not share on the same level as we had before.

The family I was staying with was going to a community church, so on Sunday evenings I would go with them since we did not have a service at that time. They had a fairly new pastor there, who had been a missionary in France for ten years. He was an encouragement to me. The Lord opened doors for me to get involved in that church. They were able to meet needs for me that my home church just did not meet. I nearly left my home church, but I didn't feel the Lord leading me in that way.

Besides the adjustments with churches, I had to get a job, find a place to live and buy a car. I am thankful that I did have the month of December to do all this. This was the first time in more than six years that I was in the secular work force.

In the Philippines it is common to point at something with your lips. I did that a couple of times at work. The first time I was totally unaware of what I had done. The second time I was quite embarrassed. Someone thought that I was flirting.

Both at work and at church I found it hard to understand what people considered important. Most people take so much that they have for granted. I had to work at not judging them or complaining about them.

I would never have thought that two furloughs could be so different!

FOR FURTHER UNDERSTANDING
The changes back home from one furlough to the next can bring devastating results. Fortunately for this missionary, with each reentry, he spent some time with friends on the West Coast. Decompression time, it could be called—a time to relax, shift gears, and allow his body, soul and spirit to make the transition into another time and cultural zone!

Further, he always had someone to talk with and he was not shy about doing it. He also had a strong confidence in God's ultimate provision. And God used that pastor's sermon to remind him of His care.

The "great peace" he carried to the East Coast was

in the midst of uncertainty. This is truly the peace Christ gives—not the peace of this world. Almost everything that had provided strength and encouragement on his first furlough was absent on the second. Yet, he remained faithful to his church and to his calling. His lack of resentment toward a pastor who had changed in his absence is another evidence of his strength of character. He is back on the field—through an agency, as his pastor requested.

FOR FURTHER ACTION
- There are clear signs of Christian maturity in this missionary. Reread the story. Underscore (or highlight) the statements that reflect this maturity.
- When your friend comes home, will he demonstrate the same strong confidence in facing his reentry challenges? Are there Bible studies you could be doing with him now—via mail, e-mail, or realtime chat room correspondence, that would help to strengthen his character?
- Church splits! The lack of stability in today's church is epidemic. And indicative of a society without strong moorings. Will your friend be coming home to a church life or structure greatly different from the one he left? Are you taking the time to prepare him for those changes? Not through the "gossipy rumors," but through a straightforward telling the "truth in love," share the changes that will certainly affect him.
- Little, if any knowledge of reentry care seemed to be evident in this missionary's church. Reread his story. Underscore the areas of stress that he experienced on his second reentry?

NINE AREAS OF STRESS
| Physical
| Professional
| Financial
| Cultural
| Social
| Linguistic
| National/Political
| Educational
| Spiritual

- Are you becoming prepared to help your returning missionary through the maze of reentry stress?
- Are you becoming prepared to educate your

church in the awesome, privileged responsibility of a church family to receive their missionaries home?

### I ORDERED A $3 BAKED POTATO!

I remember very well my first time back in the States after two years ministering in South America. I had been working with a church whose congregation was made up of middle- to lower-class people. During those two years I had come to be more like those among whom I lived.

Knowing it was time to go home for a break did not make it easier to accept the extreme materialism I faced. My family met me at the airport. After some rest and clean up, the next day my family wanted to treat me to dinner. We all got ready and they took me to the Chart House Restaurant. It wasn't so bad until I looked at the menu. Most every plate was in the $20-$25 dollar range. I wanted to leave. I wanted to cry. How could anyone spend $20 on a dinner? Twenty dollars is what many families used to feed their entire family for a month where I had just lived. What was I supposed to do? Well, I told them what I thought and I ordered the baked potato for $3. I had a hard time even eating that! Three dollars for a baked potato! When we got home, I went to my room and cried. They had no way of knowing how I felt or how my friends in South America lived.

A few days later, a couple of girlfriends invited me over to their home to chat (fellowship). I clearly remember a conversation where my dear friend started complaining about her wallpaper and how she was looking forward to getting new wallpaper put up in the fall. She had the colors picked out so it would go with the decor. "New wallpaper!" I thought inside myself. "Be thankful you have walls!" Of course, I thought of the families who went to my church in South America who had walls made of thin plywood and aluminum pieces somehow nailed together. And this color coordinating of decor I could not relate to. Needless to say, I didn't partake much in this conversation. My friend was excited to get new wallpaper; I was grieved thinking of my brothers and sisters who never complained about their plywood, aluminum, and cardboard walls. They were content to be together as a family.

When I first came back, the Home Fellowship that had "adopted" me wanted to hear what the Lord had been doing on the field. I shared some highlights and as the Holy Spirit had put on my heart to "speak the truth in love," I began to share how I myself had been in need many months. The real reason I moved ten times in two years was because I couldn't afford rent. Those in the Home Fellowship thought that the church was supporting their missionaries. They thought the $20-$40 they sent a month was for extra things. I told them "No, that's what I was living on."

After the meeting was over, everyone gathered around a table of goodies. I wanted to scream and run out the door. An abundance of chips, dip, cookies, brownies, and all kinds of junk food were available and I'm thinking of the beans and rice the families I'd minister to would graciously and humbly share with me. There were many times when I would see pieces of bread, or a bit of leftover good food thrown out. I wanted to reach into the trash can and pull this food out. How could people be so wasteful? At home, if I didn't finish what was on my plate, I'd put it in a small plastic container and save it for later. My family and later, my roommates, thought this was odd! To this day, I save anything that's still edible. We live in such a wasteful society.

I think one of the things that saved me was that I talked and cried… and shared and cried… and prayed and cried… with a friend who had spent the first year out on the mission field with me. She had gone through cross-cultural shock the year before. She was there for me and knew exactly what I was going through.

I think that having a friend who's been through it is one of the greatest helps for those returning.

FOR FURTHER UNDERSTANDING

There is no doubt in my mind that materialism— whether we have the wealth or are just lusting for it—is one of the most difficult aspects of life!

Every Christian has to come to grips with his management of the resources God has given him. And this returning missionary has clearly expressed how it has affected her on this brief furlough. There is a delicate balance between receiving graciously at the hand of caregivers and lamenting the extravagance of a materialistic society.

FOR FURTHER ACTION

• We can be sensitive to the internal reactions our missionary friend might be having in dealing with the materialism that seems so normal to us.

• We ask our missionaries to live a frugal lifestyle on the field. Is it possible for those of us who serve as senders to more wisely manage our resources at home? An excellent book to help you get started in a better management of His wealth entrusted to you is *Living More with Less* by Doris Longacre.

• On the other hand, all missionaries do not minister to "down-'n'-outers!" Although the United States poverty level is in the ninety-sixth percentile of world wealth, there are a few wealthy people to be ministered unto cross-culturally. It is possible you will have to help your missionary friend adjust to a downscaling of lifestyle when he returns home.

A friend worked directly under the President's wife of a Latin American country. She was the Minister of Children. As the director of an orphanage, my friend's involvements often had him in the President's palace!

• Did you notice another issue in this missionary's reentry? Two of the key steps to a full integration are clearly mentioned; another is alluded to. Reread the story. Underscore her expressions of this care.

> STEPS TO REENTRY
> Know it's time to go
> Go to home church
> "Abide"
> Rehearse "all"
> Fully integrate

### I THOUGHT I'D EXPERIENCED IT ALL

I was told this was coming, but I didn't really know how bad it could get. Reentry culture shock! Aptly named, I'm afraid.

After spending a year preparing to go to the mission field for the first time, you'd think I'd experienced it all: The crisis of faith as I faced securing my own financial support through donations, basically jumping off a cliff into God's waiting, yet invisible arms; a professional crisis as I resigned a stable job and abruptly changed careers in mid-life; a crisis of independence as I sold, gave away, or in some way abandoned, most of what I had worked twenty-five hard and lonely years to acquire; a crisis of belonging as I turned my back on family, friends, church, shopping centers, roads, restaurants, television, bookstores, various psychological crutches and escapes, and my own culture and language; an identity crisis as I shed my old self and my old home—the world—for a promised new self I'd yet to meet who would abide in a completely different reality—the Kingdom of God.

You'd think I'd experienced it all!

Then there was the mission field—Russia. And a year experiencing a new culture and language. Culture shock! A year of working with a team of people I didn't know and several of whom I didn't like or who didn't like me—impossible relationships, impossible odds. Running to God in a complete panic, begging for help, for succor, for understanding and wisdom—for a shoulder on which to cry and a gentle hand to dry my tears. Slowly, almost imperceptibly, the Holy Spirit, the great Comforter, brought order into my chaos and beauty into my nightmare. And I discovered God, for the first time in my life, it seemed. I was filled with purpose and joy in my work. In the intimacy of that relationship, I'd finally fallen into love with my patient Lord. I fell in love head over heels, eternally with my Lord Jesus. I was complete and I would never turn back! I would never give up this wondrous intimacy that no poem could ever describe. Surely the angels envied me!

You'd think I'd experienced it all!

It came time to return "home." I wasn't sure what home was anymore. And throughout the year, few from home had communicated with me. Only now and again, when I purposefully reached out and asked for some news, just a crumb to help me stay linked to my friends, my family, my church. I was certain I would hear from so many of my dear friends. After all, we had e-mail! I wrote stories of my experiences and sent them home. I was extremely faithful to communicate and stay connected to my loved ones and supporters.

Yet, only one remained faithful and consistent—my friend and sister in Christ. How I cherished her messages and the phone calls she arranged with other Christian friends who sang to me from back home! But what of my family, my church, my other friends? Didn't they know my need? Didn't they know how desperate I was to hear from them, to know they had not forgotten me? A Christmas card, an Easter card—little more. Nothing personal. And now it was time to return home, and I was sure of only one person—only sure that one friend would be there to welcome me and be happy to see me.

My father said I could stay with the family while I got on my feet, but I had to ask for that! However, they were going to the beach and my staying in their house alone "was not possible." Why? I didn't dare ask. The answer had to be more painful than the question. I would have stayed in Russia if I could have, rather than return to this unknown. And yet, my greatest fear was yet to be faced. I knew returning to the "busyness" of America would challenge the intimacy I had come to enjoy with my God, my great love, Jesus. I feared losing that more than anything.

I completely lost my footing upon my return and I sank into a deep depression. Again I experienced the crisis of identity, of belonging, of profession, of independence. I had no job and no home, no car and no possessions.

**FIVE REENTRY PATTERNS**
⌐ Alienation
│ Condemnation
│ Reversion
│ Suicide
└ INTEGRATION

My church didn't seem to know what to do with me after the potluck and the report. They kept asking me when I'd be returning to the field or would say, "It's so nice that you are visiting with us." No one had time for me. There was no one "like" me for miles and miles. I felt lost and alone, more afraid than I ever remembered being. I was a different person and everything I saw or experienced and every relationship I tried to rekindle had changed as well.

And I couldn't find God. I couldn't feel Him. My greatest fear had come to pass. It was as if I'd left Him behind in Russia. I tried to pray, but didn't seem to be able to connect. Suddenly, my experience with God became "locational." I was in the wrong location. I was alone.

**NINE AREAS OF STRESS**
⌐ Physical
│ Professional
│ Financial
│ Cultural
│ Social
│ Linguistic
│ National/Political
│ Educational
└ Spiritual

It's been a year since I returned, and finally I have returned to the precious intimacy I experienced with God in Russia—and then some. It took all of this time for Him to teach me that He is everywhere—that He is the same wherever I am—that I can be the same person here as I am in Russia or in any other part of the world.

I have learned a lot and made many important decisions. I have chosen to be a career missionary and hope to spend the rest of my life serving God wherever He wants to send me. And I've learned never to ask "why" but to merely accept what is given and work within the realm of that reality. Most of all, I've learned that I'm at home wherever God is. Maybe that way I can "stay" home instead of "going" home. Home is now the Kingdom of God. We are, after all, foreigners in this world! And the Kingdom of God is within us.

No, I haven't experienced it all. I've only just begun!

FOR FURTHER UNDERSTANDING
You'd think she *had* experienced it all! She clearly outlined the crises of going to the field. She certainly grappled well with the issues of ministering cross-culturally. And she went all the way to Russia to find that satisfying relationship with her Master, Lord and intimate Friend, Jesus Christ.

But reentry: "I completely lost my footing...and sank into a deep depression." How could this happen? How could she be so unprepared? One clue she could have recognized was the lack of communication from home. The tragic saying, "Out of sight; out of mind," is often jokingly used as a legitimate excuse for losing contact with a person. Those committed to a communication support team cannot even think this way!

AREAS OF
SUPPORT
Moral
Logistic
Financial
Prayer
Communication
Reentry

From her part, she did secure a financial support team. But did she gather all the "players" necessary for a successful "game?" It does not seem so.

Nor was the church educated in their part of providing an "intensive care unit" for her preparing to go, while she was on the field, and definitely now upon her return. In her words, "My church didn't seem to know what to do with me after the potluck and the report."

A critical key to a successful reentry is keeping in contact with the people back home while on the field. If the church had kept the people informed (she certainly was doing her part in sending back stories of her experiences), they would have known what to do "after the potluck." They would have been able to ask intelligent questions instead of "When are you going back?" Or, "So glad to have you visiting us."

And her greatest fear came upon her. In her frustration, she lost that intimacy of relationship with her Lord—until a whole year passed. But that relationship has now been strengthened, for she has grasped the truth of "the Kingdom of God is within!" I *am* home wherever He is. And He is everywhere!

FOR FURTHER ACTION

• This missionary had "one friend who remained faithful and consistent to communicate." What did she do to try to expand her friend's communication support team? Find the statements in the story. Underscore them.

• If your friend wrote you from the field saying that communication support (except for you, of course) had broken down, what could you—would you do to bridge the gap? Is there a communication liaison person you could talk to? If that person has tired of the responsibility (fallen in battle) can you assume that position? Is there a church communications secretary who could pick up the ball?

• Again, it is repeated in story after story! A missionary has only two needs upon reentry: *Abiding* and *rehearsing!* Reread the ninth paragraph, beginning with, "I completely lost my footing...." Underscore (or highlight) the phrases that indicate her need for "abiding...a long time." I found five. Maybe you will find even more.

> STEPS TO REENTRY
> Know it's time to go
> Go to home church
> "Abide"
> Rehearse "all"
> Fully integrate

• How about her need for "rehearsing all...?" Her "crises of identity, of belonging, of independence" certainly speak to the need to dialogue with someone on a personal level. There are other phrases in that same paragraph that suggest her need for "a listening ear." Can you find them? Underscore them? Are you ready to listen to the heart of your friend to discover his areas of need? And help him find and resolve each issue?

• Have you found that deep intimacy with our Lord? Could you help your returned friend maintain his spiritual vitality in the midst of the frustrations of clashing cultures? Could you help restore him if that position of fellowship has been lost?

### TEN MINUTES TO SHARE TWO YEARS!

It was time to spend a few months "back home." That term by itself sounded funny, since about half of our married life had been spent "on the field."

As we prepared to return, we had the usual fears. We wondered, "What will we find? Will we know anyone in the church? Will anyone know us? Will anyone want to know us? Do we belong there? Will we be welcome? How will we be welcomed?" We didn't know the answers.

Though these were the feelings that really concerned us, we realized the main immediate issues were housing, finances and transportation. But before we could resolve them, we faced our first shock—one that would continue through our time in the States.

Our best friend and the missions pastor picked us up at the airport. That was a very pleasant surprise! However, we had had breakfast at the hotel in Paris (an all-you-can-eat buffet), breakfast on the plane, dinner on the plane and sandwiches for a snack. By the time we landed, food was the last thing we were thinking of. But the first thing they were thinking of was to buy us a "good ol' American dinner!" Ugh! We ate shrimp at the Sizzler, and when we got to the house, the hostess called out, "Should I call for pizza?" No!!!

Housing: God provided a room with our best friends. In fact, they said the room is ours every time we return. That kind of security made things much easier.

Transportation: The next morning we were taken to the church and given the keys to a car that one of the church members had donated for our use "as long as you need it!" We were able to use it the whole three months. He even gave us his pager number in case something went wrong so he could get to us quickly. That's what I call a blessing!

Finances: Our monthly support had to be used to care for the ongoing expenses on the field. No one mentioned how we were expected to live while we were at home. But on the same day we were given the car, one of my close brothers came up and handed me an ATM card and said, "Just enter your pin number. There's one thousand dollars to help you get by!"

Could these three acts of kindness be any more reflective of God's love? Our fears were literally obliterated! Our immediate needs had been met. However, our debriefing did not go so well. On our first Sunday at church, I was asked to share. "The whole service is yours!" I had been told. When we got there I was informed that they were going to show a "short" film clip before I started. The service is ninety minutes. After a longer-than-usual worship (thirty minutes), the film ran for fifteen minutes. I was also asked to do the communion and to "plan twenty-five minutes for that." Our whole time to share about two years on the field was down to twenty minutes! "Oh, yes, we'll need ten minutes for welcome and announcements." Ten minutes left to share two years!

We were told we would be given another service later, but it never happened. It gave us the idea that they weren't "really" interested. What else could we think?!

FOR FURTHER UNDERSTANDING
There isn't too much "between-the-lines" uncertainty in this story! He has quite clearly spelled out his needs: both his "abiding" needs and his "rehearsing all" needs.

Did anyone say...food? We "love" to eat! And because our missionary has been "surviving" on those strange foods (All missionaries eat strange foods, don't they?), we may sense an urgency to feed them a "good ol' American dinner!" "Fatten them up!" As you can read, this was not a priority for this couple. Nor is it for most missionaries, for they have come to enjoy the cuisine of their host culture.

Particularly if your friend has been away for some time, extra care must be given to the resumption of his home country diet. While his digestive system has gotten used to handling the "bugs" of his host culture, it is going to have to build up a resistance to those of his new home culture.

FOR FURTHER ACTION
• His questions in the second paragraph give you an outline to follow—a checklist to mark off as you tend to the issues of your returning missionary "that really concerned us." In other words, get the list that really concerns *your* friend.

• Prepare the church for your friend's return. Devote a bulletin board to a current picture of all the family members. Even include the pictures of the support team so others in the church can ask them questions about "our" returning family. Have extra copies of their most recent newsletters and a video of their ministry available. Prepare a "Welcome Home!" banner. Have people write personal notes on it for your missionary to read as he is up in the middle of the night, not able to adjust to the time change. Let the church know that "a part of us—the Body of Christ"— is returning.

• Housing, transportation, finances. Again, how

succinctly could his immediate needs be identified. Though these three needs had been tended to ahead of time, the missionary didn't know it. Know your friend. Will he appreciate being surprised? Or do you think he would feel better being assured before he leaves the field that these things have been cared for?

• Can you imagine Paul and Barnabas having only ten minutes on "Sunday morning" to share their two years of ministry? Unthinkable! Yet, our fast-paced agendas do not allow us the "luxury" of sitting a spell to rejoice with our missionary as he rehearses all that God has done in and through him. What can you do to break this pattern of "busyness?" Will you set a number of small group meetings with a variety of venues at which your friend can speak? Will you help him edit his slides or videos for optimum showing? Will you make sure each meeting is hosted by a person who knows about the speaker: Who he is, where he has been, how long he will be here, if/when he is returning to the field?

Home, on furlough! To some missionaries those are most dreadful words. However, with this new knowledge you have, you can change that for your missionary friend. By applying the understanding and action suggested in these stories, you will create an environment of care and encouragement for him while he is on furlough.

Don't be hurt or surprised if your friend is a bit hesitant at first to cooperate with your plans. Being well-cared-for on reentry might be an additional shock to him! But do it anyway. This is a shock he will gladly accept, once it hits.

## TO GO HOME OR NOT TO GO HOME

A corollary issue to "on furlough" is a missionary's concern: Do I need to go home?

Certainly Paul the Apostle was a travelling man. His travel vouchers would have frustrated the home office!

On the other hand, following the dispersion that resulted after the martyrdom of Stephen, Philip the deacon fled to Samaria. Apart from his Gaza strip experience with the Ethiopian eunuch, we hear of only one other move—from the city of Samaria to another Samaritan town, Caesarea.

And today there are those who have spent their life in a country other than their birthplace. Their children have been born there. They have grown up there and married nationals of that country.

When we were in Brazil we fellowshipped with a family in which six of his seven children had married Brazilians. There was no way that the parents were going to go "home!" They *were* home! Their children and *grandchildren* were there.

Some missionaries so fear the challenges of coming home that they try to put it off. One single missionary with whom we were communicating obviously needed to come home. She needed to develop some perspective of her work on the field as well as rekindle relationships with her support team.

All was set. She would live with us for the three months home. Then one day, we received her letter. In it she listed all the "reasons" why she didn't need to come home. This produced the shortest letter I have ever written! It said: "Sue! Get home!" She came... and was reacquainted... and returned to the field better for her home experiences.

As you read this one story, however, seriously consider how you would counsel your missionary friend if confronted with the decision, *to go home or not to go home!*

## I DON'T WANT TO GO HOME!

Because of some fairly serious health problems, complicated by old age, we are faced with the decision of returning home or not. I am trying to analyze the situation to better understand why I don't feel like going "home." I think there are several reasons for this:

1. We were not "sent." We felt a great desire to be able to do something for the Mexican people, but knew that we were not qualified to go as "missionaries." Our denomination had some guidelines for candidates and we definitely did not qualify. We understood this and knew that they were right.

Knowing all this, but still feeling a strong desire (which we later knew to be a "calling" of God), we decided that maybe we could go and live there and be of help to missionaries in whatever way they needed us.

We did not stay in Mexico at that time, neither did we go back home, but rather we settled in Texas to be close to the land that we loved. Little by little, over a period of 12 years, the Lord prepared us. We finally became pastors by founding a church just across the border.

Again, we were not sent. Our church in Texas, being of the same denomination, could not really send us because we still did not "qualify." The pastor was very good to us. He and many of our friends in that church helped and still support us financially. But there was no one that took the authority to direct us, to help us plan strategy, to help us define our calling or direct us for further training. I do not blame anyone, there just was no one that understood the need or was qualified to do this. We did not know what we needed so we did not look for it.

As a result, our work has evolved, but not as a part of the program of the denomination or with a team working together. Then our pastor in Texas passed away. The new pastor doesn't really know us, and many of our friends are not there anymore. It would be hard for us to return there and become a part of that church again.

2. Mexico cost us a lot and we don't want to leave it behind. Because of our lack of qualification, our limitations, lack of preparation and lack of financial support it was very "costly." Financially it cost us everything; physically we gave lots of effort, the best years of our lives. We gave our son to Mexico; he married a national, of whom we are very proud. They are now the pastors of the first church we founded. We are now looking forward to being there for our grandchildren. Mexico is our life.

3. Financially. We have no health plan and no retirement plan. We would probably have to go to work or go on welfare. We don't qualify for much pension because we did not live in our home country long enough, nor did we live in the U.S. long enough to build up many Social Security benefits.

4. There is much left to do. We still feel the call to missions and we see *"the fields are white unto harvest."* We want to get out to do all we can, in spite of being more limited by health and lack of energy.

The question we face is: *To go home or not to go home?*

FOR FURTHER UNDERSTANDING

When Jesus said, *"Go into all the world...,"* He never said anything about coming home. Yet, His twelve and seventy returned to Him. Paul and Barnabas returned to their sending church in Antioch. And through the ages *most* missionaries have been able to return to their home country. Today, with air travel so available, missionaries are coming home for—what some would consider—even unjustifiable reasons!

The four expressions of concern by this missionary are all valid. But I believe his statement, "Mexico is our life!" sums up his reason for frustration about going home. Years of ministry, developing deep relationships, not knowing where "home" would be if he did return and "there is still so much work to do" are arguments that tug at the hearts of many missionaries. And cause some of them to remain on the field.

One missionary, giving reasons for staying on the field, asked for this to be put on her gravestone: "I lived and worked with you; I laughed and cried with you. I am buried with you. And I will rise to meet Him in the air with you!"

FOR FURTHER ACTION

- Would you counsel this missionary to go "home"? To which "home"? His birthplace? The U.S., where he spent twelve years? Or, is he "home"?!

- Discuss this with some of the senior citizens in your church. Try to understand the "sense of belonging" that develops by living for years in one place.

- What questions would your missionary friend ponder if he were considering staying on the field? Are you prepared to listen and probe and help him sort through those issues? Or insist he come home, as I had to?

- Corollary to this is an issue you might encounter with a returning youth. His mother is American. His father is Canadian. He was born and raised in Brazil. Until eighteen, he has been able to keep his three citizenships. At eighteen, however, he must relinquish one. He sees himself as Brazilian. But maintaining that birthright requires compulsory military service. If he keeps his Brazilian passport, does he "deny" his mother's heritage? Or his father's? Beyond the family concerns are the ramifications of health insurance, taxes, retirement, a place to live, grandkids!—and much more!

Chapter Ten

# _Home, Not By Choice_

There are various and sundry reasons for missionaries to come home from their fields of service before the end of their term of commitment. The tragedy of human experience brings some home. Others return for reasons of discontent on the field. Still others discover that they should never have gone to the field in the first place! (Unfortunately, not enough of these come home!) Though an extensive and exhaustive study has been done on missionary attrition, one simple conclusion they reached was that, despite which reason was recorded in the files, it is very difficult to know the real reason why missionaries come home.

When ministry has gone well, national leadership has been raised up and it is obvious that it is time to move on, reentry is easier. Paul, in Acts 20, expresses his feelings about leaving the churches in the care of those whom the Holy Spirit had told him to ordain for leadership.

However, when the environment is rough, ministry is not going well or interpersonal relationships are boiling out of control and one is _sent_ home, it is not as easy to deal with. We don't know the exact circumstances of John Mark's _"departing from them and returning to Jeru-_

salem" (Acts 13:13), but from later Scripture, it would seem that the reasons were not positive. (See Acts 15.)

In this brief collection of stories, some of the reasons are very clear. In others, not so clear. A "first step" in a successful reentry for your "early" returning missionary friend is to discern the real reason in terms that he can understand and deal with.

And it is always good to be able to come to the point that the early disciples expressed in their prayer in Acts 4:28: ...they (the enemies of Christ) were gathered together *"to do what Your hand and Your counsel had determined before to be done."* We serve a sovereign God. Ultimately we will see all things from His perspective. The more quickly we do, the greater the ease in coming home, though not by our choice.

### FLY THE PLANE

We went to Africa to fly with a small mission. Our plan was to stay indefinitely, as we were the only pilot/mechanic in the country with that organization. Five months later we were told to return to the U.S. to take a maintenance course at Bell Helicopters. So my wife and I and our one-year-old son came back to Texas for three weeks.

Our director was not an easy person to work with or make contact with. After the course, we had trouble getting together with him to talk about returning to Africa. We spent several frustrating weeks wondering what was happening, while we lived with our parents.

Finally, the director came to where we were staying and we had a very frustrating talk with him. Sparing the details, he basically said that he didn't want us to return to Africa!

So, here we were with no place to call home, no belongings, and everything we owned was in Africa except what we had in our suitcases. We had no job, and wondered what the future held.

Through God's provision I got a job flying, and eventually we joined another mission in need of pilots. With all our pre-field requirements met, we went to France for language study, then on to our home in Africa. It was good to be back. Shortly after arriving, though, my wife became ill. For the next six months her condition worsened and no one could diagnose the problem. Finally she ended up in the hospital for a week and the doctors said to go back to the U.S. to determine what was wrong.

Only six months in Africa! Our personal belongings had just arrived and we were unpacking the barrels and moving into an apartment. Now the doctors were telling us to return to the U.S.

I had to hurriedly make flight reservations for the five of us. We had to repack our barrels with what to sell and what to have shipped back to the U.S. in case we didn't return. We then boarded a plane for the arduous trip back to the States.

That whole ordeal was just a blur of airports, several plane changes, several customs, a very ill wife, three young tired children, and questions running through our minds. Probably the biggest question was, "What are YOU doing, GOD?" Forty-eight hours later we arrived. It was late at night and we were bone weary and emotionally exhausted with more questions, but still no answers.

Our agency had no reentry program. Everyone was expected to fend for themselves. So we did.

We soon discovered that my wife had a chronic illness, which meant not returning to the field. So once again we were back from Africa with all we owned in five suitcases and no place to call home. Our dreams were shattered and we needed to learn how to live with a chronic illness.

People in our home church helped as they could,

but most really didn't know what to do. *We* didn't even know what to do, or what we needed. We were in shock from the whole experience. We were on our own. No one came alongside, either in or out of our mission to see if they could help us plan for the future. You know how independent missionaries are supposed to be? And tough? And resilient? So we persevered. We survived. What else could we do?

As a pilot, the first thing you do in an emergency is "fly the plane." So, as the husband and father in this emergency, I had to "fly the family." I was determined we were not going to crash and burn. We were going to stay in the air. We were going to survive!

By late summer, we were assigned to the mission's Stateside headquarters. We drove out West in time to get our two oldest children into school for the start of the term. We found an apartment and started our lives over once again in another place. I adapted to a new job. We were learning to live with a chronic illness. We were surviving, but sometimes just barely! No one ever took us aside and said, "You folks need to work through your grief, the death of your dreams."

The next few years weren't easy. There was a lot of anger on my part. But time and the Lord brought healing. Four years later, in cooperation with the churches in our region, we began a reentry program to help returning missionaries make a better landing, to offer some of the fruit of our experiences. That was very fulfilling for me. But as I moved on to other responsibilities, the program died. I believe with all my heart that mission agencies need to provide a reentry program as part of their member care.

FOR FURTHER UNDERSTANDING
We have said again and again that the mission process is a shared responsibility of the Church and the mission agency. They both should be working aggressively

in developing care for a returning missionary.

Did you count the times this family tried to move forward in what they sensed God had for them to do? Have you considered the financial commitment of these thwarted plans? The emotional energy expended? The spiritual searching for reasons?

A key paragraph in this story—to identify the dilemma of the reentry process—is: "People in our home church helped as they could, *but most really didn't know what to do.*" He continues: *"We didn't even know what to do."*

The sheer ignorance of this "closeted" issue could not be more vividly expressed than in this and the following stories.

FOR FURTHER ACTION

• With the passion of one who has had returning missionaries cry on his shoulder, I challenge you to make sure that your church—you—are attending to the needs of your returning missionaries.

(I just now got off the phone with a pastor. I was encouraging him to reach out to a returned missionary from his church. I happened to know she is having a "rough" time. His answer: "Yes, I left a message for her to call me." Before we were through, he agreed to call *her!*)

• I encourage you to contact the agencies through which your missionaries work and discover—in practice—what they do for their returning cross-cultural workers.

• Nobody knows what to do! You have heard this excuse repeated time and again in this collection of stories. It does not have to be your excuse! Do your homework. Educate yourself. List five things you could do to help this family, even just knowing what you have read in this story.

• *"No one came alongside...."* There are four levels

of relationship on which the "come alongside" help can be initiated:

1)    The missionary, as the leader, can form the relationships among those who commit to his team of caregivers. This needs to be done *before* he leaves for the field. He needs to build in them an "ownership" of this mission, a passion for this mission equal to his, a solid commitment to the task to which they agree, a faithfulness to teamwork and an attitude of "it is a *privilege* to be about our Father's business."

2)    The mission agency can initiate the process through partnership development training and resources. This training and these resources must encompass not only the financial, but also the other five areas of care. (See summary at the end of Chapter Three.)

3)    The church missions leadership can make sure—again, *before* their missionary goes to the field—that there is a team established in the various aspects of care.

4)    Personal friends of the missionary who have learned the importance of caregiving can initiate the process of team development.

In which category are you? Do your part in making sure there is a team developed.

• Let's assume you step into this situation at any one time of their frustration, hurt or anger. Think about and discuss with your study group various options open to you. Do you have the time—will you *take* the time—to study and be prepared to listen and care?


**OUR MISSIONS OFFICE IS "USER FRIENDLY"**
Amid the lamentable disparity between the need for reentry care and viable solutions being used, it is a breath of fresh air to read about a church that has given itself to this challenging issue.

Mary is the Missionary Care Coordinator for her

church. She writes: "I enjoyed the *Serving As Senders* Seminar I attended over a year ago. I use the book with every missionary and their support team coordinator."

Two observations that have become foundational to our reentry ministry:

1. Mission work is usually done in community. The reentry experience also needs to happen in community. It cannot be accomplished alone or through isolated experiences. In the last year we have had six missionaries return—some forced from their country, others on scheduled furloughs. That is why I started a reentry group that meets twice a month. In this group, we share our stories, have a short devotional time and spend a good portion of time praying for each other. We have kept a prayer journal to write down our prayers and God's answers.

2. The reentry experience is different for everyone but depends largely on the family and support structure awaiting the returnee. The following examples help illustrate this.

### A Missionary from Africa

The woman who has had the easiest time reentering spent six years in Africa and had to evacuate under violent conditions. As I have observed her, I realized that her family of seven sisters, two of whom are missionaries, have provided wonderful, warm and loving support, and an effective safety net for her. Our church helped out by providing her with a car on her return. It would not win a beauty contest, but it has been reliable and allowed her to immediately look for housing and a job. She also chose to find a roommate rather than live alone—a good choice, in my opinion. She immediately made church attendance a priority and created "structure" for herself. She openly shared her sorrow at the loss of her mission life and the tragic news that the infant daughter of her co-worker had died of starvation because this co-worker had lost her job when the missionary had to evacuate. That is a huge load to carry, but she was able to carry it with the prayer and listening ear of her family and the church support group.

## A Missionary from Asia

The woman who has struggled the most returned from nine years in Asia, for a two-year leave at the recommendation of her mission agency. She came "home" to a very critical and dysfunctional family who are not believers and feel this woman is wasting her time in missions service. Her friends also seemed to be overly "needy," wanting this missionary to be there for them instead of seeing how they could serve her. Our reentry group has been her major support. We also were able to provide her with a car, but her employment situation as an ESL teacher has not been very stable.

After watching her struggle for two months, we recommended and paid for her to spend a month at Link Care in Fresno, California (See Resource Section for contact information.) for more intensive reentry assistance. When she came back, a family with a ministry to missionaries took her in for two months. Then she chose to live alone in a small apartment in the city, making it a lovely home of her own.

What has been a positive turning point for her has been in the last two months when she became involved in ministry. She is now attending a Chinese church, a Chinese Bible study and serving in several ministries of that church. This newfound ministry has helped her maintain her language skills, sharpen her vision and know that she is making a significant contribution, even while she is far from her adopted country.

## A Missionary from the Orient

This missionary returned after four years in the Orient. She returned with a defined purpose—to get a master's in ESL for further ministry. Her family had fallen apart while she was away. Her parents had gotten a divorce, her mom had moved to Europe and her father had a new girlfriend living in the house where she had grown up and came home to live in. This was a tough situation for a relatively happy and well-adjusted young woman. She came through it by finding community in the church support group, by finding a job suited to her skills and mission heart (with international students at a community college) and immediately focusing on her long-term goals of further training and mission service. She also requested help with her new family structure. She meets with a woman every week and has found this relationship with an older mother-like friend to be invaluable to her process.

Mary continues: Yes, we have had missionaries evacuated at a moment's notice. However, in cases where we knew the person was leaving the field, I sent them a copy of *Re-entry* by Peter Jordan (YWAM publishing) and a workbook published by LIFE ministries, a month or two before they left. Everyone who received these resources told me that they really helped them, especially to work on reentry even before they left their adopted countries.

We make every attempt to make the Missions Office at our church a very welcoming place for returning missionaries. The missions pastor takes them to lunch soon after they return and I am available to them for many hours of "chatting" and prayer. We arranged a wonderful weekend retreat for the reentry group. Since the participants were all women, I was able to focus on truly pampering them with flowers in their rooms, an elegant high tea, and lots of extra touches. We had a significant time of Bible study around the theme of "Clarifying Future Direction." This retreat is probably the most significant thing we have done with our reentry ministry. The women told me over and over how healing it was to be made *to feel special* and *to belong* for a whole weekend. We shared funny stories about the weirdest things we had ever had to eat or seen others eat. We read children's bedtime stories that were relevant to the shared experiences of feeling like outsiders. And we provided time for prayer and counseling with a woman who has a prayer ministry and came on the retreat just to be available.

FOR FURTHER UNDERSTANDING
It is important to realize that reentry is different for each individual. Even within the same family, one member will respond radically different from another—even to the same experience. Therefore, caregiving must be tailored to the individual.

Note that in this church there is a Missions Pastor, Mary is the Missionary Care Coordinator and each missionary family has a Support Team Coordinator. Would you not expect good care from the people of this church? And, lest one would say, "Our church isn't large enough for that," care for your missionaries is imperative! I would go so far to say, if you do not have the people to care for your missionaries *while they are preparing to go, while they are on the field* **and** *when they return home*, don't send them out! How structured a program of care you provide is not the issue—personal care is. And a missionary needs care in all six areas.

AREAS OF
SUPPORT
Moral
Logistic
Financial
Prayer
Communication
Reentry

FOR FURTHER ACTION
• Your church, no matter its size, if it is going to take the responsibility of sending out missionaries, must accept with equal responsibility the awesome task of seeing them through the process of reentry to full integration. (Did I just say that? It bears repeating!) To

whatever degree of influence you have on your church mission leadership, make sure caring people, including yourself, are ready to help your missionary reenter.

- If you can not stir the hearts and minds of others to action, take it upon yourself (in cooperation with your missionary friend) to establish the safety net for his reentry. If he says, "No big deal! I'm just coming home," you're on your own! Still be ready for him. For, with that attitude, you can expect an even greater task.

- Be aware of needs greater than you can handle. Become knowledgeable of other resources that can offer care. See the Resource Section for some materials and agencies that are available.

## A DISGRACEFUL RESIGNATION

We were commissioned by our local church in the States to develop a university discipleship program in Africa. We were to work through an indigenous agency there. Our Stateside church processed any contributions, but we raised our financial support far and wide.

Five weeks after we were married, the church gave us a good send-off with a "God bless you!" I'm sure they also prayed for us. But oversight, interactive communication and direction were really lacking. On two occasions our pastor did include a few days in his world travels to visit us.

Because we were the "experts in discipleship" (according to the general secretary), we were left without counsel and leadership from the local agency, as well. Over the eighteen years we were in Africa, we worked hard. There was plenty of success to give us confidence that the Lord was with us, but a number of emotional issues developed in my life through those years that led to more and more burnout and depression. This led to poor working relationships with the nationals, which eventually resulted in my resignation. In the few months it took to prepare to leave, our relationship with the agency went from bad to worse.

During those months of trauma, however, our home church in the States communicated more frequently. We felt "hugged" by them from afar. They were prayerful and supportive, though a team of elders led them at the time rather than a pastor. At one point, the most senior elder wrote a letter to the agency director in support of me. I felt our coming home would be good.

When we returned home, we were totally broken. The elders suggested we "just rest." No further direction! At that same time there was a crisis in the church.

A number of long-term members began to disagree with various things that were happening there, and many left; some of these were our friends. We also did not like the multiple eldership concept, but I believed we should remain loyal. We were caught in the middle. My wife had inquired about a ladies' Bible study but was given the impression that she wasn't welcome. She did not feel comfortable going to church there anymore and neither did I, but I felt that we should continue.

For more than a year the church leadership did nothing more than recommend a family counselor, whom we visited a few times. A few friends that still went there did invite us over for dinner. Even a few of the friends who had left invited us from time to time, but there was no support (other than financial), or direction, or counsel from the leadership of the church.

During this time we also attended a workshop on missionary care. I was in tears. I realized how much we had missed. Fifteen months after our return, the leadership began to realize they had let us down. They called us in to meet with them and expressed their love and regrets for letting us down. We forgave them and things have been better since.

I feel fine now toward the church leadership and still consider it my church home. My wife still doesn't like the leadership style (elders without a pastor) and the preaching style (which is shared by elders and others). She still can't feel comfortable there. She's told no one else about the rejection from the ladies' Bible study. Very few of our friends of 21 years ago are still in the church, having scattered in 20 different directions.

We are supposedly getting ready to return to Africa. To date, the elders of the church are standing with us in prayer and support, but there is some concern that it might be some time before we go. Ever since committing ourselves to return nine months ago, we have faced obstacles every step of the way, but we are in God's hands! For this, we give Him thanks!

FOR FURTHER UNDERSTANDING
Whether or not he realized his need in those early years on the field, his statements of reflection pinpoint a major problem: Lack of accountability. The church failed in "supervision and interactive communication." And the indigenous agency left them "without counsel and leadership." Few missionaries have done well as "Lone Rangers" or "Superstars." Keeping a missionary accountable is the shared responsibility of the sending church and the mission agency.

Where was the church or agency when "a number of emotional issues developed" in his life? Could they not (did they not want to) see the burnout and depression coming? To save "programs," missionaries are sometimes sacrificed!

Consider the feelings this missionary must have sensed in seeing his eighteen years of hard, successful work be terminated in an awkward resignation and a break in relationship with the agency.

A bright spot in those final months was that the church leadership seemed to be on track for this family's reentry. But then they arrive home. The husband admits burnout and depression. The sum total of their "interactive communication" was "just rest!"

Unconscionable! What went wrong? Did they not know what to do when they saw their missionaries "totally broken?" Were they too distracted by the "crisis in the church?"

FOR FURTHER ACTION

• If your church is serving as the sending agency for your missionary friend, are you aware of their policies on accountability through communication and reports? Is your friend submitting accountability reports regularly? Has your church established relationships with a responsible pastor or worker in the field who is able to send independent reports?

• Does your church leadership have the personnel to hear your missionary say he is "totally broken?" Do they have the personnel to assist him? Do they have resource agencies they know will help? Become familiar with the resource agencies mentioned in Section III.

• Reread this story. Use the skill of discernment that has been developing in you as you study this book to underscore the areas of stress that this couple faced over the course of their missionary experience. I found multiplied statements in seven of the nine areas. And you?

> NINE AREAS OF STRESS
> Physical
> Professional
> Financial
> Cultural
> Social
> Linguistic
> National/Political
> Educational
> Spiritual

• The emotional roller coaster this couple rode in those two years (probably the whole nineteen-plus years) before the leadership acknowledged their responsibility was unnecessary. Find out from your missionary friend the name of his Core Team Leader. With his permission, keep in touch with that person. Make it your business to know that all segments of care are functioning well. Did you notice that he is not aware of the six areas of care? In his last paragraph he says the church is *"standing with us in prayer and support."* By support he means *money*. So he caught two of the six areas.

- No Core Team? No Core Team Leader? Guess what? You've got a job! If you will accept it! Graciously.

### THE LONG ROAD HOME

After being home a year, I was asked, "How long is this reentry stuff supposed to last, anyway? When are you going to get over it?" That hurt deeply.

For me, reentry has been a long road. There was anger in me that would rear its ugly head in absolute frustration when faced with difficult situations. Life in the work-a-day world was so unrewarding. Going to work each day to make fat cats fatter was so meaningless after the ministry I had been involved in. Facing the greed and corruption of the world head-on was horrific! I went into a very stressful and demanding job that sucked me dry every week and that left me exhausted. The stress, along with the frustration of living what appeared to be a meaningless life, caused the anger to burn at times.

For example, in a sales meeting we were being given another piece of paper to fill out, just one more among all the other meaningless papers we fight with, and my frustration lashed out in a verbal clash with the sales manager. It was very unpleasant and definitely very un-Christian!

The following week I was faced with asking for a meeting with this manager to apologize for the terrible behavior I had exhibited in that meeting. The manager had developed a good relationship with me, so my outburst had done a lot of damage. (He confessed that to me at the end of our time together.) The manager was a backslidden Christian, so he had some idea of where I was coming from. The meeting ended very positively with the manager asking me to keep the lines of communication open. He also admitted that he had never had anyone take the time to apologize that way before.

The "long road" continues. Just recently a close friend spoke to me about what possibly seemed to him to be bitterness in me toward a pastor of the church we attended here. I discussed this with him and shared that if there was any bitterness anywhere it was towards a particular pastor who had chewed me out on my return to the field to close up our home there.

As I shared this with him, a deep sadness came over me, which showed me that there was something there I had not dealt with. I now have to work through this! Perhaps it is the cause of the anger and frustration I have had to deal with for the last two years. Now that I am recognizing these things, I am able to start dealing with them.

### FOR FURTHER UNDERSTANDING

To illustrate the contrast in family members' abilities to handle the stress of reentry, this is the father of the MK who concluded, "I'm kind of outgoing, so I can adapt when I want to!" Possibly a major difference was that the son was home by choice, whereas the father had wanted to remain on the field.

LENGTH OF TIME FOR REENTRY
How long on field
Degree of change at home
Degree of change on field
Attitude of church
Time to prepare
Time to get home
Uniqueness of personality
Disadvantaged position
Attitude of denial

Note also his realization that the anger and outburst against the paperwork probably had more to do with the bitterness he held toward the pastor than the frustration with the sales manager. It cannot be overemphasized that any interpersonal relationship issue that is "buried" in one arena is going to "resurrect" in another area.

### FOR FURTHER ACTION

• In light of this story, it would be good to review again the nine possible reasons for a lengthy reentry. Think of your missionary friend. What are some possible scenarios that could affect him. What can you do to help him avert them?

- Notice the friend's approach: *"...what seemed to possibly be...."* I hear gentleness there, meekness, a non-judgmental attitude. But on the other hand he took a risk, for *"faithful are the wounds of a friend"* (Proverbs 27:6).

- Are you prepared for the "long haul" with your missionary friend? True, preparation for reentry makes it easier and quicker. However, you cannot depend on statistics. Your friend is an individual, with individual challenges and individual needs. Your work is complete when he has satisfactorily grappled with the nine areas of stress.

NINE AREAS OF STRESS
Physical
Professional
Financial
Cultural
Social
Linguistic
National/Political
Educational
Spiritual

- Reversion was this man's reentry style. He needed to get right back into the work force. Did you notice that there was no indication of "abide" and "rehearse all?" Add that to his wanting to remain on the field and it spells "a long haul!"

STEPS TO REENTRY
Know it's time to go
Go to home church
"Abide"
Rehearse "all"
Fully integrate

Hang on! It could be a rough ride! But, *hang on!* He is your friend.

### THE *REAL* REASON

Drawing us aside from the large welcome committee at the airport, our pastor looked into our eyes and asked quietly, "So, what's the *real* reason you are home?" His words cut like a knife. Ten years later, they still hurt just a little.

The real reason we were home, after only 18 months on the field, truly was what we had written home. The field leadership had miscalculated our projected quota. Living as frugally as possible, we still fell short each month during our first year on the field. We discovered that the quota worksheet page entitled "Project needs" was completely blank. What a mistake! Thinking we had raised 100% of our financial needs before initially departing for Africa, we were actually only at 51%. Apologies were made by the agency and accepted by us. Now, what to do?

We wrote a prayer letter immediately, explaining the situation to our supporters and prayed that God would bring in the remaining 49% through the mail. He didn't. God had other plans. And so, after only 18 months in this exciting Bible translation project, we came home to speak in churches and raise the funds in person.

Within nine months the funds were in and we returned to the field, buoyed by more than twice the prayer support and 49% more financial support. We were extremely blessed and aided by an outstanding team of partners in our mission, our families and our churches. Those who encouraged, prayed, gave and helped in many ways are too many to number. Thank God for the Body of Christ!

So, why is it that one pastor's words resonate clear as a bell ten years after he said them? Shouldn't they have faded into oblivion? He was only one man, one among hundreds of others who never voiced such suspicions. I believe he loved us, yet...?

FOR FURTHER UNDERSTANDING

Note that the "understood" quota was financial. They would never send a missionary home if they were short on their moral, logistics, prayer, communication or reentry support! Can you imagine an agency saying, "We didn't realize what a difficult assignment this would be. You better go home to build up your prayer support team."

The bulk of the middle of this story does not relate specifically to the issue of the pastor's hurtful words. But it does clearly describe a very positive attitude portrayed by the family—including the children—during the nine months of travelling.

This puts that one short sentence, "So, what's the *real* reason you are home?"—eight simple words—in stark contrast.

FOR FURTHER ACTION
- With them adjusting to their time home so well, why would that careless question hurt so much? From this story we can't know. But your sensitive spirit, I trust, would be able to help her through to a resolve.
- Practice your communication skills with your friends at home. Be prepared for your returning friend. Realize that all the culture stress he is experiencing will make him more sensitive. Be careful with your words!

## THE BANDANA SCARF

We had just returned to the field, uneasy about leaving my mother because she was experiencing some blackouts. But now back on the field, we jumped into a major project. Two Catholic nuns from a neighboring country came to help in the project, as it would be written in their native language. Two months into the project, we got a phone call that my mom was going into surgery for a brain tumor, but she said for us to remain on the field and my brother would keep us posted. When my brother called, the news wasn't good. When they were trying to remove the tumor and couldn't, something happened that put my mom in a coma.

We hurriedly made arrangements, and I returned to the States. The nuns agreed to stay and help care for our boys, ages two and four. I had always had a hard time driving the freeways, and now, back in the U.S., I had to drive every day in a borrowed car through a metropolitan "nightmare" to be with my mom. It was terrifying. For two weeks I made the dreaded drive. Only once did a friend take me. It was such a relief not to drive that time.

Then my mom passed away, and all of a sudden, I was left with decisions to make about funeral arrangements. Because my mom's head had been shaved for the operation, a person at the funeral home suggested using a scarf to cover her head. It never even occurred to me to buy a wig. My mind and emotions were in a blur. I remember trying to drive home the day my mom died. My eyes were filled with tears and I had to pull off the freeway several times, feeling I just couldn't go another mile.

At the funeral, some people became very irritated over the scarf bandana saying, "It makes her look like a washer woman." Those hurtful words devastated me. What help it would have been to have had a home church that would have rallied around me in my time of need. Even those who helped didn't understand that I was suffering reverse culture shock as well as the grief of my mother's death. If there had been someone to just give advice about the funeral arrangements, dressing my mom, and what was expected in U.S. culture during a funeral, it would have been so helpful.

After the funeral, I returned to the field and to the work, but the hurt has never gone away.

FOR FURTHER UNDERSTANDING
"Sticks and stones may break my bones, but words can never harm me!" (For those of you too young to know it, that was a saying we learned from childhood!) But the experiences of life have taught me that it was incorrect! Reality taught me: "Sticks and stones may *break my bones*, but words *just crush my soul!*" Does not James give us a real tongue-lashing about the unruliness of our tongue? It is like a tiny spark that can set the whole forest on fire. A drop of poison...! (See James 3.)

One thing about words is, once spoken, they cannot

be taken back. (With writing it is different. You should see all the scratched out words on my original paper. And the editor will "scratch" some more that you will never see!) Additional words may attempt to modify or alter or clarify what was said. But oftentimes that effort does no more than stick the proverbial "foot in the mouth" further!

Oh, that all our words were spoken with grace and healing and encouragement. *"A word fitly spoken,"* said the man of wisdom, *"is like apples of gold in settings of silver"* (Proverbs 25:11). But when a word is carelessly spoken, what injury it can inflict. This, and the previous story testifies, the pain may be felt for years.

It must be remembered that these missionaries heard these careless words in the context of reentry stress. Along with the other challenges with which they were dealing (probably a combination of several), these carelessly spoken words hurt.

It is possible that at another time—in another context—they would carry no sting. Or, said to another person, they may have been a non-issue. But to these particular missionaries in their particular mindset, they became real issues that needed to be dealt with. Better with prevention of careless words, but if not, then with your sensitive healing words.

FOR FURTHER ACTION

- Even in normal circumstances, church people are usually there for the grieving family. What could you do in practical ways to help your friend. Hint: Reread the story. Underscore the things she said would have made this time easier for her.

STEPS TO REENTRY
- Know it's time to go
- Go to home church
- "Abide"
- Rehearse "all"
- Fully integrate

- Educate yourself to be a speaker of kind words. Ask God for help in the control of your tongue. Think, before you speak! Use Ephesians 4:29 as a guide to the control of your words.

- Consider ways you could help to restore such a one. Could you be a "Barnabas" to take this offended sister by the hand and bring her to her offender? To be a peacemaker? Is that even necessary for a resolution?

## JUST HANG AROUND THE OFFICE

After one year on the mission field, we returned home, intending to return to the field in two months. We knew we had some personal financial challenges ahead of us. We had anticipated these and were trying to have confidence that God would take care of them.

We also had some physical needs. My husband's back had gone out and he was in a lot of pain. Upon arriving at the airport, we discovered the ticket for the last leg of our journey had not been arranged, though we had the assurance of our sending organization that it had been. We fortunately were able to phone our church and they ordered tickets with a credit card, but we spent eight hours in an airport, about 1-1/2 hours from home, waiting for the next available flight.

The next day, our first day home, our lawyer called us requesting an immediate consultation. We weren't quite prepared for this. We spent the next few weeks preparing for a court hearing. My husband was getting no relief from his back pain and was in quite a lot of turmoil spiritually and physically. We were blessed with the use of a car, which was great, since we had sold ours before leaving.

Not knowing quite how these things work when you return, my husband went into the church office for a debriefing. He talked of the year, of his plans and of his insight into some of the mistakes made, especially by well-meaning Christians. Generally, the year had gone well and our pastor was pleased. He did not quite agree with our insight into the mistakes of the sending organization. My husband was encouraged to just come into the office and hang around. No mention was made of financial assistance, just a vague "We'll see what the Lord provides," No desk or chair was readily available for him to use. I suppose he could have hung out in the sanctuary.

After our remaining funds were completely depleted, we asked if there was any money left in our account for us. We were given a check; again, no accounting, no planning, no assurance of another. We were left feeling uncertain and didn't know if my husband should just get a job, which would have been difficult because of his bad back.

Meanwhile, we were seeing our lawyer every day and bills were mounting. A court date was looming, but the only question anyone ever asked us was, "When are you going back? We have to make plans!" We had no idea how this court thing would turn out. My husband was getting more and more stressed, which just increased his back pain.

He went into the office a few times with really nothing to do and no guidance or relationship-building going on. He decided that he could write a letter to our sending organization and express our concern for some of (what we believed to be) their detrimental procedures. It was a loving letter, strong but supportive in the end. The leader of this organization got the letter and promptly called our pastor.

Our pastor then relayed to us that we had pretty well ruined the relationship our church had had with this organization and that my husband had greatly disappointed him. My husband left devastated. He never went into the office again. The relationship with our pastor and all ministry leaders was almost destroyed in my husband's mind. He did not know what to do from this point. He began working to pay for our needs.

Because of a combination of financial setbacks and spiritual devastation, we did not return to the field.

That left a greatly hurt Body that was waiting for us in Europe, damaged relationships here and spiritual paralysis in my husband's life. Six years later I am just beginning to see signs of restoration.

FOR FURTHER UNDERSTANDING
Unfortunately, misunderstanding regarding flight schedules is not uncommon. My personal experience occurred in Germany. I had been assured that though I had a confirmed flight on one day, if I showed the ticket at the Frankfurt airport two days earlier, I could get on the earlier flight. On the strength of the agency's word, I had given all but a few of my dollars away. I arrived at the counter, presented my ticket and passport. "I am able to get on this flight, aren't I?" Their blank stare made me wonder if they didn't understand me, didn't know what to do with me, or just hoped I would go away! Two days and nights of conservative spending on airport food and restless sleeping on my luggage prepared me for my flight home! But then again, Paul had some rather unusual travel experiences!

And, unfortunately, misunderstanding within a church of how they could receive their missionaries home is not uncommon. But the devastation in this family's lives was largely avoidable. Again, had there been knowledgeable caregivers (as you are becoming)!

FOR FURTHER ACTION
• As you read and reread this story, highlight the points where you as an individual, or you as a part of a missions committee or caregiving team, could have done something to turn these situations around into a time of rejoicing, and the returning of this family to the field. (Hint: Consider the interrelationship of the six areas of care.)

AREAS OF SUPPORT
Moral
Logistic
Financial
Prayer
Communication
Reentry

• Imagine, note or jot down how effective serving in

the other five areas of caregiving would have made this story—no! not a story, but the life experiences of your missionary friends—dramatically different.

*   Secondly, assume you just joined this church at the "six years later" time. Lay out a scenario of several approaches you could use to help this family. Discuss these ideas with your study group.

### AM I CYNICAL? YES!

We are tentmakers, but have periodically received gifts from churches and individuals. We intentionally kept our living costs (and thus our tentmaking) at near subsistence level as we tried to spend significant time in our Christian ministry. It got to the point, however, that I could no longer find jobs to make enough money to support my family. My best options had been with UN agencies that now insisted upon an "advanced degree," which I didn't have. We married late so we have young children (a good time to be overseas), but also elderly parents (a bad time to be overseas).

Finally I decided to bring my family to the U.S. to be with my aged father and to pursue a graduate degree in computer science. I could not find a job, and the intensity of my studies proved that holding one was not a reasonable extra burden. I am embarrassed to say that I borrowed money to get through the last semester of school. (I had never borrowed money in my life!) People around us had been blissfully ignorant of our needs. Or, at least, no one at our church gave us any gifts (outside of one doctor giving free medical consultations).

Virtually everyone owned their own home. We owned none. Others had a shiny car. We borrowed my dad's old clunker. Most frequented restaurants. We hit McDonalds or Burger King for a rare treat. Many owned recreational vehicles of various sorts. We had none.

We could not afford health insurance, so I had to pay for two skin cancer surgeries for my wife out of our savings. We have never asked for money (it seems those are the people who get it), or been explicit about our situation, as the Lord does supply our needs. But not always our wants!

We love and serve Him. It seems the average Christian in America is chiefly interested in the approval of their religious clique and the tax deduction they can gain. It sometimes seems that the Holy Spirit has very little to do with their giving.

Am I cynical? Yes! Am I ready to become a professional beggar and give up on the Lord's quiet provision? Never! Nevertheless, I'm sure many Christians are foregoing a blessing by being so mechanical about their giving.

FOR FURTHER UNDERSTANDING

The sorrowful cynicism in this man's heart is so sad. The god of this age has certainly blinded the eyes of not only the people of the world, but unfortunately, the eyes of many Christians. As wrong as may be the attitudes of some Christians about financial care of missionaries, there is no way we can defend this man's cynicism! This story certainly paints a clear picture of how such a destructive attitude in the church can transfer into a destructive attitude in a missionary.

I again remind you of the deathly silence I get when I approach the Financial Section of the *Serving As Senders* Seminar. "My hard-earned money," we proudly boast. Written on every Christian's paycheck stub should be the words of Deuteronomy 8:17-18: *"You who say in your heart, 'My power and the might of my hand has gotten me my wealth'—You would do well to remember the Lord, your God: For it is He who has given you power to get wealth."*

It has been calculated that there are more recorded

words of Jesus in the Gospels on the subject of money than any other! So, realizing this is no new problem, we still need to grapple with it, and then deal with the cynicism that can develop in a missionary who was not well-cared-for in this area.

Nothing needs to be added to his paragraph where he makes comparisons of lifestyle based on relative financial resources. It is a most difficult challenge for those of us who live "behind the lines" to live the austere battle-lifestyle we expect of those on the front line to live.

How fortunate is the missionary who has a good core group to head up his team of caregivers. It is much easier for the missionary's financial liaison to bring up the details of this subject than the missionary himself. Communication in both directions is better facilitated by a go-between.

Consider: A person has made a $50 per month commitment to his missionary friend. After several months—his friend is now on the field—he loses his job (or some other unexpected financial hardship strikes). It is much easier for him to tell the financial liaison of this turn of events than to write to his friend. Likewise, when the missionary on the field sees that for several months in a row his friend has not sent the amount to which he committed, it is much easier for him to contact his financial liaison person, asking him to see what's wrong, rather than writing to his friend.

FOR FURTHER ACTION

- Your own financial resources are already delegated. Your church's policy does not include financial contributions to tentmakers. How could you help this person? Is it being a "professional beggar" to offer your friends the opportunity to expand their investment portfolio to include some eternal investments?
- Before rereading the story, it would seem that his

concerns center on money. Reread the story. Consider what his more basic needs might be. Hints: To whom is he accountable? Is cynicism *ever* a spiritual attribute? Could you share the "truth in love" with your friend?

- Do you have a right perspective on the resources God has entrusted to you? Can you help your friend do a "reality check" on his attitude?

- Because most mission committees deal primarily with finances, discuss with them these behind-the-issue-of-money issues.

**Author's note:** This next story might be the most difficult one in this collection that I am asking you to consider. A prayer for God's mercy and grace and protection might be appropriate before you read on.

The human dilemma—beyond all that the medical and legal and psychological communities have propounded and expounded and confounded about it—is still a human dilemma. Now that may not be too profound a statement in itself, but it is true!

Does one who is sensing a friend is drowning, ask others for help, and then end up in an argument with them over how to do it? I realize there is probably a "First-Aid correct" answer. But, STOP! Wait! Where is that friend? Still in the human dilemma of drowning!

And it is no different for the friend caught in the human dilemma of homosexuality. I do not believe God gave this man the courage to write this story for me to discard it in a pile of Christian "untouchables!" I do not agree with this man's doctrine or his "understanding" of the Word of God, but as this issue is more and more affecting the Church, I believe we must face it head-on. Cry with me as you read about his reentry experience.

### MY CHURCH RECEIVED ME HOME—QUIETLY

I became born again at the age of 42, after a lifetime as a nominal Christian, having done little about my faith since going to a Billy Graham crusade in the U.K. at age 16. About eighteen months after my true conversion, I was asked to go to India to teach beekeeping at a Christian Institute. While there, I sensed a call to mission work among the poor. On my return home, I joined an organization with a ministry among urban poor. They recommended a three-year Bible college course, and there a life-dominating problem, my homosexuality, was dealt with through counseling at Exodus Ministries. I was cleared as being fit for ministry as any single heterosexual planning to go to work in the slums. After two years of preparatory work in my home church, I was sent to join a team of about 12 workers in the slums of a major Asian city.

I had four-and-a-half years of ministry in that slum area, and though often being tempted to sin, I had been blessed with the strength to withstand, and had had many converts attending the local church. We had three house groups in the slum at one stage. However, eventually the married friend of one of my converts perceived my orientation, and in a moment of unguarded vulnerability due to the loneliness and stress of the living situation, I allowed myself to be seduced in a moment of unfulfilled passion.

As a result of that incident, I knew I would fall again and again in the promiscuous and liberal sexual mores of that metropolis. So, in spite of my fellow team members wanting me to stay and receive counseling to deal with it, I asked for and received their support to go home to socially safer shores.

My church family received me back quietly, with an acknowledgment of my return, but most people knew "something had gone wrong." Being refused any opportunity to share the positive aspects of my ministry from the pulpit did not help the feelings of shame and disgrace. In the five years I had been away, the church had been through a traumatic time of losing their senior pastor, and was admittedly in a fragile state, still without a senior pastor. Many of my friends had moved on, but it was a large church, and I still had many acquaintances and some friends left.

Some asked me to come 'round for a welcome-home meal, and an evening of fellowship. These were followed by a more generalized invitation, "You know you're welcome anytime." As a result of my life-dominating sin, and its recent eruption on the mission field, I had a severe self-esteem problem, so I didn't respond to these casual invites, though anyone who said, "Come next Tuesday," had an eager guest!

My mission organization, sensing my struggles to resettle, did offer at one stage to pay for me to have counseling, but I had a negative response to this. I felt counselors only told you what you didn't believe to be the truth, and told you repeatedly until you gave in and accepted their version of perceived reality. Self-esteem doesn't get rebuilt on the psychiatrist's couch, but in the loving and understanding acceptance of positive friends.

I felt rejected by my church and couldn't make the effort that was needed to force my way back into the social slot I had previously enjoyed, and which in my five year absence had, of course, disappeared without any apparent trace.

After the initial run of invites had ended, I was left with only about three families where I felt a real and genuine welcome home and received ongoing specific offers of fellowship. I persisted in attending the large fellowship of about 400-500 folks, but after six months of generally feeling worse every time I came out from worshiping in the church, I decided I needed to change to a smaller congregation. My missions committee chairman said he "understood." Inside myself, I felt that the church was glad to be rid of me, though this may not have been true. They certainly didn't seem to know what to do to help me resettle.

A few of my friends were at a smaller daughter church of ours, so I started going there. Initially, I enjoyed the worship, maybe because there was less knowledge among the congregation there of my history, so I felt slightly more comfortable. However, it was still extremely hard for me to come to grips with developing relationships. Looking back, I can see that the whole of my first two years home were times of depression, varying from mild to severe. So after a further five to six months at the smaller congregation, I left the act of nominal fellowship and worship, just as they were trying to gently get me immersed into some forms of involvement in the church.

During the first two years back, I'd made several unsuccessful and unfulfilling attempts to rejoin the work force. Who wants a 55-year-old ex-missionary, ex-teacher? Then I was offered a chance to purchase a three-acre macadamia nut grove in the center of a dairy farm some long-time friends of mine were purchasing. This, I thought, would be an ideal interest to involve myself in, as I had always been a keen organic gardener and into self-sufficiency.

So, my third year has been further removed from my past, and I've had plenty to do on my three-acre paradise. When we arrived out here my friend and I spent some weeks doing the circuit of churches. He settled in a local church that had a good program for his kids. I ended up going back to my denominational roots, and worshiped there for another five to six months.

During this time, the feelings of rural isolation and low self-esteem increased in spite of the enjoyment of the physical work I was doing. I didn't have the energy needed to push into the new church. After five months, I had not received one specific invitation to a meal, so I went to a nearby home group, which had been set up for younger families. Most were very accepting of me, but it only took one young wife to comment that she felt it would be better to keep the group as intended—for younger folks—to put me off from ever going again. When the leader asked why I hadn't returned, I couldn't tell him about it, and just mumbled something about feeling that it was not right for me at that time.

Several of my Christian friends have known of my struggle, and have been praying specifically for this area of my life over the past seven years or more.

As all this was going on, I was doing a lot of self-searching about my sexuality and faith. As part of my spiritual and personal journey, I started to get some information from the Internet about the homosexual movement and homosexual Christian support groups. After what has been the hardest three years of my life, I have now come to a place where I can be comfortable with my true self and with my relationship with God. That is still intact, in spite of my church relationship having dissolved. And, finding a spiritual home where there would be an acceptance of this theology is in itself a new challenge in my rural three-acre setting.

The feelings of isolation and rejection are still here, and I have known how easy it is for returned missionaries to feel so badly about themselves that they contemplate, and some actually undertake suicide as a way out.

The church has to come to grips with acceptance of failure. To have tried to undertake a ministry that God has called you to, even though it ends in sin and disappointment, must surely be better than to have never been obedient to the call in the first place. The hard, judgmental attitude of those who stayed comfortably at home is surely not an example of Christ's compassion.

FOR FURTHER UNDERSTANDING

Sometime during His forty days with His disciples after His resurrection, Jesus stated the parameters of His Great Commission: *"Both in Jerusalem and in all Judea and in Samaria and unto the uttermost parts of the earth"* (Acts 1:8). Today, the Jerusalem, Judea and the uttermost parts can be understood quite easily. But, Samaria! Why did Jesus say, "Samaria?" There were other districts around Judea. Why didn't He name one of them?

I believe He said Samaria because of the relationship the Jews had with them. The feelings were mutual—a deep hatred. Remember James and John wanting to call fire down from heaven to "burn them up" because they wouldn't rent Jesus some rooms? (See Luke 9:54.) To the Jews, these "half-breeds" were the unloveables of the world.

There is no doubt in my mind that each of us in our Christian journey has come to the time and place of having to face and deal with the "unloveables" in our lives. For many, homosexuals have been relegated to that unloveable—don't go there—closet of secrecy.

However, those who have chosen that lifestyle are not allowing us to ignore their issues any longer. And they are bringing them right into the church.

Though my own abhorrence for this sin is overwhelming, I grieve over the dilemma of this man. Did you note the several times he acknowledged his actions as sin, yet also declared he has become "comfortable with my true self and with my relationship with God." Yet, even after that statement, in his closing paragraph, he says, "To have tried to undertake a ministry that God has called you to, even though it ends in *sin* and disappointment, must surely be better than to have never been obedient to the call in the first place." To me, it sounds like he is crying out for help.

Did you note the several times churches seemed to

not know what to do with him? Yet, also the several groups that tried to reach out to him, he rejected? I have to wonder if his home country provided the "socially safer shores" he was hoping for. Might his ministry team have been in a better position to help him?

And, do not overlook his final sentence, for whatever the moral issue might be that brings your missionary friend home, a judgmental attitude is not going to minister healing and restoration.

FOR FURTHER ACTION
* What is the depth of our spiritual resources to help our returned missionary friend? Jesus had the reputation of being a *friend* of prostitutes and sinners. Does our reputation equal His? Can we find ourselves befriending a homosexual?
* After three years back, he has "come to a place where I can be comfortable with my true self and with my relationship with God." Do you have the compassion of Christ exemplified in His dealing with the woman taken in adultery?: *"Neither do I condemn you. Go and sin no more!"* (John 8:11).
* In reading that list of sins in Romans 1, we must not fail to continue reading into Chapter 2:1-11. Could you enter a non-judgmental dialogue with him (though still hating the sin)? He once found help through Exodus Ministries. Would he return to them for help? Would you accompany him? What is your level of commitment to your friend who is returning to his home culture? Can you help him deal with whatever issue he is facing?
* God forbid that your missionary friend (and this issue is no longer mainly male) would face the struggle of homosexuality. However, the more "acceptable" sexual sins of fornication and adultery are no less sinful. Are you prepared to give wise counsel? Are you prepared to make a correct referral?

- I passionately believe that if we are going to help restore missionaries who are sent home because they have fallen into moral sin, we must face the issue of "my unlovables." Thus, I have included as Appendix E a personal journey of facing one of my "unlovables."

### I STRONGLY DISAGREED WITH MY HUSBAND

From the beginning, the hardest thing about being a missionary was to travel back home. The trips were so difficult because they meant an interruption in the work and an interruption in our family life. Even two or three weeks of going from city to city and house to house with an energy-packed preschooler totally broke our personal routines. I found that my personal devotional time also suffered each time we came back.

And then there were the gadgets! I couldn't get over it! Each time we came back, (which was every six months to renew visas), all our friends had some new gadget, (answering machines, portable phones, personal computers), things that we'd never seen. On our way back to our home, we would decide on the "gadget of the trip!" What these gadgets represented to us was a very visible example of the level of materialism that had seemingly consumed our friends at home. These were things that we were quite content to live without and felt a little strange around.

I also remember vividly struggling to have a right perspective as we would come home and see what seemed to us great opulence in so many Christian friends. I was grateful for a friend who took me aside at one point and reminded me that it wasn't them who had changed; it was I, and they could not be held accountable for the light that I had received. That made it easy to go to the Lord and ask His forgiveness for my harsh judgment. But I was still more than ready to return to the simplicity of our lives in Mexico.

We started several Bible studies and soon we could see the tiny beginnings of a new church. Alongside this new church that was being birthed, there also was another new life coming into being. I was going to have a baby! About midway through the pregnancy, though, the doctors advised us that due to complications, I should return to the States prior to our child's birth.

About the time that we were to leave, my husband shared with me that he felt the Lord might be leading us back to the U.S. after the baby was born! Nothing could have shocked me more! I gave a thousand reasons why it couldn't be so! I cried, I prayed, I probably even begged. He assured me that he wasn't doing anything yet, but that he sensed he was hearing the Lord and that I needed to pray.

We returned and despite a very difficult delivery and four frightening first days, God gave us a beautiful daughter. He also began to confirm to my husband from several sources that we were to remain in the States. I watched it happening and felt I was in a dream. It didn't make sense. We had just begun. We had several studies and new believers and, even more, I had a heart burning with a vision for this work. I could see it as if it were already done. How could we leave it?

This became the hardest test of my Christian walk. This was my husband of fifteen years. This was the man that I so loved and admired, and he was taking a course that I vehemently disagreed with. And then there was the Lord! Where was He in this whole thing? Why was He allowing it? Why had He given me such clarity of vision for something that He now was allowing to be jerked away from me?

I cried more than I ever had in my life. I would dream of Mexico and the work and friends there and be so happy and wake up and cry when I realized it was just a dream. Our son was also having problems readjusting, (probably in part due to his mom's condition).

He considered himself more Mexican than American and missed his friends and the culture that allows children to be children.

At one point, after being back for nearly a year, we took a drive out to the barren desert. It was a good family day and we were having a pleasant time, but as we drove through the absolute barrenness, I began to cry. My husband was shocked and asked what was wrong. "This is where I have been living spiritually for the last year," I replied. I knew that I had to come out of my desert experience, but I didn't know how.

Shortly after this time, we moved and started a new church. I loved the people. I loved ministering alongside my husband. The place was beautiful. My children were beautiful. God was blessing but my heart still pined for my adoptive home country. My husband was very patient and was always there to talk with me and pray with me about it. He apologized for the hurt, but said he knew he had to obey what he believed was God's voice. As things progressed, I too knew that he had heard from the Lord.

It has been more than fourteen years since we came back. I can't say when I began to understand the why, but as time went on, the Lord began to involve our little church in missions in ways that I never would have imagined. And He began to expand our hearts beyond the great love that we both have always had for Latin America, especially toward India and Asia.

I think that the Lord has taught me through those very hard years that the place I most want to be is in the center of His will and that the vision I most desire to have is His vision for my life. It so far surpasses my own narrow scope. He knows me! He loves me!

FOR FURTHER UNDERSTANDING
There are a dozen or more passing comments in this story that give us insightful glimpses into the life and

thinking of this missionary: "I found my personal devotional time suffered." "...a culture that allows children to be children." "I knew I had to come out of my 'desert' experience, but I didn't know how."

Reread the story to find more statements. It is by reading and rereading the experiences of returning missionaries and by listening and listening some more to their stories that you develop a sensitivity to their needs. "Practice" on missionaries who have been home even for some time. They will be happy to share.

FOR FURTHER ACTION

• Reread the second and third paragraphs. Do you have the courage and the right perspective to "defend" American gadgets? We, as reentry caregivers, must be careful to not develop the attitude that we are to only "pamper" our returning friends. Scripture says: *"Faithful are the wounds of a friend."* Sometimes we will see wrong attitudes developing in our friends. At times like that, a "word fitly spoken" might even be a rebuke!

• It cannot be overemphasized that the first step to a quick and successful reentry is knowing that it is time to come home. And in the issues of this chapter, Home, Not By Choice, that seems impossible to believe. Is your confidence in a sovereign God who says, *"For I know the thoughts that I think towards you; thoughts of peace, not of evil, giving you a hope and a future"* (Jeremiah 29:11). Can you assure your friend of the same?

STEPS TO REENTRY
1. Know it's time to go
2. Go to home church
3. "Abide"
4. Rehearse "all"
5. Fully integrate

• Some issues are for ladies ONLY! I trust you realize that the issues this lady was dealing with were of such a nature that if you, a man, were brought into them, you would have had the wisdom and humility to defer to a woman to be her "listening ear."

Likewise, there are "men" issues that must be dealt with only in a male context.

### AMAZON HEARTBREAK

My wife and I met in Peru and we married there. While on the field, we came to realize that we could not work with the mission my church had sent me to. They were abusive and controlling, were causing grief and harm to the Peruvians as well as to us, and were obviously wrong theologically. In light of this spiritual abuse, we decided we could no longer devote time and energy to their teaching.

There was also severe sexual abuse of underage girls at the highest levels of leadership at the mission. We discreetly shared our knowledge of this with a spiritual leader. There had been some counseling but until recently the leader continued to lie and claim that he had never even kissed a girl. There were never any public confessions, apologies, nor any consequences. Though this leader has left a trail of broken lives, he continues to lead.

The mission, instead of allowing us to leave quietly and peacefully, immediately attacked us and sent back outright lies, misinformation, and stories of rebellion to our sending church. They said that they didn't have problems until we came along, and that *we* were the problem. I was also told that I had demons of division and rebellion; that since I was leaving the mission, the devil would get my whole family—that the ground would open like it did to the sons of Korah and swallow me and my family. The church never asked us to confirm or deny allegations, but assumed that they must be true, coming from a "respectable" mission. At one point I called collect to the church elder who was supposed to be our contact and told him that we had to talk, that there were serious things happening. "Can't you send me a fax?" was his reply, and our conversation ended. He later called and talked to a leader of the mission for hours. He never did talk to us other than by fax.

We asked our sending church to allow us to go to another mission, any mission, and gave them information on several options, including one where two families of the same denomination were, including one couple from that very church who had previously left this mission for the same reasons! That request was denied and we were told to submit to the mission or our support would be cut off. We reiterated that we could not, in good conscience, work with that mission. We were labeled as rebellious and slandered before the whole church.

Since our support (almost wholly from that one church) was subsequently cut off, I took a job as a translator for another mission, but it did not pay much. We were ordered to return to the U.S., but had to wait for a visa for my wife, who is Peruvian. It took eight months and more than three thousands dollars in travelling expenses to obtain. We ended up selling all our possessions, all of our wedding gifts, our computer, cameras, everything that we had of any value. The church refused to help pay for all of our airline passages, though they had given us an agreement before I left that they would pay for airline tickets, among other things. They did pay for one ticket. We charged the other.

When we got back, there was supposed to have been money to help us get relocated and get a job. We were told it was spent on the ticket. Our reputations were tarnished since the church passed on the stories from the mission. Even now, five years later, we don't know everything that was said about us. We were unwelcome in our own church, and ended up leaving the church in disgrace. We had nothing but debt, nowhere to go. We stayed with a relative for two uncomfortable, imposing months, and borrowed more money to get an apartment and to get a car so that I could get a job. The spiral of debt continued and ended in bankruptcy.

My wife had a very hard time adjusting to the American culture. We were accustomed to having a houseful of relatives, of company and friends. We found the American culture very isolated and solitary, and my wife went through severe depression and panic attacks until she was dramatically healed in a service at our new church.

It has been five long years. We are out of debt, have been through counseling for the spiritual abuse, and we have cautiously ventured back into low level leadership roles in our new church. We are now raising support to return to South America as long-term missionaries, as we have always known that was our calling. It has been a long road of pain, healing, grace and mercy. Sometimes I still cry when I think of what that mission, and our sending church, put us through. Sometimes I still get angry and I repeatedly have to seek strength to forgive, even now.

We looked to our church to protect us, but the people we trusted and loved for years, turned away from us. That was what hurt the most, I think. Those that we expected to shelter and nurture us back to health instead picked up stones or walked to the other side of the road to avoid our crumpled, bloody bodies. Thank God, our current pastor took us to the "inn," and helped with our healing.

FOR FURTHER UNDERSTANDING

It is tragic how a breakdown in other areas of support can affect reentry. This "reentry problem" begins long before the couple returned home. If moral, communication and prayer support had been open and intense for the situation this couple was in, it would have been difficult for the church to take the stance they did.

AREAS OF SUPPORT
Moral
Logistic
Financial
Prayer
Communication
Reentry

It is incomprehensible that church leadership would

respond as they did without *"hearing the whole matter"* (Proverbs 18:13). In issues as delicate and sensitive as this, it would seem appropriate for someone in leadership to even come to the field to observe first hand. As the situation escalated, it touched the financial support! Cut off! Ending in their bankruptcy.

But the most hurtful was the lack of protection emotionally and spiritually. In his words, "The people we trusted and loved for years, turned away from us."

FOR FURTHER ACTION
• Keep communication open with your missionary friend. If the areas of care are clearly separate, i.e., one part of the team does the communication, another the prayer, another reentry, etc., then the core leaders must communicate with each other. The communication support core leader, knowing that your friend is experiencing these hard times, will let the reentry caregivers know. Thus, you can be prepared for your work of "sheltering, nurturing us back to health" that this couple acknowledged they needed.

• Assume you are a member of their sending church, but because you took time to listen to their story and you found it credible, how would you have been supportive? Again, could you have been a "Barnabas" to take them to your church leadership and say, "You must listen to their story. It is truthful."

• Assume you are a member of the church to which they move. (For this is often the place where poorly-cared-for returning missionaries will show up— or not at church at all!) You see a couple, obviously hurting from—something! Are you prepared to approach them? Develop a relationship? Do you have a listening ear to allow them to share their story of sorrow (as did Jesus on the Emmaus Road)? Have you the patience to sort out the details? Do you know how to get an independent verification of their story?

### REFLECTIONS OF A "LINE ITEM"

A local post office has many options for sending packages overseas. Usually I send packages having little monetary value or little urgency by way of surface mail. While there is a risk of it getting lost, it usually gets there—eventually. However, when I send something of greater value, I use first-class or even certified mail, to ensure the package reaches the desired destination.

The question I have been asking myself is: "How are we sending our missionaries? Are we sending them by surface mail? Or do we make every effort to help them reach our shared destination?"

Seven years ago I was *sent* to Southeast Asia, fully anticipating a long-term career as a missionary. After a difficult and demanding four years, I returned to my home country. I immediately became engaged in six months of deputation work. Finally, while taking a break to study, I came to realize how burned out I had become. I had many deep questions about God and felt spiritually empty. So when I was faced with the decision to return, I did what I thought I'd never do—I stayed home. This was a far more difficult decision than any I'd ever made.

For the past two years I have been on "leave-of-absence," trying to put the pieces back together.

A major struggle since that decision to stay here has been: "Was I ever really *sent?*" It's really at the heart of being a missionary, it seems to me. My high school Latin reminds me that the very word *missions* is based on the Latin verb "to send." While we may talk a lot of the local church sending out missionaries, I wonder if we really "walk our talk."

While many factors determined my staying home, I was surprised how little response my decision made. My parents, supportive as always, were glad to have me closer to home. Friends and prayer partners said next to nothing about my decision. I was also confused to find my supporting churches providing little if any feedback. Perhaps they were relieved to have more funds for other "pressing needs."

My situation has brought me to think about the whole manner in which we carry out our obedience to the Great Commission, primarily as senders. Three impressions seem to clarify my thinking:

Lack of focused vision—Missions is something the church should do, and so we engage in various missions activities, often without a cohesive vision. The tendency is to atomize our missions budget and energy into numerous projects. The result leads to a lack of deep involvement with the missionaries and projects supported. It might look great to have one of those world maps with numerous pins scattered over the world marking the missionaries supported, but is that really the point?

Perhaps the most cutting phrase I heard while on deputation came from a missions committee member at a church very active in missions. When introducing me to a friend she said by way of explanation, "He is one of our line items." Is that all missionaries become—a *line item*?!!

Lack of focused care—At a recent mission conference I heard a message from a ministry that focuses on missionary care. They provide (at a price many missionaries can't afford) a place where they can debrief, relax, receive counseling or whatever might be needed.

While I listened to him, I appreciated the work they were doing. Yet I still questioned the larger perspective. Why must one go off somewhere to receive a listening ear and a relaxed atmosphere? Shouldn't the local sending church be the primary care group of the missionary?

Lack of focused financial support—The bane of missionary life is raising financial support. Probably no other topic touches more "hot buttons" than this. While

I was blessed with full financial support through my term, there remained an uneasy feeling. Having several different churches and individual supporters scattered over thousands of miles made keeping in touch difficult, to say the least.

I don't know the answer for every person's situation, but I believe I would have been served (and the cause of Christ would have been served) if I'd had *one* supporting church, which knew me and was behind me in success and failure. While I recognize my own failures and short-comings in building that kind of close partnership, I feel the current practice of having many churches provide the financial base encourages this lack of focused effort.

These are my musings. I simply hope that perhaps some others will reflect on how we send missionaries—by surface mail or by certified!

FOR FURTHER UNDERSTANDING
We have said it once; we will no doubt say it again. And again! The church cannot—must not—leave the responsibilities of missions to the care of mission agencies. There must be a cooperative relationship—the church doing the things it can do best and the agency doing its part.

This missionary had planned "a long-term career" as a missionary. While on furlough, he was anticipating returning to the field. But he didn't! The missions community "lost him!" What happened? What went wrong?

He had had a "difficult and demanding four-year term." He was immediately thrust into the daunting task of making the circuit to "several different churches and individual supporters scattered over thousands of miles." Only when he "took a break to study" (Actually, he probably came down off an adrenalin surge!) did he realize that something was wrong. He was "burned out!" He was "spiritually empty!" He was even questioning deep issues "about God!"

Fortunately for this man (though apparently without the help of anyone), he was able to sort through his dilemma. Out of his analysis of what went wrong, he has provided us with three excellent insights: Focused vision, focused care, focused financial support!

FOR FURTHER ACTION

• The first thing that struck me in this story was the hurt he experienced at the careless words of a missions committee member. Can you relate? After four difficult and demanding years in Southeast Asia, he is immediately thrust on the circuit of partnership development. Certainly he has to tell all the great stories of success. It doesn't seem that there was any one to help him process his deep questioning about God. And then—and then! "Mary, this is Bill. He is one of our *line items!*"

In the first place, you will never be so insensitive to do that yourself—even if you are the accountant! But what if you are at his "next" church? Do you have a relationship with your missionary friend that would make it easy for him to tell you of this hurt? Build that kind of rapport. It may save your friend from "crashing!"

• Research the three recommendations he made about focusing missions endeavor. Then, to the degree that you can influence the missions leadership of your church, challenge them to consider a more focused approach. Though I am not sure full financial support from one church is the answer, I certainly agree with his "more focused" approach.

• You can participate proactively with your missionary friend to prevent many of the negative things that may happen upon reentry. This missionary did not become "spiritually empty" in one instant. Did you "read between the lines" to see the signs of it?

The gas gauge of a car has markings of three-fourths, one-half and one-fourth full. Then the indicator hits the red section. Then the warning light or buzzer comes on. Even then the car can continue for many more miles before it sputters to a stop.

Unfortunately, the difference between your car and the spiritual "gas gauge" is that the spiritual gauge is not mounted on your friend's forehead. With the practiced "Amen!" and the "learned prayers"—even with the appropriate vibrato—and the "plastic smiles," your friend may fool you (and even himself) into thinking the tank is full! And he'll add the convincing "Praise the Lord!" for good measure.

• Pray for the discernment to feel along the surface of his spiritual heart and discover the cracks and fissures that need mending. And pray for the wisdom and understanding necessary to help.

### OUR LIVES HAVE COME FULL CIRCLE

Our passion to serve the Suffering Church was bathed in prayer for twelve years before my wife, our three preteenagers and I were able to go to Asia in frontline ministry.

During this time, we helped found a non-denominational church, and served in leadership capacities. Our support was raised quickly. It came almost exclusively from within our own congregation, since we were respected and trusted, and people believed our call to missions was genuine. We believed it too. So off we went.

While overseas, we started receiving letters and phone calls from our church friends back home, complaining about the church and wanting to leave. In every case we encouraged people to stay with the church through its difficulties, telling them things like, "Just because the ship's in a storm, don't jump off into the water." Unfortunately, more than 100 people (about one third of the congregation) left the church.

Not only were we concerned about our friends' spiritual health, but also about the state of our church. Even before we left there were signs of increasing legalism. We wondered: Would our church continue to support us in prayer and finances? What about those people who had personally committed to pray for us, hold us before the congregation, raise funds for us and distribute our newsletter? Would they still be there for us? Would there be a church for us to return to someday? This is when we thought, "We probably should have itinerated a little more outside of our own church."

After four years on the field, a terminal illness in my family brought me home for about six weeks. When I returned to Asia, my wife and I decided to spend a year back in the States taking care of my mother, checking out the situation in our church, building prayer and financial support, and getting a little rest. So within a month, we sold or gave almost everything away to other missionaries, packed up the remainder of our stuff, and flew home.

We never thought we'd live in the States again, but here we were, cutting our missionary life short and coming home—to what?

1) To a church that had changed considerably, both in spirit and in membership. When we left, we knew everybody, and everybody knew us. Now it seemed like we had walked into a strange place. Was this still our church?

2) To a family that had just suffered a devastating death, which inexplicably changed my relationship with my brothers and sisters. For the first time in my life, we didn't seem close to one another.

3) To an uncertain job market, shared housing, American schools for the kids—an unwanted furlough, in general. It seemed as though we would never get back on the field. And we haven't!

### Does anybody hear us?

I guess we thought we'd be treated like heroes upon our return. After all, we had given up our belongings, careers, comfort, position and stability to enter a life filled with uncertainties. And now was our time to be refreshed, exhorted and uplifted.

As we entered the doors of our home church our first Sunday back, we figured we'd be swarmed, hugged, patted on the back and generally praised. It *almost* happened. People were quite warm to us, hugged us and welcomed us home, but there was something missing.

Nobody really wanted to go any deeper. Our friends seemed to be more interested in what kind of weird food we had to eat in Asia than what kind of ministry work we did. It hurt more and more as time went on.

We also expected to be able to share from the pulpit on a Sunday morning with the people who had supported us financially for four years. I asked on four separate occasions if we could speak, and every time we were told there were no openings. A guest speaker from out of town, however, gained access to the pulpit! This only increased our alienation from our pastors, and added to our deepening discouragement.

### A growing disillusionment

Over time, my wife and I both became very disheartened. Not only did we seem insignificant in the life of the church we had helped to build, but the messages and doctrines coming forth from the pulpit sounded legalistic and condemning. The spiritual atmosphere was not what we needed to be refreshed and encouraged.

My discouragement was apparently visible, because one of our pastors soon approached me, wanting to have a talk. Immediately, he accused me of not walking with the Lord, and that I should seriously consider "getting myself right." I was stunned. All I could say was,

"You don't really know me, do you? Even after all these years, don't my faithfulness and loyalty and leadership within this church mean anything to you?"

I let him know that my discouragement didn't stem from my personal relationship with the Lord, but rather the way my family and I were being treated.

Several months later, in the middle of a Sunday service, the condemnation became unbearable. We decided to leave the church. We needed to seek healing and solace somewhere else.

We felt we owed it to our former pastors, however, to give them an explanation, so we requested an exit interview. After three hours of being accused of listening to the devil, we knew without a doubt that we were making the right decision, and we were free.

**Paying the price**
Setting up our lives again was an agonizing process, and we didn't get much help. Our church had abandoned us, our friends had been told not to associate with us because we were "listening to the devil," and family members were even accusing us of not caring properly for my mother.

At that point, I can honestly say that I was as close to suicide as I've ever been. There really didn't seem to be much hope for anything anymore. And financially, we were flattened. I was making very little money, so I secured a couple credit cards to finance our new life, and quickly became mired in debt.

The weight was overpowering. I started to get mad at God. "Why did you call me to the mission field?" I screamed at a blank sky. "Was it just to toy with me? Why have you abandoned us in our greatest time of need, especially after we gave *everything* for You?" I felt alone, betrayed, depressed, angry and hopeless. "Is this what missions is all about?" I thought. "Will this nightmare ever end? Will there ever be any answers?"

## It's not just me

It was difficult to remind myself that I was not, in fact, alone. There was my wife, right beside me, and beat up just as badly. There were our children, who now faced reentry without the support of a good church, coupled with the fact that their mom and dad were severely wounded. How would they handle all this? Would they continue to love God through all this? Had we allowed our pain to wound our kids' faith too?

My wife dealt quite differently with the whole process than I did. Where I tended to get angry and rant and rave, and cry and moan, she pretty much kept it all in. She said that she forgave those who had hurt her, and I had no reason to doubt her word. But deep down, it was hard to believe. I knew she was hurting more than she acknowledged.

FIVE REENTRY PATTERNS
Alienation
Condemnation
Reversion
Suicide
**INTEGRATION**

Thinking about our kids' spiritual state really started to tug at our hearts, too, and gave us a reason to get our own lives in order. Our two sons and daughter were now teenagers. We sent them back to the Christian school they'd left four years earlier, and hoped that their old friends would help them adjust and fit in. We asked the principal to have patience with our kids, and to understand that they'd been living in an Asian culture for four years. We warned him that they may not be as "in step" as he'd like (he was very authoritarian).

He assured us that everything would be OK, but unfortunately things didn't go very well. The kids didn't seem to fit in, and the rigidity of the school's administration definitely worked against them. They had a pretty tough year, probably in part because the school was affiliated with our old church, so their old friends had all heard from their parents that we were "having problems."

The following school year, we placed the kids in a Catholic school near my mother's house, where we were still living. I think they learned some new things about drugs and drinking that year, but we were still pretty caught up in our own problems, and didn't notice everything that was going on.

By summer, we were tapped out financially, and couldn't afford to keep them in private school, so we moved to a suburb with a good public school system, and enrolled the kids there.

Our oldest son was entering his senior year in high school. In fact, he had attended four high schools in four years, and was pretty unsettled. Little did we know how unsettled.

One evening, as we prepared for supper, I called to him. He came in the room groggy and totally disoriented. He didn't even know his name. I questioned him, and he said something about taking a bunch of pills, which blew us away!

How could this happen to a good Christian family? Especially us? At the hospital, after his stomach was pumped and charcoal was fed in through a tube to soak up all the poison he'd ingested, a psychiatrist told us, "Your son has no hope. I recommend that we place him in the adolescent psych ward here."

We were stunned, and didn't quite know what to do. We followed the doctor's advice, with feelings of guilt and shame. We really thought we'd caused all this, and were lost as to how to get out of it. All we could do was love our son at that point, and hold on.

### Coming home again

We had started attending a new church a few months previously, and were being regularly fed with grace and mercy, through the teaching of the solid Word. Our pastor was an extremely gifted man, but humble. He came to the hospital, prayed with us, encouraged us, and helped us through this traumatic time in our lives.

He also sincerely reached out to our son, which

made a tremendous difference in his life and walk with the Lord. That was four years ago. Today, he has a degree in applied science in vehicle design, but is currently serving God on a missionary ship, travelling all over the world. He has grown very close to God, has found his own faith (not his parents'), and desires to be in full-time ministry.

Our second son stayed pretty quiet through all this. In fact, he says now that he doesn't even remember most of it. I'm convinced that's not totally accurate, but he does seem to have handled reentry fairly well.

He finished his associate's degree in graphic and commercial design, and has just been accepted into a very prestigious art school. He's a hard worker, has a wry sense of humor, and recently finished his first seven-day fast, initiated all on his own. He really prayed hard about art school, and sought the Lord heartily.

He did go through a period of rebellion for a year or two, but I don't know if that was due to reentry or just normal teenage stuff. He seems to have come out of it, however, so my wife and I are very hopeful for the way his life is going.

While we were overseas and our daughter was about twelve years old, she told us that she wanted to become a missionary doctor in Africa someday. We were thrilled, but also realistic enough to know that it would take a lot of hard work and dedication. We assured her of our support for her dream, but let her know that we wouldn't pressure her. This would be her dream, her goal, her life.

She is now entering her third year of college, taking pre-med classes, intent on becoming a pediatrician. Only God knows how far that will go, but I've rarely seen anyone work so hard. I'm confident that whatever she decides to do, she'll be a great success. Amazingly, I was privileged to take her with me on a trip to Africa. The kids there followed her around like the Pied Piper.

You see, my wife and I are now the Missions Directors of our church, deeply involved in world outreach, but now as mobilizers and senders. We have led and sent several teams to Africa, and were thrilled to lead a team to China just a few months ago. That trip opened up a whole new vista of opportunity for our church. Our oldest son is the first full-time missionary sent out from our church, and several others are now preparing to go.

Our lives have come full circle! God has been very gracious to us, and allowed us to continue on in the passion of our hearts—missions.

FOR FURTHER UNDERSTANDING

"Our lives have come full circle," he summarized. From a dismal beginning to a tragic suicide attempt to rejoicing in the graciousness of God. This story somehow brings into focus many of the issues expressed in the other stories: Discord among family members who stayed at home, a legalistic, unsympathetic church leadership, uneducated people within the congregation given to gossip, children not able to function in a Stateside (authoritarian) school, economic hardship, alienation, condemnation, reversion, suicide, death to their passion to minister cross-culturally, questioning God. What aspect of this family's lives wasn't touched?!

Yet, this story also exemplifies the gentleness of a pastor caring for them—helping to restore them. It tells us of a faith in God settled deep in their hearts that provided a strong mooring for each of the family members. It certainly bears testimony to God's Word through Paul, *"For we know that all things work together for good to those who love God and are called according to His purposes"* (Romans 8:28).

FOR FURTHER ACTION
- Reread the story. Yes, it will be good for you to

reread this one several times. Underscore the phrases that allude to the nine areas of stress. You might begin with, "Would our church continue to support us in prayer and finances?" Add to that the next several questions of doubt. Can you make sure your missionary friend has a solid support team, headed by a committed Core Group

**NINE AREAS OF STRESS**
Physical
Professional
Financial
Cultural
Social
Linguistic
National/Political
Educational
Spiritual

to "steer the ship" of missionary care? For, by now we know that difficult reentry usually follows lack of care in the other five areas. If your friend doesn't have such a team of people, in cooperation with him, can you begin building his team?

• One church, after they had about thirty missionaries on the field, discovered the concepts of caregiving. While each of the home fellowships was studying the book, *SERVING AS SENDERS*, the missions pastor contacted each missionary. After they read

**AREAS OF SUPPORT**
Moral
Logistic
Financial
Prayer
Communication
Reentry

the book, they were to identify one or two people back home whom they wanted to assume the role of Support Team Coordinator. Though more difficult to do in your missionary's absence, it can be done!

• Identify the positive and negative phrases regarding the five steps to reentry. You might begin with "My wife and I decided to spend a year back in the States." That *sounds* positive. Yet, in the

**STEPS TO REENTRY**
Know it's time to go
Go to home church
"Abide"
Rehearse "all"
Fully integrate

very next paragraph: "We were cutting our missionary lives short." Be sure to note the phrase "an unwanted furlough." Sometimes clear decisions that seem right at the time become clouded when circumstances don't line up with our expectations. They began to doubt their decision that it was time to come home. Can you listen for the same ambivalence in your missionary friend? Can you identify it? Can you help him "hang on" to his moorings of faith in God's plan for his life?

- Underscore the phrases that point to the five reentry patterns. Remember, the roots of wrong reentry behavior patterns begin to grow long before they surface in visible symptoms. Thus, I would suggest the beginning of each of their patterns could be rooted in the paragraph: "I guess we thought we'd be treated like heroes upon our return. After all, we had given up our belongings, careers, comfort, position and stability to enter a life filled with uncertainties." This suggests to me that they did not go *to* the field with the attitude of "It is a *privilege* to be about our Father's business." Or, more to Scripture: *"We rejoiced to be counted worthy to suffer for His Name"* (Acts 5:41). Thus, they came home *from* the field hoping for a "hero's" welcome. When that didn't happen, seeds of discontent were sown, sprouting up through each of their personalities to produce a different reentry behavior. Are you aware of your missionary friend's attitude of service? Of his personality? What are his expectations on reentry?

> **FIVE REENTRY PATTERNS**
> Alienation
> Condemnation
> Reversion
> Suicide
> **INTEGRATION**

- Can you help your friend to find his rightful place, *"seated with Christ in the heavenlies"* (Ephesians 2:6), so that he may have a broader perspective of his circumstances?

- Did you note that the pastor of their new church played a significant role in this family's recovery? Are you on the lookout for hurting missionaries hoping to find refuge in your church? Are you in a position of leadership in your church to educate the Body in developing such a watchful eye?

Our missionaries are too valuable to lose. They need a proactive team of reentry caregivers at this critical time in their lives. Find your place of influence in the missions community. And become a radical facilitator of missionary care. Focus on the five steps of integration used by the Antioch church for those First Century missionaries, Paul and Barnabas.

# Section III

## Resources

# *Further Thoughts*

## APPENDIX A

I. You may have been challenged to consider involvement in cross-cultural ministry by...
   A. The Perspectives Course
   B. A Missionary Biography
   C. A Missions Conference
   D. A Visiting Missionary
   E. A "New" Understanding of the Bible

This puts before you the consideration of...

## EIGHT POSSIBLE "NEXT STEPS."

II. "Missions is great, but... **NOT** for me!"
This is an OK response (as much as I wish it weren't)! Missions isn't for everyone. There are other ministries in the Church. Just make sure you find what your place in the Body of Christ really is.

III. "What about short-term teams?"
Short-term teams are finding a strategic place in

the scheme of world evangelization. These teams are sometimes finding an entrance for the Gospel where long-term missionaries are finding difficulty. Also, short-term teams often pave the way for longer term involvement.

IV. "When can we go again?!"
You may see that there is a place for you as part of future short-term trips.

V. "What about leading short-term trips?"
You may find your abilities and giftings in the area of forming, training and leading a team, and mobilizing into further cross-cultural ministry those who go with you.

VI. "Who are our long-term missionaries?"
You might be motivated to become an active part of a missionary's care group, joining with a team who are serving as senders.

VII. "How can I help with the church's mobilizing team?"
You may be motivated to become part of the coordinating ministry of missions in your home church.

VIII. "Don't a lot of internationals live among us?"
You may be challenged to minister to any one of (at least) nine groups of internationals who live in your city. Internationals who live among us are maintaining their cultural ways. To reach them for Christ requires bridging those distinctive characteristics.

IX. "How do I get involved long-term?"
You may catch the vision of your personal involvement, long-term in another country and culture.

## APPENDIX B

### WHO I AM/WHAT I DO

My personal experience in missions, as I have pursued the call of God with a whole heart, has included many times of sudden transition from home to mission field and mission field back home. I once rated myself on a stress indication test. You add up certain numbers of "stress-points" for changes of location, changes in diet, death in the family, and so on. A score of over three hundred is supposed to put you in the high-risk (90%) category for getting sick. My score that year, based on the changes I had experienced in moving from a country to home again, was around eight hundred! The fact that I'm still sane and going strong for God is an indication of His grace, but it is also the result of a very important lesson I have learned and applied about the issue of my identity in relation to my calling.

Now it is very important to measure what we accomplish for God and to make sure that our lives and choices result in lasting fruit for the Kingdom of God.

However, our calling and our identity are not the same thing. Paul makes a beautiful and liberating distinction when he introduces himself to the church in Rome: *"Paul, a servant of Christ Jesus, called to be an apostle..."* (Romans 1:1). He makes a distinction between his *identity*—a servant of Jesus, and his *calling*—to be a missionary.

Paul never suffered from an identity crisis. Preaching to crowds, healing the sick, rebuking high priests, getting shoved around like a pawn by politicians, shipwrecked, rescued, on trial, in jail, out of jail—if there was ever a missionary who experienced traumatic and unplanned change, it was this man. But we don't hear him complaining of reentry stress on his release from prison! I believe that part of the reason for this is that Paul knew *who* he was and what his *calling* was, and didn't mix the two issues.

When we get these two things confused, we set ourselves up for some major insecurity. When we derive our sense of who we are from what we do, we set a trap for our own sense of identity by linking it to something that is temporary—what we do. When we return from the mission field, what we do changes. And if my sense of identity of who I am lies in the fact that I'm a missionary, then who am I when I'm not a missionary any more? In my observation, this error is at the root of a large portion of the negativity of the experience we call reentry stress. Overcoming this deception will free us from much of the pain of significant life changes.

What is the answer? God is our reference point. He is the only unchanging thing in the universe. My identity is this: I am His kid. Even if I were to lose both arms and both legs and be unable to feed myself or do anything else for the rest of my life, I would still be His kid, and He would still be my Daddy. My inability to do anything would not change who I am for one second.

On the other hand, if my ministry is my identity, when God wants to bring change to my ministry, or when it's time for me to move on to make room for other people to grow in that ministry, or when I go home from the mission field, I will find myself, consciously or unconsciously, having to deal with a crisis in my sense of identity.

When I have travelled overseas, I have always gone for purposes relating to the Kingdom and to missions, and usually it has been for periods of at least three months. When I buckle up on the plane ready to take off, it hits me. I'm going to a new place. Sometimes I don't know anybody there. I have no idea what the environment or the accommodations or the people or my co-workers are going to be like. Everything in my universe is going to change. Except for one thing—my Daddy. Because of this, I can rest secure.

When I get on the plane to come home, I'm in exactly the same situation. I don't know if anybody in my church is going to understand or even care about what I have done for God, what I have seen, the precious people I was with who are now so dear to my heart, or even whether they will notice that I was gone. But my Daddy knows. He's coming home with me, and because of that, I am in no danger. There is no threat to my emotional life or my sense of worth or of who I am. Even though I go from employed to unemployed, from working for God to "looking for work," I know *who* I am.

With this truth in my heart, I can honestly say that reentry stress has never been a problem to me. Confusion, disorientation, not knowing where to buy things or how to get to places, sure. Misunderstanding or indifference from friends and spiritual leaders, yes. It's par for the course. But as long as I know who my Daddy is, as long as my sense of identity and worth come from the security of that relationship and not from what I do (or don't do or can't do), reentry becomes a new adventure. It becomes part of my calling. That, I have the grace to handle.

~~~Mark Burnard

## APPENDIX C
## SEVEN CHALLENGING WORDS

Reentry can be a greater challenge than going to the field. Seven Biblical challenging words come to my mind:

INTEGRITY—This is one of the greatest words in the English language. It involves openness, honesty, purity and reality. It means we will not exaggerate what we have done or seen on the field. It means we will be especially careful about the sins of the tongue. It means we will be open and honest about finances.

GRACE—I urge you to read Charles Swindoll's book, *The Grace Awakening*. This book, together with the book, *Re-Entry* by Peter Jordan, could be a major factor in helping you face, in the power of the Holy Spirit, the challenges and difficulties that are bound to meet you when you get home. They will help you to be big-hearted when people ask you silly questions, or no questions at all!

This revolution of grace will help you to accept people and forgive people when they seem selfish or vision-less. We especially must learn how to graciously agree to disagree. We must learn how to be aware of the most subtle forms of pride, even missionary pride. It will also help us to keep forgiving ourselves when we fail or sin. Grace will keep us in the center of God's "highway of holiness."

DISCIPLINE—It has been proven thousands of times that "grace without discipline can equal disgrace." After a tough mission experience that demands hard work and discipline, it is easy to drop our guard in this area. Outside a team situation and leadership structure, we will have to shift gears into more of a self-discipline mode. In attempting to do this, it will be easy to miscommunicate and fail to find the balance. Some mission situation experiences leave people with a lot of pent up sexual drive, and when they get home in a loose and promiscuous environment, it is easy to let one's moral guard down and end up in a real mess.

Some people quickly reject missionaries and don't want contact, writing them off as "super-spiritual" or ascetic. Efforts to prove otherwise don't always succeed and feelings of rejection easily come. The enemy will do everything to discourage us because when we are discouraged the door to other temptations is very easily opened.

REALITY—I find that some who return from mission events have a rather fantasy view of the Christian life. We can fail to realize that no matter how filled with the Holy Spirit a person is, they are still very, very human. If we are realistic, we know that good people (committed Christians) can and will say and do very wrong and sinful things.

Terrible things also happen to good people. We love the Psalms and sometimes read Proverbs, but seem to forget that those two great Books are preceded by Job.

FORGIVENESS—Have you really forgiven those who have hurt you on the field? What about yourself? Have you forgiven yourself for blunders, mistakes and sins that you have committed? If so, you're on a good road because now you will forgive those who hurt you back home.

Beware of unrealistic expectations, especially in connection with your mission agency and your home church. If you are greeted at the airport and given a royal reception, then praise the Lord. If not—still praise the Lord. Let your first source of joy and satisfaction be the Lord. Let human love be the water over the top of the glass.

You must learn to love and accept people back in your home culture, just as you accepted those new people in their foreign culture. We need to be grateful for those who have supported us through prayer and finance. We need to esteem the senders and realize that they have an equal part in this great missions task.

Do not be critical or negative about your local church, which can happen so easily if they did not help or support you that well. Try to listen and discern their situation and some of the struggles they went through while you were away. Remember Philippians 2:3, *"...but in humility consider others better than yourselves."*

VISION—We must battle hard not to lose the vision God has given us. We should become senders and mobilizers, making every attempt to pass on to others, in reality and humility, what God has taught us on the field.

Sometimes it may just be one person at a time that you will be able to love, influence and help on the road to becoming a World Christian. Try to make good use of the tools, like books and cassettes that can help people grasp what it's all about.

You also need to stay in touch with people on the field, especially people you have helped come to Christ. Try not to break *any* of the promises you made to them.

Try to fellowship, even if necessary, by phone or e-mail with like-minded people. Keep the fire burning in your heart.

PRO-ACTIVE—How easily, especially under pressure, it is to become re-active. Reaction is generally negative as the hard blows of life and people seem to "hit below the belt." Let's remember I Corinthians 15:58: *"Therefore, my dear brothers, stand firm. Let nothing move you. Always give yourselves fully to the work of the Lord, because you know that your labor in the Lord is not in vain."*

We should stay active in prayer and evangelism. We can seek out those who are living among us from the countries where we have been. We need to affirm that the mission field is everywhere, and keep the missions vision alive. Keep on keeping on!

~~~George Verwer

## APPENDIX D
## GUIDELINES FOR SHARING

I. Share Your Experiences - Acts 14:27
  A. Sunday AM/PM
  B. Sunday School
  C. Home Fellowships
  D. Prayer Groups
  E. Mission Fellowship
  F. Civic Groups
  G. Public & Private Schools
  H. Other Churches
  I. Share in as great a variety of groups and venues as become available. This allows you to process your experiences many times. You will remember the good and the "bad." You will put your experiences into a realistic perspective.

II. How & What to Share - Mark 5:18-20
  A. Sharing is *not* preaching or talking down to those who did not go. Sharing *is* telling what Jesus has done in and through you. Jesus said, *"Let* your light so shine *before men that they see* your good works *and* glorify your Father *in heaven"* (Matthew 5:16). The first two parts of that verse are not too difficult to do. We all have a tendency to let people see what *we* have done for the Lord. But to follow the third part of that verse takes a bit more effort—that He might receive *all* the glory!
  B. Be prepared! (Boy scout, or not!)
    1. Know what you are going to say.
    2. Write yourself notes.
    3. Practice what you are going to say.
    4. Tailor what you are going to say to the specific group.
  C. Share essential and eternal things.
    1. Avoid "travel-log-ism." (Tour guide)
    2. Talk about "real" people. Give names.

3. *ALWAYS* avoid superlatives!
4. Stress needs and opportunities that still remain on the field.
5. Share specifics that represent the whole; don't tell everything!

D. Share failures as well as successes.
1. Be honest. Let them see your humanness.
2. Give all glory to God! II Cor 4:7; Luke 10:17-20; Luke 17:7-10

E. Share with enthusiasm! "En-*theos-iasm*"—God in you; you in God! That's where the word comes from. Share from the perspective that it is a privilege to be about our Father's business.

F. "A Picture is Worth a Thousand Words!"
1. Use good, sharp slides.
2. Use *edited* slides and video!
3. Let the pictures tell the story.
4. Avoid details that are not of general interest.

G. Share thankfully.
1. Thank the people and pastor for their faithful prayer and financial support.
2. Thank God for the opportunity to share.
3. Stress that you hope you and others may go on another mission.
4. Keep you presentation to the time allotted. Do not extend your question & answer time more than seven minutes. Dismiss, and let them come to you for more questions.
5. For non-formal sharing, develop a one-minute, five-minute and twenty-minute answer to the question, "How was your trip?" (Whether you were gone two weeks or two years, many will call it a "trip!") Be sure to put a "hook" at the end of each answer. This will have them asking for more.

## APPENDIX E

### FACING MY "UNLOVABLES"

Until the experience I am about to share happened to me, when I even heard the word "homosexual," I was headed in the opposite direction! Don't talk to me about it! I'm out of here!

Over a period of time, a graduate of a ministry school I directed kept inviting me to visit a ministry she had joined in San Francisco. When I ran out of excuses, arrangements were made for them to meet me at the conclusion of a Mission Board meeting I was attending there. "And, oh yes, I'm sure our director would want you to bring a devotional word of encouragement before we go out to Castro Street to witness to the homosexuals!" I couldn't believe her words. But there was no "back door" for me.

That Sunday morning I shared the most hypocritical "encouragement" ever given! Not only was I having to share these "uplifting words," but in a few moments I was going to have to join this team on the street!

The sight of these men parading their lifestyle was nauseating. I tried to join in conversation. I found it easier to be the "silent prayer partner!" That is, until Michael, the evangelist came strutting down the avenue! He was boldly declaring how much better he could proclaim the love of Christ now that he was free from the guilt others placed on him because of his lifestyle. "After all, the cultural implications of Biblical times and the misinterpretations of Scriptures in the original language, etc., etc.!" Lies of satan, all of it!

In the middle of our conversation, attention was drawn to one of the team members who had been shouting Scriptures on the street corner. But this time he digressed from Scripture: "And the judgement for your lifestyle is...!" Before he could get the word "AIDS" out of his mouth, he was struck in the face. We ran to the corner. He was being cared for, but the man who had struck him was standing to the side by himself, shaking. I approached him. His story was that he worked in a lab trying to understand this HIV/AIDS issue. (This happened just as the United States was beginning to realize the magnitude of the epidemic on our hands.) Further, his man friend had just died of AIDS. He knew his time was fast approaching.

After returning to my conversation with Michael, he invited me to his church—just down the street. With permission from the team leader, I went. Sparing the details of our meeting with his bishop, God broke my heart for men caught in this human dilemma. Is the sin any less repulsive to me? NO! But now when I read the sins that Paul states in II Timothy 3:2-5, I know the "proud" and "untruthful" are in the same list as those "without natural affection!"

To punctuate this newfound compassion for lost sinners, God allowed another situation: The following Sunday evening, being an elder in my church, I was at the altar praying with various ones. Moving from one to another, I looked to see a heavy winter coat leaning over the altar rail. Its sides were heaving with sobs. Its long hair was disheveled. Not until I put my arm around this "human dilemma" did I realize it was a man.

In that instant, God revealed to me that he was trapped in the lifestyle of homosexuality. I began weeping with him. "It's so awful! It's so awful!" he lamented. Through tears, I said, "I know! I know!" We prayed and talked. I committed to help him tell his wife, the next step he needed to take to wholeness. You see, his wife was pregnant with their second child, he was "involved" with her ten-year-old brother, and he was the choir director in a neighboring church!

*May God give to each of us a love for whomever we (secretly) label "my unlovables!"*

# Resources for Reentry Care

## BOOKS

*Crossing Cultures: How to Manage the Stress of Re-Entry*, The Salvation Army, 140 Elizabeth Street, Sydney 2000, Australia.

*"Fishers of Men"—Coming Home*, by Howard & Bonnie Lisech, Deeper Roots Publications, 2100 Red Gate Road, Orlando, FL 32818. E-mail: HLisech@aol.com Web Site: http://members.aol.com/HLisech/Deeper Roots

*Living in The Zone: A First-Term Missionary Reflection*, by Mike Sloan, WEC Press, Fort Washington, PA 19034. E-mail: 76145.1774@Compuserve.com Web Site: www.wec-int.org

*On Being A Missionary*, by Thomas Hale, William Carey Library, PO Box 40129, Pasadena, CA 91114. Phone: 1-800-MISSION. E-mail: orders@wclbooks.com

*Re-entry*, by Peter Jordan, YWAM Publishing, PO Box 55787, Seattle, WA 98155. Phone: 1-800-922-2143. Web Site: www.YWAMPublishing.com

*Reentry Guide for Short-Term Mission Leaders*, by Lisa Espineli Chinn, Deeper Roots Pub; See address above.

*Serving As Senders*, by Neal Pirolo, Emmaus Road International, 7150 Tanner Court, San Diego, CA 92111
Phone/Fax: 858 292-7020
E-mail: Emmaus_Road@eri.org   Web Site: www.eri.org

*Staying A Missionary*, by Hudson Deane, Impetus Communications, Bible College of New Zealand, Private Bag 93104, Henderson, Auckland 1231, New Zealand.
Fax: 64-09-8367801

*The Art of Coming Home*, by Craig Storti, Intercultural Press, PO Box 700, Yarmouth, ME 04096.
Phone: 1-800-370-2665

*The Missionary Team*, Ian Benson, Missionary Training Service, 18 Aston Way, Oswestry, Shropshire SY11 2XY, United Kingdom.
E-mail: coord@missionarytraining. org.

*Too Valuable To Lose*, William D. Taylor, editor, William Carey Library, PO Box 40129, Pasadena, CA 91114.
Phone: 1-800-MISSION.  E-mail: orders@wclbooks.com

## ORGANIZATIONS

Alongside, Inc., Steve Maybee, 870 Sunrise Blvd, Mount Bethel, PA 18343. Phone: 570 897-5115
E-mail: contact@alongsideinc.org
Web Site: www.alongsideinc.org
   Restoration and growth programs for missionaries.

Barnabas International, PO Box 11211, Rockford, IL 61126.   Phone: 815 395-1335
Web Site: www.barnabas.org
   The mission of Barnabas International is to edify, encourage and strengthen servants in ministry.

Canterbury Member Care Network,
Web site: www.cancare.org.nz
   CMCN is a network to develop relationships and resource sharing among the mission community.

Consultation on Debriefing and Renewal, and Debriefing and Renewal, Tom Eckblad, Mission Training International, Box 50110, Colorado Springs, CO 80949. Phone: 719 594-0687
E-mail: info@mti.org. Web Site: www.MTI.org
Various seminars and workshops to assist mission leaders and missionaries in reentry.

EXODUS International, Bob Davies, PO Box 77652, Seattle, WA 98177. Phone: 206 784-7799
E-mail: info@exodusnorthamerica.org
Web Site: www.exodusnorthamerica.org
EXODUS International is dedicated to helping individuals overcome homosexuality and other sexual identity struggles.

Fairhaven Ministries, Director Kevin Swanson, 2198 Roaring Creek Road, Roan Mountain, TN 37687. Phone: 423 772-4269 E-mail: fhmin@aol.com
Web Site: www.fairhaven1.com
Retreat center and/or counseling for returning missionaries

Heartstream Resources, 101 Herman Lee Circle, Liverpool, PA 17045. Phone: 717 444-2374
E-mail: Heartstream@compuserve.com
Residential programs with professional services.

Link Care Center, Pastor Ken Royer, 1734 West Shaw Street, Fresno, CA 93711. Phone: 559 439-5920
E-mail: Info@linkcare.org Web Site: www.linkcare.org
Residential programs to help families or individuals to focus on leaving and grieving, transition, adaptation, closure and action planning.

Lisa Espineli Chinn, 1113 Velvet Leaf Drive, Madison, WI 53719. E-mail; LEChinn@aol.com
A resource person in reentry research and short-term mission reentry.

Mental Health & Missions Conference, Dr John Powell, Mission Training International, Box 50110, Colorado Springs, CO 80949. Phone: 719 594-0687
E-mail: info@mti.org　Web Site: www.MTI.org
This annual conference is for those committed to serving and supporting a healthy missions community.

OSCAR, Mike Frith, E-mail: info@oscar.org.uk, Web Site: www.oscar.org.uk
OSCAR is a network of resources. Many deal with reentry issues.

Resources on Missionary Furlough: Web Sites:
* Debriefing Form - www.geocities.com/CapitolHill/5645/Questionaire.html
* Furlough Resources - www.iteams.org/ITeams/resource/crdb/Topic-Furlough.html
* Maximizing Missionary Furloughs - www.acmc.org/furlough.html

Third Culture Family Services, Elsie Purnell, Director, 2685 Meguiar Drive, Pasadena, CA 91107.
E-mail: empurn@aol.com
Support groups for adult MKs; consultation on MK care.

Third Culture Kids. The following web sites focus on care for children of career missionaries:
* http://mksafetynet.cjb.net　* www.mknet.org
* www.webring.org/cgi-bin/　* www.tckworld.com
* webring?ring=mkschools;list

### OCCASIONAL PAPERS
*In Touch*, Peter Jordan, editor, PO Box 1295, Sumas, WA 98295. Phone: 604 826-9937　E-mail: Intouch@cnx.net
This paper is a ministry publication to ex-YWAMers.

# Index to Reentry Stories

## MISSION ACCOMPLISHED
Nine Months to *Feel* American... 54
One Antique Piano for Sale 61
Job Hunting in the Workplace 68
Walking in God's Will 71
Our Core Group Covered Us 74
A Little Persecution Might be... 79
Securing Our Own Home 86
We Didn't Go Back to "Antioch" 90
Our Journey Back into Ministry 91
Let's Play Telephone—The... 95
Just Do It! 97

## SHORT-TERM MISSIONS
Capturing Missionary Zeal 104
I Still Grieve for My Nation 107
Reentry Stress is *Real* 109
On the Lighter Side 111
From Ecstasy to Passivity 113
I was Interrogated Like a Spy 116
I Kept My Mouth Shut 118

## LISTEN TO ME; PLEASE LISTEN
So Much to Say; No One to... 123
A Lady Reached Out to Us 128
In a Perfect World 131
All the Grief Came Flooding... 135
They Never Asked Me to Share 136
Debrief Me, Please 138
One Person Was Enough 140

## SILLY LITTLE THINGS
Forewarned & Forearmed... 145
Linguistically Speaking 148
Three Straws in the Saddlebag 149
A Little Tab Will Do You–In 151
INS, IRS and the SSA in the... 152
My Mother's Maiden Name 156
Pets 157
Lines That Divide & Separate 158

## MK'S, THIRD WORLD KIDS
Exhibit A: MK 160
Haunting Deja Vu 163
Bad is Good 169
Telephones & Drinking... 171
The Rest of Your Life 173
Lost in a Tidal Wave 175
Youth Leaders Were Afraid... 183
I'm Really *Not* American 186
But for the Grace of God 187
Happy Birthday 200
On the Street 201
Give it to the Missionaries 203
College Bound 204
Feelings Buried for Ten Years 206
What I'd Like to Tell the... 207

## ON FURLOUGH
To Work or Not to Work 212
Logistic Details 216
Cultural Identity 218
Contrast of Two Cultures 221
I Ordered a $3 Potato 226
I Thought I'd Experienced it... 229
Ten Minutes to Share Two... 234
I Don't Want to Go Home 239

## HOME, NOT BY CHOICE
Fly the Plane 243
Our Missions Office is "User... 247
A Disgraceful Resignation 252
The Long Road Home 256
The *Real* Reason 258
The Bandana Scarf 260
Just Hang Around the Office 263
Am I Cynical? Yes! 266
My Church Received Me... 270
I Strongly Disagreed with My... 276
Amazon Heartbreak 280
Reflections of a "Line Item" 284
Our Lives Have Come Full... 288

# Resources of Emmaus Road

## Publications

*Critical Issues in Cross-Cultural Ministry* is a bulletin on vital missions topics. Each bulletin is four to six pages. Reprints are available:

Series I: *Mobilizing Your Church* 15 Issues
Series II: *For Those Who Go* 15 Issues
Series III: *Serving As Senders* 12 Issues
Series IV: *Internationals Who Live Among Us* 12 Issues

*SERVING AS SENDERS: How to Care for Your Missionaries—While They are Preparing to Go, While They are on the Field, and When They Return Home.*

*PREPARE FOR BATTLE: Basic Training in Spiritual Warfare*—Making reference to over 700 Scriptures that point to victory in battle, this book drives home the importance of practicing the basics in spiritual warfare.

*THE REENTRY TEAM: Caring for Your Returning Missionaries.*

## Seminars

*Nothing GOOD Just Happens!* Seminar—This is an intense, 21-hour seminar to train church leadership in how to mobilize their Body in cross-cultural outreach ministry.

*For Those Who Go* Seminar—The sessions of this seminar help the potential cross-cultural worker look beyond the "romanticism" of missions and to deal with some very practical issues of going.

*Serving as Senders* Seminar—The lessons of the book, *Serving as Senders,* are presented in a 6-hour format.

## ACTS Training Courses

*ACTS Team Orientation*—2-10 hours of cultural, interpersonal relationship and spiritual warfare training for short-term teams.

*ACTS Boot Camp*—One week of cultural, interpersonal relationship and spiritual warfare training for those serving up to six months.

*ACTS 29 Training Course*—An intensive 10-week immersion in a second culture to learn how to live and minister in other cultures. The courses include cultural adaptation, language acquisition, interpersonal relationships, spiritual warfare, contingency training and unculturating the Gospel and teachings of Christ. This prefield training incorporates classroom study and community experience with living in the home of a national family.

*Mini-ACTS 29 Training Course*—A 4-week modified schedule of the 10-week Course.

### ACTS Video/Audio Training Tapes

*Prepare for Battle: Lessons in Spiritual Warfare*—This 9-hour video or audio training tapes program comes with 19 pages of Student Notes and Assignments and a Study Guide for Groups or Individuals.

*Building Your Support Team*—This 2-hour audio training tape is the counterpart of the book, *Serving as Senders*, instructing the missionary in how to develop relationships in the six areas of support.

*Solutions to Culture Stress*—This 4-hour video training tape helps prepare a short-term missionary for the culture stress of going overseas and returning home.

### ACTS Ministry Trips

ERI leads three-week trips throughout the year. Prefield training, a demanding "hands-in" experience and follow through after the trip helps the church leadership develop a consistent  involvement in missions.

### Speakers Bureau

The Associates of Emmaus Road are available as speakers on a variety of subjects, all challenging to a personal involvement in cross-cultural outreach ministry.

For more information on these or other developing resources to equip you and your church for cross-cultural ministry, contact:

**Emmaus Road International**

7150 Tanner Court, San Diego, CA 92111 USA
Phone/Fax: 858 292-7020
E-mail: Emmaus_Road@eri.org • Web Site: www.eri.org